PASTORALIST LANDSCAPES
AND SOCIAL INTERACTION IN BRONZE AGE EURASIA

PASTORALIST LANDSCAPES AND SOCIAL INTERACTION IN BRONZE AGE EURASIA

Michael D. Frachetti

UNIVERSITY OF CALIFORNIA PRESS
Berkeley   Los Angeles   London

University of California Press, one of the most distinguished university
presses in the United States, enriches lives around the world by advancing
scholarship in the humanities, social sciences, and natural sciences. Its
activities are supported by the UC Press Foundation and by philanthropic
contributions from individuals and institutions. For more information,
visit *www.ucpress.edu*.

University of California Press
Berkeley and Los Angeles, California

University of California Press, Ltd.
London, England

Library of Congress Cataloging-in-Publication Data

Frachetti, Michael D.
    Pastoralist landscapes and social interaction in bronze age
Eurasia / Michael D. Frachetti.
        p. cm.
    Includes bibliographical references and index.
    ISBN 978-0-520-25689-7 (cloth : alk. paper)
    1. Bronze age—Eurasia. 2. Pastoral systems, Prehistoric—Eurasia.
    3. Excavations (Archaeology)—Eurasia. 4. Antiquities,
Prehistoric—Eurasia. 5. Eurasia—Antiquities. I. Title.
    GN778.28.F73 2008
    950.1—dc22   2008015855

Manufactured in the United States
16 15 14 13 12 11 10 09 08
10 9 8 7 6 5 4 3   2   1

The paper used in this publication meets the minimum requirements of
ANSI/NISO Z39.48-1992 (R 1997) (*Permanence of Paper*).∞

Jacket illustrations: above, the Dzhungar Mountains of eastern Kazakhstan,
photograph by the author; below, Bronze Age rock-art motifs of the Eshkiolmes, after Mar'yashev and Goryachev.

For my parents

CONTENTS

ACKNOWLEDGMENTS

In acknowledging those who have contributed to the development, execution, and writing of this research, it is unnatural for me to separate them into categories of "friends" or "colleagues," or some other designation; most if not all are both in various contexts and at different times. This work reflects over a decade of ethnographic and archaeological research among nomadic societies ranging from Sami reindeer herders in Finnish Lappland, Berber and Tuareg herdsmen in Tunisia, and of course, Kazakh mobile pastoralists of Kazakhstan and Xinjiang (China). Therefore, I would first like to thank the pastoralists: Hasan, Bolatai, Erlan, and many others, who opened their communities and lives to me and included me in the interactive arenas of their contemporary pastoralist landscapes. Without this experience, my understanding of Eurasian pastoralism would be deficit.

Throughout the growth of my research, a number of world-class scholars have encouraged and supported me. At the outset, I must acknowledge the immense role and contribution of Professors Ezra Zubrow and Renata Holod. Both represent formative figures in my professional development and have inspired me to pursue challenging intellectual problems. In addition, it is rewarding to offer this study to a community of scholars for whom I have great respect, gratitude, and who together form a dynamic community that drives research in the Eurasian steppe. Among others, I thank David and Dorcas Anthony, Claudia Chang, Perry Tourtellot, Sandra Olsen, Bryan Hanks, Phillip Kohl, Fredrick Hiebert, Karl Lamberg-Karlovsky, Colin Renfrew, William Honeychurch, Thomas Barfield and Adam Smith. These individuals have contributed variously to this research by sending me their most recent work, reading and reviewing chapters, and unselfishly discussing ideas with me.

This study developed substantially from my dissertation work at the University of Pennsylvania, where a number of individuals (in addition to those named above) played a role its development. I am grateful to Gregory Possehl, Victor Mair, Clark Erickson, Holly Pittman, Naomi Miller, Robert Dyson, and Bernard Wailes for their interest in and guidance of my research at Penn. I am also grateful for the financial support provided by the Louis J. Kolb Society at Penn, the George F. Dales foundation, and the American Councils for International Education. Without these contributions, I would not have managed to spend so much time in Kazakhstan or have been afforded the requisite time to explore the wide array of topics and languages this study demanded.

In Kazakhstan, I am indebted to Dr. Alexei Mar'yashev, Yuri Peshkov, and Alexei Rogozhinski, who were instrumental to my archaeological and ethnographic field experiences. Without them, my knowledge of the archaeology and language of Kazakhstan would not have developed . I also would like to thank Professor Karl Baipakov, the director of the Institute of Archaeology in Almaty, for his support in making my research there a reality and for developing international relationships in Central Asian archaeology. In fact, everyone at the institute in Almaty played an important role in making this research a success, and I am grateful to them. Also in Kazakhstan, I would like to acknowledge Bulat Aubekerov and Saida Nigmatova at the Institute of Geology for their collaborative work concerning paleobotany and geology and for their key roles in the planning and execution of stages of the fieldwork. My field research in Kazakhstan was supported by two grants from the National Science Foundation (#0211431 and #0535341).

I would also like to thank a number of European scholars, whose research expands the breadth of Eurasian archaeology, and from whom I have benefited greatly. I first thank Professor Elena Kuz'mina. Her corpus of research on Eurasian archaeology is astonishing and worthy of admiration. While researching this book, I had the opportunity to visit and talk with Professor Kuz'mina in Moscow. She invited me to dinner at her home, which contains an amazing library of Bronze Age Eurasian archaeology. From our conversations, I understood that although I am presenting an alternative view of the evolution of Bronze Age steppe societies, my approach is possible only because of the comprehensive work conducted by scholars like Kuz'mina and her contemporaries. I can only aspire to one day have such an impact on future generations of scholars. I would also like to thank Natalia Shishlina for her guidance in Moscow and for introducing me to Russian theatre and culture there. In Ukraine, I would like to thank Yuri Rassamakin, Yuri Boltrik, and others at the Institute of Archaeology in Kiev. This study also benefited from a nine-month research stay at the Eurasian department of the German Archaeological Institute in Berlin. I would like to acknowledge the director Professor Hermann Parzinger, as well as Sven Hansen, Nicholas Borofka, and Norbert Benecke for their help and contributions to my work there. I am also grateful to Elizabeth

Fentress for lengthy conversations about composition and content, and for offering the most wonderful setting in Italy where I drafted a number of chapters.

Large portions of this book were written at Washington University in St. Louis, where I have benefited greatly from the contributions of my colleagues in the Department of Anthropology. First, I would like to thank Professor Lois Beck, who read drafts of this manuscript at various stages and contributed to its organization. In addition, I thank Professors Fiona Marshall and David Browman for inviting me to participate in a seminar concerning world nomadism in 2006. In the course of the semester, our fruitful discussions of nomadic landscapes beyond Eurasia further informed my ideas in the final stages of writing this book. I must also acknowledge my students: Taylor Hermes, Brandy Trimble, Dan Kandy, Nicholas Efremov-Kendall, Robert Spengler, Lynne Murone-Dunn, and Paula Doumani, who were very helpful in the editing of this manuscript. Finally, I must thank Dr. Sarah Rivett, who was a supportive sounding board for ideas and issues as they arose throughout the writing of this book. Her role as a primary reader of chapters as they came out was fundamental to the organization and shape of this work.

Finally, I would like to thank my family and parents, to whom I dedicate this book. You remind me that no matter the expanse of your mental map, there is continuity at the heart of it.

NOTES ON TRANSLATION

All non-English quotations cited throughout the text were translated from the source language by the author, unless otherwise noted. Where a quotation is from a work that is itself a translation of the original into a language other than English, the language of the mediating source is noted. All Russian placenames, proper names, and toponyms have been transliterated using the BGN/PCGN 1947 romanization of Russian. Dates are presented in calibrated years before the Current Era (BCE) or Current Era (CE), unless otherwise indicated.

PROLOGUE

I began working in Kazakhstan in 1999, eight years after the collapse of the Soviet Union. At that time, Kazakh people[1] were economically and socially adjusting to the free-market system and capitalist enterprise they had chosen (or had been handed), less than a decade earlier. In Almaty, still the de facto capital at that time, Kazakhstan seemed to be more a part of wider Russia than of Central Asia. Communication and business were conducted almost exclusively in Russian, and the mode of life was still effectively Soviet. With ironic grins, local colleagues and friends often described the decaying housing blocks, transportation system, cafeterias, and general nature of social life as "Sovetsky." Although these contexts reflected the political wake of state communism, they also stood in contrast to the rapid progress and emergence of "newly independent" Central Asian identities.

In the late 1990s the urban, political landscape of Almaty was being recast in the light of new Kazakh nationalism. Regardless of the comparatively small percentage of the total population affected, the emerging twenty-first century Kazakh identity was to be intricately tied to modern global interaction indexed by Mercedes-Benzes, Italian designer suits, cell phones, international banking, the oil industry, and other commercially globalized commodities.[2] Yet in contrast to the growing national pride and meteoric trajectory of development and reconstruction in Almaty, I commonly encountered a seemingly pessimistic phrase among everyday people: "Before, it wasn't like this."[3] This phrase expressed a form of nostalgia for Soviet times when life was somehow simpler, at least in the collective memories of many Kazakh citizens.

In fact, in rural territories such as the Koksu River valley of Semirech'ye, I experienced a distinct, alternative image of "New Kazakh" identity. Here existed a population that before the Soviet era could be described as largely nomadic and tribal (Khazanov 1994). Three generations of Soviet technological change in the form of large-scale collective field modification, the introduction of mechanized farming and social and ethnic resettlement introduced fundamentally new structures into the practical lives and social networks of rural Kazakhs. After decades of Soviet collectivization, this reorganized system failed and rural Kazakhs were left with little state support for the survival of their agricultural and pastoral villages. The abrupt introduction of new economic policies in the early 1990s left a financial and productive vacuum in the rural sector, which made recovery a seemingly impossible prospect in the minds of many in Kazakhstan's agrarian population.

Thus, as the tractors sat without gasoline in the 1990s, many people abandoned their former *kolkhoz/sofkhoz* villages to seek employment in larger cities and regional centers. This was evident by the rows of men waiting along major roadways on the outskirts of Almaty, hoping to be picked up as day laborers for the large-scale construction projects in the city. At that time, it was common to see women who had traveled into the center from surrounding villages to sell berries, eggs, or other domestic products. Most of Kazakhstan's agrarian Russians, Germans, Poles, and Ukrainians had gone back to Europe, exchanging their defunct Soviet passports for "new" national identities.

Those who remained in the rural villages were predominantly ethnic Kazakhs, especially in Semirech'ye. Their task was to redefine their communities and their agro-pastoral way of life under the pressures and uncertainties of the new political, social, and economic order. This social setting helped to illustrate the malleability of the Kazakh pastoral way of life and highlighted the historical continuity and strategic variation that are central themes in the formation and character of Eurasian pastoralist landscapes in history and prehistory.

In 2007, herding is the basis of the economy in the village of Begash (located in the heart of the Koksu valley), followed by modern agriculture. The character of the village is distinctly pastoral with nearly all working-aged individuals engaged in the primary and secondary production of pastoral products. Although nomadic pastoralists have exploited the Koksu valley for more than four thousand years, the modern pastoral system reflects a reconstruction of Kazakh pastoral identity derived from three distinct sources.

The first and most obvious component of pastoral strategies in villages like Begash is the continuity of a herd-management system institutionalized during the Soviet period. In Soviet times, villagers in state settlements like Begash were collectively engaged in the production of milk, meat, and wool based on the environmental setting and the pastoral history and working skills of the local population. Carried over from the Soviet system, the current coordination of collective herd management continues to revolve around a small village herd consisting of a few animals from each household, managed through a shared work rotation among the villagers. This type of pastoralism operates essentially like a collective ranch. Yet, without the Soviet redistribution system and state salaries for work as herdsman, this form of collective herd management is effectively a small-scale subsistence endeavor for the individual families in the village, and the herd is typically less than one hundred cattle or two hundred sheep. Given that these animals are distributed among roughly forty households, this system of herding does not provide villagers with viable incomes, wealth, or status.

The second element of the pastoral system in Begash has recently emerged under the new economic and social conditions of the post-Soviet era. In the mid-1990s, some families in the village were more readily able to negotiate the competitive arena associated with farm privatization and took advantage of opportunities for growth by drawing on social and economic networks for capital. Extended families pooled their financial resources; others drew on friendships and social alliances to establish themselves as independent farmers and herders. Thus, even by 1999, it was not uncommon to encounter individuals with privately owned herds of cattle, horses, camels, sheep, and goats. This mixed herd structure has been characteristic of wealthy Kazakh nomads in the region for centuries and, after the collapse of collectivization, family-organized pastoralism was making a comeback.

Herders in 2007 have compounded their animal investments, and a new class of rich pastoralists (*chabany*) is emerging. Nevertheless, this kind of pastoral wealth falls into the hands of very few families, since it means breaking away from the collective village system and ranging more extensively in response to the herd ecology. Often hired herdsmen and extended family members, who are paid a small salary plus a few animals per year to work under the social protection and support of the local "big-farmer", drive these larger mixed herds on longer migrations. Although this system reflects a strategy born in the new climate of capitalism and entrepreneurship for few individuals, the structure that blurs extended family and economic relationships is not wholly unfamiliar. One cannot help but see this system as a contemporary form of the traditional segmentary system that dictated social interactions and herding practices of Kazakh nomads for centuries before the Soviet era (Masanov 1995, Bacon 1958).

In addition to the modern refitting of ex-Soviet economics with a generally capitalist system of economic growth, the pastoral system in Begash in 2007 draws heavily on a third component: the historical memory of local nomadic practices and social relationships carried down by the older members of the village. In fact, local herders described the social contracts and community structure that are integral to the success of the modern pastoral strategy as "traditional"—as if the Soviet period was a short deviation in their long history as Kazakh herdsman. Of course the system in 2007 exhibits significant deviations from the pre-Soviet pastoral system, but these deviations have been absorbed in the contemporary pastoral strategy; so there is little distinction between historically continuous practices, practices developed in the Soviet years, and the novel strategies that have recently emerged to enable individual success.

The pastoralist landscape of the Koksu valley is constantly being reconstructed in the minds and experiences of the Begash herdsman to accommodate a contemporary system that fits the conditions of their current social, political, and economic context. For example, in the highland summer pastures, land is no longer allocated according to long-standing tribal divisions, but because there is plenty of open pasture territory, local social and economic relationships determine the pattern of settlement and range use. For example, Kazakh pastoralists can easily distinguish the differently shaped yurts of immigrant Chinese Kazakhs, and sometimes choose to locate their summer settlement (*aul*) away from these newcomers. The impact on their pastoral migration pattern is reflected in a minor relocation of summer settlement areas five to ten kilometers to more distant pastures, perhaps to a historically used pasture zone now reclaimed under current conditions. The mobility patterns and social interactions among native and immigrant Kazakhs are derived from their extended social histories and their shared tradition of mobile pastoralism, an identity integral to the perceived cultural geography of their region for centuries.

This book does not delve deeply into the contemporary pastoral system in the village of Begash or the Koksu valley. In experiencing the redefinition of the pastoral system over the past decade in contemporary Kazakhstan, however, I witnessed the complex dialectic between sociopolitical structure and individual agency in the lives of mobile pastoralists and saw how variable strategies within a particular pastoral system can reflect larger-scale socioeconomic histories. Living among Kazakh herders, I observed how they move about their territory, where they choose to locate their summer yurt camps, where their animals graze, and how they implement diverse strategies in particular places structured by the geography and ecology of their territory. I also saw how their strategies include a complex network of interactions which define the extent and significance of their social landscape while also enabling them to develop innovations in their way of life. Experiencing the reiteration and changing shape of contemporary pastoral landscapes informed my perspective on the prehistory and long-term evolution of pastoralist systems in the region while also complicating my historical perception of steppe nomads and their catalytic role in globalizations throughout the past.

In this study, I have tried to disentangle the knotty perceptions of Eurasian pastoralism by tracing a few exposed threads of data in a particular study zone: namely the environmental history, ecology, ethnography, and archaeology of pastoralists of the Dzhungar Mountain region of Semirech'ye. I present these lines of evidence in detail and in regional context to characterize the emergence of pastoralism as a dominant way of life on the steppe and to understand the evolution of this socioeconomic strategy from a regional and long-term perspective. Taken together, the environment, ethnohistory, and archaeology illustrate how the historical structure and strategic variation of pastoral groups framed a complex network of interaction over time. I also rely on this case study to help reweave the larger fabric of Eurasian pastoralist landscapes using fresh analytical threads, and to offer a new paradigm for understanding local evolutions of Eurasian pastoralism as generative forces in the broader geography and history of Eurasia.

The scientific knowledge we have about the Eurasian steppe zone was largely collected and presented by scholars living in the USSR. The limited research prior to 1917 represents a footnote to the archaeological work carried out in Soviet times. The archaeological work of the mere sixteen years since the collapse of the Soviet Union has made substantial contributions and is the current framework through which my own critique of Soviet archaeology is filtered. Yet just as American archaeologists build on the intellectual history of their discipline, so also Russian, Ukrainian, Georgian, and Kazakh archaeologists (among others) build on their histories. Since I am neither a Russian nor a former Soviet citizen, I feel that my use of this archive demands a few words of qualification.

I have made an attempt in this book to recognize and contextualize the scholarship upon which my own research relies while also extending fair and rigorous critique consistent with the scope of the current global academic arena. In order to understand and critique the Andronovo Cultural paradigm, for example, I must engage with the history of Soviet science so as to appreciate better the intellectual climate within which steppe archaeology was formulated. While it would be inaccurate to conflate post-Soviet and Soviet archaeological theory, it would be equally wrong not to recognize their relationship and the enduring Soviet paradigms through which the prehistory of Eurasia is currently understood—both within and outside the former Soviet Union.

It is undesirable to plaster over eighty years of paradigmatic study with a foreign trowel just as it is equally undesirable to deconstruct eighty years of research with a blunt instrument. My attempts to contextualize Soviet scholarship are meant to filter the dominant body of previous research through a contemporary understanding of Eurasian prehistory rather than relegate it to a past ideology. I have attempted to disentangle the archaeological record from its original scientific historical setting so that it can be effectively reused within another setting. That this task is possible is a testimony to the objectivity and rigor of the original researchers, and it is with humility that I stand on the shoulders of my predecessors to offer this study.

MDF, St. Louis, 2008

INTRODUCTION

Were the history of the Turko-Mongol hordes confined to their expeditions and obscure skirmishes in the search for new pastures, it would amount to very little, at least as far as present interest is concerned. The paramount fact in human history is the pressure exerted by these nomads on the civilized empires of the south, a pressure constantly repeated until conquest was achieved. The descent of the nomads amounted almost to a physical law, dictated by the conditions prevailing in their native steppes.

GROUSSET 1970, XXV

GEOGRAPHY, HISTORY, AND ARCHAEOLOGY OF EURASIAN LANDSCAPES

The geography and history of Central Eurasia are inseparable. Together they reflect the formation of Eurasia's diverse landscapes through time. Thus, a geographic perspective underlies this book's thesis regarding Eurasian pastoralism. Through the negotiation of social institutions, ecologically variable regional geographies, and historical events (i.e., social interactions), Eurasian pastoralists have constructed enduring local landscapes that have shaped a dynamic constellation of socioeconomic exchanges, reformations of social identity, and political economies across Eurasia over the past four thousand years. Pastoralist landscapes represent the foreground contexts for historical events in the Eurasian steppe largely because social interactions (the catalysts of historical change) have been fundamentally structured according to the temporal and spatial rhythms of pastoral ecology of the steppe. Furthermore, as populations moved and interacted locally and regionally, their crossings and exchanges set the stage for a dynamic history of political consolidation and collapse, economic shifts, and material diffusions. Therefore, the landscape of the steppe is conditioned both by changes and continuties in socioeconomic strategies, which alter the shape and extent of interactive networks among pastoralist communities.

In this study, I illustrate how pastoralist strategies served both to redefine the extents of local cultural landscapes and to promote a network of interconnections among regional groups. This network functioned in response to the routinized spatial and temporal patterns of local seasonal migrations and was extended and reshaped by periodic changes in those routines. From this perspective, pastoralist landscapes are essentially formulated at a local scale and enfold a condition of "ordered variation", wherein routine structures fluctuate in response to a variety of pressures including environmental variation, political change, economic opportunity, and currents of ideological affiliation to generate a simultaneously durable and flexible structure of interaction.

Viewed at a wider scale, the interleaved geographies of Central Eurasian landscapes can be traced to the earliest forms of mobile pastoralism in the Bronze Age (c. 3000–1000 BCE). At this time, the cultural geography of the steppe was first transformed from disconnected regional systems to a fluctuating network of articulated regional populations, ultimately defining the fundamental character of the region for millennia. As pastoralist systems changed in response to regional forces they variously contributed to the wider geography of interaction, which under specific circumstances aligned and allowed rapid "flashes" of connectivity and diffusion, and then, in the course of regional metamorphasis, cyclically rotated out-of-sync again. I argue that these stochastically connected networks take form through the dynamic practices of steppe pastoralists and are recoverable through the archaeological footprint of their landscapes.

Geographically, Central Eurasia (sometimes called Inner Asia) represents an enormous territory spanning from the steppes north of the Black Sea to the Gansu corridor in China and from Siberia to the Iranian plateau and the edge of the Pamir and Himalaya Mountains. Within this macro-region, the steppe ecotone is a broad expanse of grasslands stretching from east to west across the Eurasian landmass. North to south, the steppe grasslands become increasingly arid until they fade into the sandy deserts of the Kyzl Kum and Kara Kum. In the east the grasslands continue up the northwestern slopes of knotty mountain ranges:the Pamir, Tian Shan, and Altai. Along the northern border, the steppe gently transitions into Siberian forests, which extend into the plains like fingers along the courses of the Volga, Samara, Ural, Irtysh, and Yenesei Rivers. The analytical focus of this book is the central and eastern steppe zones of Eurasia, effectively areas west of the Volga River to the ranges of the Altai and Tian Shan Mountains (fig. 1). This book does not extend its detailed analysis to the westernmost steppes of southern Russia or farther east to Mongolia or Xinjiang, though I discuss these areas periodically in their relation to the central and eastern steppe zones where applicable.

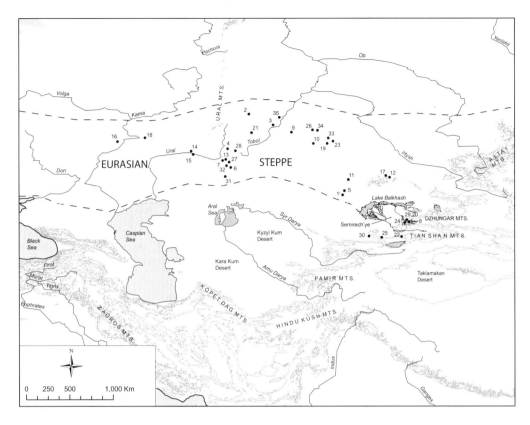

FIGURE 1

Central Eurasia, the Eurasian Steppe and principal sites mentioned in the text: (1) Ak-Mustafa;
(2) Alakul; (3) Alekseevka; (4) Arkaim; (5) Atasu; (6) Atken-Sai; (7) Baitu; (8) Begash; (9) Berlik;
(10) Botai; (11) Buguly II & III; (12) Dongal; (13) Elenovka I & II; (14) Gorny; (15) Kargaly; (16) Khvalynsk; (17) Kopa I; (18) Krasnosamarskoe; (19) Krasnyi Yar; (20) Kuigan; (21) Kulevchi IV; (22) Kul'sai;
(23) Mirzhik; (24) Mukri; (25) Oi-Dzhailyau; (26) Petrovka, Petrovka-2; (27) Shandasha; (28) Sintashta;
(29) Talapty; (30) Tamgaly; (31) Tasty-Butak; (32) Ushkatty; (33) Vasilkovka IV; (34) Yavlenka; (35) Yazevo.
(Map data source: ESRI Digital Chart of the World.)

The following chapters combine archaeological studies with (paleo) geography and
ethnohistory to present a rich dataset documenting the changes and continuities among
Eurasian pastoralists through time (and those of Semirech'ye more specifically). These
diverse lines of inquiry combine for a new characterization of Eurasian pastoral
nomadism that emphasizes socioeconomic metamorphosis resulting from strategic interaction with environment and neighbors. Eurasian pastoralists also contribute to a
long-term continuity of place and cultural geography despite variations in their extents
of mobility, political and economic transitions, or environmental change through time.
As such, Eurasian pastoralists act as catalysts of broader-scale historical change through
their ability to manipulate and modify economic and political structures at the interstices of social networks. This documentation stands apart from the still common

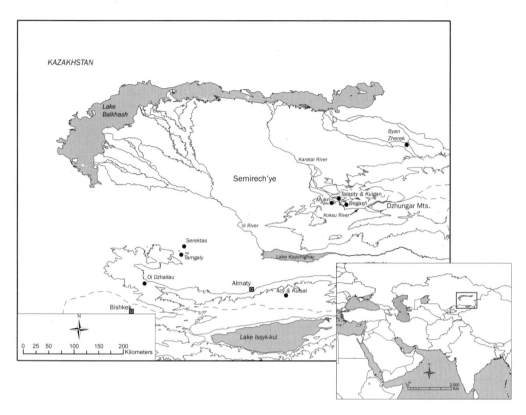

Semirech'ye, the Kosku River, and principal sites in the region. (Map data source: ESRI Digital Chart of the World.)

portrayal of steppe nomadic societies as placeless populations standing at the fringes of great civilizations and reacting to the whims of nature. The primary case study of this book examines the formation of pastoralist landscapes, starting with the earliest evidence for pastoral societies in the Bronze Age in one region of the Eurasian steppe in greater detail:the Dzhungar Mountains of Semirech'ye (fig. 2, also below).

Historically the Eurasian steppe has bridged urban and nomadic contexts as a territory occupied by tribally organized pastoralists, migratory groups, traders, transient populations, and armies (Golden 2003). But the view presented by historical records often masks the geo-cultural time-depth of local populations, whose practical histories are embedded in the geography of archaeological places that serve to map their cultural landscapes in time and space. In the early scholarship of the region, correlation between perceptions of geographic marginality and ancient historical accounts fostered a conception that the steppes and deserts of Inner Asia were the lands of unbounded nomads who lacked substantial localities of cultural investment and whose cultural ontology was known only in contradistinction to better-documented neighboring civilizations.

Historical geographers of the late ninteenth and early twentieth centuries, like Sir Aurel Stein, illustrate this conception in their descriptions of the cultural geography of Inner Asia. Stein (1925, 378) wrote, "On looking at the map [of Innermost Asia] it may well seem as if this vast region had been intended by Nature to serve as a barrier between the lands which have given to our globe its great civilizations, than to facilitate the exchange of their cultural influences." Considering the historical basis and context of Stein's remark, early twentieth century scholars knew ancient "civilizations" of China, the Indus valley, and Mesopotamia, while Central Eurasia represented a vast unknown region of social and environmental extremes: a land of historically reported nomadic tribes whose cultural geographies and history were as obscure as their way of life.

Ellis Huntington was one of the strongest proponents of the direct relationship between the marginality of the steppe geography and its population. In *The Pulse of Asia* Huntington (1907, 9) observed that "Two main types of civilization prevail [in Central Asia]: the condition of nomadism with its independent mode of life, due to the scattered state of the sparse population, and the condition of intensive agriculture in irrigated oases with its centralized mode of life, due to the crowding together of population in communities whose size is directly proportional to that of the streams." With such geographic views at the root of early historical works, a categorical polarity of the Inner Eurasian landscape emerged, "the steppe versus the sown" (Fleure and Peake 1928). The steppe was conceived as a territory of nomadic barbarism and landlessness, whereas the "sown" was the region of settled (i.e., urban) agriculturalists and therefore "civilization." Building on this underlying equation, historians of Inner Asia, supported by the biased accounts of steppe nomads by ancient historians of China, Persia, and elsewhere, constructed a broad geographic impression of the steppe territory as a vast no-man's-land of social marginality and barbarism,.

In his seminal work *L'Empire des Steppes* (1970 [1939]), Rene Grousset's characterization of steppe pastoralists resonates with the paradigm of earlier historical geographers and extends their broad impressions of the steppe zone to interpret the antique record as well.

North of this narrow trail of civilization [Central Asian Oases] . . . the steppes provided the nomads with a route of a very different order: *a boundless route of numberless tracks, the route of barbarism*. Nothing halted the thundering barbarian squadrons between the banks of the Orkhon or the Kerulen and Lake Balkhash; for, although toward the latter point the Altai Mountains and the northern spurs of the T'ien Shan ranges seem to meet, the gap is still wide at the Imil River in Tarbagatai, in the direction of Chuguchak, as also between the Yulduz, the Ili, and the Issyk Kul basin to the northwest, where the horsemen from Mongolia beheld the further boundless expanses of the Kirghiz and Russian steppes. The passes of Tarbagatai, Ala-Tau, and Muzart were *continually crossed by hordes from the eastern steppe on their way to the steppes of the west*. In the protohistoric period, the movement must have been more often in the opposite direction; one gains the impression that nomads of Iranian-that is, Indo-European, stock, called Scythians and Sarmatians by Greek historians and identified as Saka by Iranian inscriptions, must have penetrated a long way to the northeast, to the region of Pazyryk and Minusinsk, while other Indo-Europeans populated the Tarim oases, from Kashgar to Kucha, Kara Shahr, and Turfan, perhaps even as far as Kansu. It is certain, however, that from the beginning of the Christian era the flow was from east to west. It was no longer the Indo-European dialects that prevailed-"East Iranian," Kuchean, or Tokharian-in the oases of the future Chinese Turkestan; it was rather the Hsiung-nu who, under the name of Huns, came to establish a proto-Turkic empire in southern Russia and in Hungary.

Grousset 1970 (1939), xxiii, emphasis mine

In his narrative of steppe history, Grousset drew on an impressively wide array of sources from disparate epochs and geographic contexts and extended the historical record of vast steppe empires into antiquity to include the Scythians and Saka of the first millennium BCE. Art historical and culture historical work of the time seemed to corroborate this retrofit of steppe history (Jettmar 1965).

Historians have derived a picture of the steppe from specific events, largely reported from the perspective of non-steppe populations: Persians, Chinese, and Greeks among the most notable. One cannot ignore this important fact since, as is the case with most historical and geographic phenomena, the pertinence of historical characterization depends on the relationship between the documentary scale and geo-chronological generalization of the evidence. Significantly, there is no historical documentation from the local pastoralist societies who may have fielded the waves of nomadic hordes, so we are left to interpret the history of pastoralist political economies at the macro-scale of tribal conquest and population displacement rather than situate the events of history within a practical reconstruction of regionally strategic pastoral ways of life.

For early art historians and archaeologists, the essential notion of steppe nomads as highly mobile provided an apposite explanation for the observed distribution of material forms from both historic periods and antiquity (Okladnikov 1959; Jettmar 1965). In fact, archaeologists of the steppe have helped to propogate the historical notion of nomadic mobility as an analytical paradigm for prehistoric periods and perhaps extended it beyond analytical and evidential relevance (Gimbutas 1958).

Steppe archaeology has had a great impact in recycling the characterization of sweeping hordes of steppe nomads into fields such as human genetics (Wells et al. 2001) and historical linguistics by coupling general categorical conceptions of nomadic ways of life with various distributions of material cultural forms (ceramics, artwork, metallurgy, and, later, textiles), genetic variation, or linguistic trajectories. Although archaeological evidence does illustrate a considerable degree of homology in material forms (for example, among the ceramics and metallurgical styles of Bronze Age steppe populations), these archaeological assemblages must be related to the way early pastoral societies actually lived in the steppe, rather than to an historical image of Eurasian nomads.

Recent pastoral ecological reconstructions of the steppe (chapter 3) illustrate that those steppe pastoralists who did migrate long distances likely did so along north/south trajectories, and that these distant migrations were restricted to groups exploiting the arid regions of the open steppe where variation in seasonal pasture productivity correlates with substantial differences between latitudes. Elsewhere, Eurasian pastoralists may seek the ecological advantages of mountain territories where the availability of rich pasture resources can be exploited with shorter migratory orbits, typically associated with seasonal vertical transhumance (Khazanov 1978).

In recent decades, scholars have also recognized the patchiness of both the historical and the archaeological record and have done well to contextualize their studies within relevant geo-historical boundaries (Di Cosmo 2002; Rogers 2005; Shishlina 2004). Nonetheless, few have explored a fundamental question: how did pastoralists live in various regions of the steppe through time, and is this long-term pattern consistent with our historical understanding of the region's evolution and the peoples' nomadic character? Until recently, the archaeology of the steppe has reproduced aspects of the historical view of highly mobile Eurasian nomads to flesh out the otherwise scanty details of prehistoric steppe societies. This is evident both in the original Soviet archaeology and in much of the derivative western literature (Mallory 1989; Mair 1998).

I characterize the Eurasian steppe not as a vast highway of grass but as a mosaic of regionally differentiable eco-social spheres or landscapes. I present the geography of Eurasia as a jigsaw puzzle of discrete regional environmental contexts differentiated by major and minor rivers, mountain ranges, and diverse climatic and ecological micro-niches. I also characterize the cultural geography of the Eurasian steppe as complex and varied, with societies of different scales interacting to generate a dynamic rise and fall of political and economic arenas through time (Frachetti in press). In contrast to suppositions about local processes inferred through macro-scale geo-historical narratives, this study provides a focused investigation of local environments and socioeconomic systems and offers an opportunity to examine more closely the impact of local-scale pastoralist strategies on broader historical processes that define the trajectory of Central Eurasian societies through time.

THE IMPORTANCE OF THE BRONZE AGE IN EURASIA

This book is fundamentally concerned with Bronze Age pastoralism in Central Eurasia (c. 3000–1000 BCE) and the incipient role of prehistoric mobile pastoral societies in the formation of historically connected landscapes and networks across the Eurasian steppe zone through time. The Bronze Age was a key period in Eurasian prehistory when major technological, linguistic, and cultural innovations changed the way societies of Eastern Europe, Asia, and the Middle East interacted (Levine et al. 2003; Jones-Bley and Zdanovich 2002). These innovations include the proliferation of horse-riding technology and the development of wheeled transport in the form of horse-drawn chariots (Anthony 2007), the transmission and evolution of Indo-Iranian and Indo-European languages (Mallory and Mair 2000), and the widespread distribution of metallurgy and other material culture across the Eurasian landmass (Chernykh et al. 2000). The Bronze Age was also a period of marked changes in social organization with the development of social hierarchies and more complex political economies across Eurasia (Kohl 2007, Koryakova and Epimakov 2007). These innovations have been commonly associated with the widespread development of mobile forms of pastoralism in the steppe zone during the second millennium BCE among Bronze Age steppe societies, conventionally attributed to the "Andronovo Cultural Community" (Anthony 1998; Koryakova 2002; Kuz'mina 1994; Sorokin and Gryaznov 1966; Zdanovich 1984).

The Andronovo Cultural Community (*Andronovskoi Kul'turnoi Obshchnost*) is the name commonly used to describe a related body of material culture that has been recovered from archaeological contexts of the second millennium BCE across the Eurasian steppe zone (Teploukhov 1927; Chernykh et al. 1989; Gryaznov 1969; Sal'nikov 1967; Chernikov 1960; Sorokin and Gryaznov 1966). This archaeological assemblage is characterized by broad similarities in ceramics, burial traditions, and metallurgy, which supposedly were diffused or transported along with eastward displacements of people throughout the second millennium BCE. The extent of the material distribution of the "Andronovo Culture," as it was originally called, occupied an enormous territory from north of the Caspian Sea through the steppes of Kazakhstan, east to the Minusinsk Basin (southwestern Siberia), and south to the Aral Sea, Karakum desert, and Pamir Mountains. According to current models, the spread and evolution of the Andronovo Cultural Community can be seen as a proxy event for the spread of many of the innovations listed above.

Claims that "Andronovo" steppe societies were the transporters of language, material culture, and technology across Eurasia during the second millennium BCE are rooted in our understanding of the Bronze Age economy of pastoral herding (*skotovodtsvo*)[1] focused primarily on sheep, cattle, and horses. Supposedly, the increased mobility associated with the Bronze Age pastoral economy provided regional populations with the means to press across the steppe (e.g., Tsalkin 1970, 1966; Gimbutas 1965; Kuz'mina 1998; Kosarev 1981; Gryaznov et al. 1955–1956). Thus, the current explanation for the diffusion of comparable material cultural forms across Eurasia in prehistory is based on the view that steppe pastoralists moved eastward throughout the Bronze Age, although this theory may be more in tune with macro-historical views of the region than it is with a detailed analysis of regional archaeological sequences (Koryakova 1998).

This volume presents evidence that questions the degree to which regional populations migrated across the steppe throughout the Bronze Age. I do not suggest that population movements did not occur in prehistory, nor that regional cultural, linguistic, and genetic similarities must be explained a priori, without consideration of migration as a factor. Rather, I present three lines of evidence that demonstrate a more nuanced process of emergence and metamorphosis of Eurasian pastoral populations in locally durable contexts. Specifically, environmental, ethnographic, and archaeological data from the Semirech'ye region together demonstrate that the proposed theories of population displacement used to explain the wide distribution of Bronze Age material and semiotic elements are inconsistent with the ways in which pastoralist landscapes take form and are reshaped by local populations.

In order to account for the documented transmission of numerous innovations in the Bronze Age, I propose a model of regional interaction wherein localized mobility patterns associated with pastoralist strategies contributed to the construction of a diversity of contexts of diffusion within regionally confined territories. Periodic variation in the location and employment of these contexts—responsive strategies to both ecological and social variables—contributed to extensions in the distribution and dissemination of material and semiotic forms beyond the local landscapes of activity of various pastoral societies. From this perspective, the formation of wide-reaching archaeological assemblages, for example, may be attributed to irregular and stochastic interactions across fluctuating social networks rather than from either displacements of population *en masse* or a steady diffusion of material and people from particular sources. The resultant geographic distribution of anthropogenic locals in localized arenas reflects the historically embedded nature of Eurasian pastoralism and the socioeconomic organization of steppe societies from as early as the third millennium BCE.

To understand how Bronze Age materials and technology may have diffused across the steppe one must understand the nature of prehistoric pastoralism and its impact on the interactive and economic geography of societies across Eurasia. Many studies of the steppe zone have characterized various Bronze Age societies as herders (Kosarev 1981; Shilov 1975), although the extent of their mobility and exact character of economic and social interactions of different regions remain largely undemonstrated by scientific archaeology (but see Shishlina 2004). This is especially true in Semirech'ye, where no detailed studies of Bronze Age pastoralism as a specific regional problem have been conducted before the present one.

PASTORALISM IN SEMIRECH'YE, A CASE STUDY

Semirech'ye, located in present-day eastern Kazakhstan, is a territory known to have played an important role in generating the wider historical view of Inner Asian nomads because of its interstitial position in the trade networks and socioeconomic geography of the region (Bartol'd 1943, Kuz'mina 2004). Undoubtedly, the region has acted as an attractive environmental niche, trade corridor, and social nexus for more than four thousand years, in part due to its unique geographic characteristics. The Dzhungarian Gate, a wide mountain pass through northeastern Semirech'ye and the Dzhungar Mountains, has bridged western China and the steppes and deserts of present-day Kazakhstan and Central Asia for millennia (chapter 4). In medieval times, Semirech'ye was host to a northern segment of the Silk Route and the invasion path of Genghis Khan.[2] Details of ways the local populations of Semirech'ye experienced these various social, political, and economic interactions are less known. This is especially true when one looks beyond historical periods to prehistory, where our view of the environmental and cultural history of Semirech'ye is still largely undocumented.

Within Semirech'ye, the study zone of the Koksu River valley and Dzhungar Mountains was selected for several reasons. The environment of southeast Kazakhstan and the Dzhungar mountains varies drastically from sandy deserts to grassy steppe-lands and ultimately to alpine meadows within a geographic extent of less than 150 kilometers (west to east). This variation enabled a concise investigation of different ecological contexts within a logistically reasonable territory and allowed for the correlation between archaeological materials and different environmental niches. The Koksu River, one of the "seven rivers" that gives the Semirech'ye region its name,[3] flows west from its glacial sources in the mountainous border between China and Kazakhstan, down through Dzhungarian canyons and across glacially carved basins, fanning out into a fluvial delta where it joins with the Karatal river. Braids of the Karatal continue to flow across the lowland arid steppes before finally trickling together across sandy deserts to reach Lake Balkhash. In the foothills that overlook the course of the Koksu river, grassy tributary drainages lead to upland pastures, which today provide rich summer grazing for domesticated sheep, cattle, horses, and camels managed by Kazakh mobile pastoralists. Ethnohistorical and ethnographic documentation of the past three hundred years illustrates that the pastoralists of this region practiced seasonal transhumance, traveling up the valleys to high pasture in the summer and down to lower altitudes during the harsh winters (chapter 4; also Dakhshleiger 1978; Vainshtein 1991).

More intensive archaeological studies of the Semirech'ye region began in the 1950s as part of the eastern Kazakhstan expedition (Bernshtam 1952), the results of which were later included in the *Archaeological Map of Kazakhstan* (*Arkheologicheskaya Karta Kazakhstana* 1960). Of the prehistoric sites that were recorded during these surveys, only a few were excavated throughout the 1960s and 1970s (Maksimova 1961), and very few Bronze Age sites in Semirech'ye were described in the archaeological gazetteer at that time (Karabaspakova 1987). Nevertheless, these early surveys illustrated that that the region was rich in prehistoric archaeology with sites located throughout the river valleys and mountainous areas of the region, such as the Koksu River valley. Archaeological work in Semirech'ye during the late 1970s and 1980s led to the material associations of Bronze Age sites within the general classification of the Andronovo Cultural Community. More specifically, Bronze Age pastoralism is thought to have first appeared in Semirech'ye due to migratory "expansions" of Late Bronze Age (Fedorovo) groups into the southern regions of the steppe and mountain-steppe from the second quarter to the later half of the second millennium BCE (Kuz'mina 2004).

By virtue of the comparatively few known sites in the region, Semirech'ye was typically designated a frontier region of other, better-studied regional cultures areas such central Kazakhstan (Mar'yashev and Goryachev 1993; Margulan 1979). However, the current study illustrates that the Bronze Age landscape of the Dzhungar Mountains, and likely those across Semirech'ye, reflected well-populated territories before the start of the second millennium BCE and that pastoralist landscapes were forming prior to the proliferation of the Andronovo material horizon. Thus, pastoral sites in Semirech'ye provide key case studies of early independent development of pastoralist societies while offering a rich context to situate this regional development within a broader development of Eurasian pastoralist landscapes throughout the Bronze Age.

OUTLINE OF THE BOOK

I have organized this book into three parts. Chapters 1 and 2 explain the conceptual basis for the book and the scientific history and archaeological background of Bronze Age Eurasian pastoralism. Chapters 3, 4, and 5 present three key studies for the reconstruction of pastoralist landscapes in Semirech'ye: the environment, geography, and pastoral ecology; the ethnohistory and ethnography of recent pastoralists; and the archaeology of pastoral exploitation in the study zone. By way of synthesis, chapter 6 and the conclusion draw these lines of evidence together to characterize the economic and social form of pastoral landscapes in the Bronze Age and propose how we may understand the impact of local landscapes on the development of wider-scale networks of interaction.

Chapter 1 presents the conceptual elements that underpin the terms "pastoralism" and "landscape" while defining an analytical approach to studying local and global scales of interaction. I argue that the distinct character and social construction of a "pastoralist landscape" lies in the spatial and temporal variability that is fundamental to the practical employment of mobile pastoral strategies. These strategies include economic adaptations to dynamic ecological conditions; selective mobility patterns and periodic transformations of cultural identity; and the development of social histories through the long-term repetition of migratory rhythms and the establishment of interconnected locales.

Chapter 1 also outlines an approach to the study of prehistoric pastoralism that is rooted in landscape archaeology. This approach suggests that pastoralists create variable boundaries or "extents" to their experienced world, which are products of the way individuals and societies construct, animate, and exploit the habitat (social and environmental) within which they live. From this perspective, it is possible that different populations construct different landscape outlooks, even if there is considerable overlap in their physical passage over specific territories. Chapter 1 also presents a meta-narrative of regional communication that relates different groups within a network of expanding relationships, generated by the potential interactions of various societies over space and time. Specifically I propose that a practical state of "globalizing" may fruitfully explain the dialectics of local interactions in specific territories as they are communicated at wider regional scales.

Chapter 2 presents a critical review of the most recent Bronze Age archaeology of the Eurasian steppe. This chapter provides a current archaeological synthesis in order to characterize accurately what "pastoralism" means in a prehistoric Eurasian context. This essential assessment provides the reader with both the necessary background to understand the long-term development of social and economic trends in Eurasia and a critical foundation from which the established paradigms of regional interaction and culture change, which pervade steppe archaeology to date, can be reassessed.

A major problem with archaeological reconstructions of the Bronze Age of the Eurasian steppes is the reliance on the cultural-historical reality of various Bronze Age cultural groups as a basis for explanations of social and economic processes from the third millennium BCE to the beginning of the first millennium BCE. The typologically based cultural sub-divisions of the Andronovo category are based primarily on stylistic ceramic designs and formal trends in the distribution of material culture. This paradigm is approached from a critical stance; the past forty years of archaeological theory has demonstrated that "pots do not equal people." Thus, chapter 2 also delves into the history and theoretical basis for the construction of Eurasian steppe culture-history and scores a division between the existence of regional material forms and their ability to explain the processes of transmission or diffusion that facilitated their spread. Chapter 2 provides a critical repackaging of the Bronze Age archaeology of the steppe.

The landscape concept employed in this study partly relies on the premise that subsistence strategies in specific ecological niches are selected by people according to known physical conditions of their regional environment. Chapter 3 presents a detailed investigation of the physical geography, paleoenvironment, and pastoral ecology of the Eurasian steppe and Semirech'ye. Specifically, the chapter describes the productive resources of the Koksu valley and Dzhungar Mountains for pastoralist strategies and compares them to other steppe and mountain zones of Eurasia. The aim of chapter 3 is to establish and calculate the potential productivity of the study region for herding strategies and produce a spatial and temporal template of the available resources in different places and times according to the seasonal climatic dynamics and geography of the Dzhungar Mountains.

Chapter 3 is both a review of existing work and a contribution of new ecological analysis. The pasture productivity of the Dzhungar Mountains has not previously been calculated in terms of herding economies, thus, the chapter presents the capacity of the region's pastures and meadows to support herds of various domesticated animals. These original calculations are based on algorithms and units common to Russian and American agro-science, such as fodder quality of pastures, agricultural yield potential, and availability and dynamics of seasonal grasses. The calculations of these resource spheres are assessed without bias and lead to an optimization assessment of the region in terms of land-use strategies and economic productivity. Chapter 3 provides a detailed investigation of the impact of environmental and ecological variation in conditioning the structure and variability of pastoralist landscapes.

The nature of pastoralist social interaction is intricately tied to the creation and history of particular places as well as to the contingent environments that support their use (Koster 1977). Thus, the reiteration of social connections in both spheres is fundamental in the archaeological investigation of prehistoric pastoralists. Chapter 4 presents ethnographic and ethnohistorical accounts of pastoral strategies and social interaction in Semirech'ye to show how ecological conditions and historical contexts influenced the construction of pastoralist landscapes and affected the selection and practical employment of various loci of interaction in recent history. Chapter 4 also addresses the dynamic shaping of economic and political arenas across the Dzhungar Mountains and explains how this territory was structured by pastoral interactions throughout the last five hundred years. Ethnographic and ethnohistoric investigations of the way populations have lived in the Dzhungar Mountains provide a vivid insight into the factors that affect patterns of mobility, trade, and interaction and further improve our ability to contextualize archaeological data vis-à-vis a select set of ethnographically observed social and economic models.

Chapter 5 delves further into the pastoralist archive of the Dzhungar Mountains and Semirech'ye by presenting archaeological evidence spanning more than four thousand years to illustrate the dynamic shapes of pastoralist landscapes in the study region from a longitudinal perspective. More than 350 newly discovered archaeological sites in the Koksu River valley form the core of a detailed investigation of local pastoralist landscape from 2500 BCE and provide the archaeological basis for the thesis of this book. Archaeologically, the survey data serve to establish the extent of the Bronze Age and later pastoralist landscapes. Pastoralist land-use patterns and changes in the distribution of burials, ritual contexts, and settlements are derived from this data. The geography of pastoralist sites is also used to propose the scheduling of certain activities within a structure of both seasonal or temporal change and spatial relocation. The survey data provide material evidence to assess the degree of mobility, pattern of land use, and variability of pastoralist ways of life as they are imprinted on the landscape. Archaeological sites in the study zone also illustrate the chronological and geographic continuity between prehistoric and later strategies from both ecological and social vantage points.

On the basis of the archaeological data as well as the environmental background and ethnohistory presented in chapters three, four and five, chapter six presents a new synthesis of social interaction among Bronze Age pastoralists. Chapter 6 illustrates how the formation of "ordered yet variable" networks served to shape the economic, social, and ritual landscapes in the study zone during the Bronze Age, while contributing to broader developments further afield. Variations in local practices as well as the distribution of non-local materials and technologies are contextualized in light of a detailed reconstruction of pastoral mobility strategies and modes of interaction based on the Bronze Age archaeological record.

The conclusion offers a wider spatial and temporal perspective on the development of interlocking pastoralist landscapes and the central role of social interaction in the formation of larger regional networks and longer historical trends in Eurasia. This section also expands the scope of the analysis to situate the book's thesis in a wider discourse concerning institutional and social change in human history.

1

CONCEPTUALIZING PASTORALIST LANDSCAPES

Does the snowgoose, airlifting itself from the warming shores of Chincoteague Island, visualize the Arctic tundra toward which it is heading to breed? Does the bee, radar-beamed to a particular tree in an apple orchard, have a conscious dream of yellow nectar in the unfolding white blossoms? Does the beaver, felling his first trees across a narrow stream, have a mental image of the pond that will rise behind his dam?

DANSEREAU 1975, 67

THE NATURE OF PASTORALISM

Dansereau's question is compelling because fundamentally it asks us to differentiate between human cognition and animal perception. Bees surely recognize the existence of the blossom and are well adapted to exploit its nectar with inherent deftness, but a more complicated philosophical inquiry is whether bees perceive their own ontology through the spatial and temporal geography of their socioeconomic practices.

At the core of the concept "landscape" is precisely the idea that humans do perceive their own ontology: mental maps allow humans to conceive and socialize their environment. Our landscapes, therefore, are emblematic of our historical accumulation of knowledge and ability to conceptualize our behavior and interactions at a variety of scalar extents. This chapter presents the definition of mobile pastoralist landscapes through a discussion of three integrated concepts: pastoralism, landscape, and interaction at local and global scales. I argue that mobile pastoralists of Eurasia generate landscapes across temporally and spatially protracted scales through their strategic negotiation of variable social and environmental contexts. Locales such as seasonal pasture zones, settlements, and ritual sites shape a broad geography of interactions, which, I suggest, frames the most distinguishing ontological reality of pastoralist populations.

Nomadic pastoralism is most commonly understood as a social and economic strategy predominantly based in routined (such as seasonal) migratory management of domesticated herd animals (Lattimore 1940, 54; Barth 1964, 4; Khazanov 1994, 17).

Etymologically, the words "nomadism" and "pastoralism" imply pasturing or raising of herds (Salzman 2002, 245). A number of scholars, such as Barfield (1993, 4), note that the term "nomadism" is also used in association with other mobility strategies (such as hunting/foraging) (see also Barnard and Wendrich 2008). Thus, "nomadic" is commonly used as a referent to movement or mobility, and "pastoralism" refers to a productive economic strategy: "raising livestock on natural pastures" (Salzman 2002, 245).

Much of the earliest ethno-historical work concerning pastoralists was guided by the categorical inclusion or exclusion of particular societies as "nomads" (Myres 1941; Bacon 1958). Although arguably more sophisticated, the categorization of socio-functional types of nomadic systems can still be found in contemporary literature (Khazanov 1994) and its critique has also been prolific (Ingold 1985). Archaeological studies of nomadic pastoralism have been hindered by reductive modes of classification as well. Roger Cribb (1991, 16) astutely notes that the archaeologist's ability to document the origins or emergence of nomadic pastoralism, for example, has depended largely on the identification of defining attributes, such as extent of mobility or inclusiveness of agriculture, to index typologically a population along an arbitrary continuum of nomadism.

Salzman (2002, 249) characterizes nomadic strategies as highly variable and flexible, rather than typologically distinct. Over thirty years ago he noted how early western scholars struggled to appropriately define "nomadism" (Salzman 1967, 115–118) by overstating the reliability of typological categories of pastoral nomads.

> Throughout the literature, particularly plaguing general discussions, we find repeated references to "pure nomadism," "semi-nomadism," "transhumance," and the like. Each ideal type is based upon a combination of characteristics, usually including type of animal, degree and/or pattern of movement, participation in agricultural activities, [or] type of housing. These ideal types invariably obscure through oversimplification and rigidity the variables at play because they ignore the many subtle and gross variations along the dimension of any given variable and because they presume a very limited number of possible value-combinations of different variables.
>
> Salzman 1972, 67

Since then, decades of ethnography have provided a more nuanced understanding of the range of pastoralist systems. For this reason, typological categorization of nomadic pastoralism in current ethnography has been superseded by more focused attention on the historical and practical particulars of "mobile pastoral" ways of life (Humphrey and Sneath 1999, 1). Kavoori (1999, 14) optimistically remarks that "we are well past the earlier sterile typological concerns that sought to classify pastoralists as nomads, seminomads, transhumants, and so on."

From this ethnographic legacy, we learn that community-level mobility and reliance on domestic herds are archetypical and variable traits of most pastoral systems. Mobility strategies commonly associated with raising herds—often in marginal environments—are also continuously changing according to opportunities and risks presented by social, political, and economic interaction among pastoralists and their neighbors. Consequently, the variable geography and timing of interaction among mobile pastoralists widens the realm of strategic options available to them, helping them succeed under often uncertain ecological and social pressures. For pastoral populations, interactive geographies alter the range of practical possibilities for negotiating risks and opportunities and contribute to their social identity. Thus, interaction presents a key dialectic catalyst for the growth and metamorphosis of pastoralist social networks. I propose that the adaptive vitality of such interactive networks is a function of the maintenance of links between nodes, or specific sites, which pastoralists achieve predominantly through strategies of mobility.

This study uses the term "mobile pastoralism" (Humphrey and Sneath 1996, 1) as a general phrase to describe those societies whose subsistence economy (direct and indirect) is structured by patterned yet variable mobile management of domesticated herd animals and whose social, political, and ritual practices and interactions are associated with, and co-generated by, such mobility and pastoral emphasis. Mobility here describes a generalist strategy of patterned movement, drawing attention to the practical differentiation between migratory pastoral populations and groups whose way of life demands a sedentary strategy. Although mobility for pastoralists can be variable through time, I emphasize how patterned movements across local terriories—even if variable—fundamentally shape the extent to which social and economic institutions are stretched across a framework of interactions. This study explores the ways mobile pastoralists form durable contexts of interaction as well as the flexible employment of those contexts across space and through time. I apply this model to the region of Semirech'ye to illustrate that Bronze Age pastoralists, for example, periodically altered the extent of their mobility patterns as well as their degree of investment in fixed loci. Yet, the structure of these interactive networks is shown to be durable long after the Bronze Age, ultimately shaping pastoral ways of life in Eurasia for millennia.

The definition of interaction used in this study is broad in both a geographic and temporal sense, in that there are many conditions through which contact and communication can occur (Stein 2002). These scenarios include face-to-face contact, symbolic exchange through signs and monuments, trade or economic exchange, kinship relationships, war and conflict, and many more (Schortman and Urban 1987). At its most general, interaction is defined as communication and social interface through numerous forms of person-to-person (or group-to-group) discourse. Discourse is structured by the practice[1] of agents who are socially and economically engaged within a co-experienced territory and through the selective coordination of activities in space and time (Giddens 1984, 132; Stein 2002, 906). This is what Giddens calls "focused interaction" (1984, 72). Interaction in this study also includes what Giddens calls "unfocussed interaction" or unintentional communication, contact, or conveyance through physical co-experience of a context, without an explicit choice to coordinate activities (1984, 72). In this case, specific contexts may be occupied by interacting parties but interaction does not demand that people be at the same place at the same time. Archaeological monuments such as burial or rock-art sites are exemplary settings for this form of interaction, and foster a condition of communication and interaction through their symbolic representation and significance of place between parties even when both parties are not simultaneously present.

The archaeological remains discussed in this study evince both aspects of interaction and illustrate the economic and social practices of individuals and groups in specific places and across a localized territorial extent. Giddens's concept of interaction as active and non-discursive patterns that span spatial and temporal scales is crystallized, in my view, through a nuanced focus on localized relationships where iterative and elemental interactions function to condition social, political, and economic networks at larger scales. The dialectic between interaction at the local scale and its structural impact at the macro-scale is fundamental to the role of mobile pastoralists in the trajectory of regional political economies.[2] Mobile pastoral systems also reflect highly heterogeneous institutional structures for managing social and ecological demands within a variety of environmentally, politically, and ideologically dynamic contexts (Irons 1974, Salzman 1972).

Even though the terminology used to classify mobile pastoral systems is frequently equivocal, archaeologists may benefit from the ethnographic observation that societies engaged in mobile forms of pastoralism commonly construct a social landscape that reflects consistent strategies for herd management across predictable ecological contexts while also eliciting a variable set of strategies for negotiating social, economic, ritual, or political conditions. Archaeological investigations of pastoralism to date, however, have yet to shed fully the categorical view of nomadic societies, thereby hindering our ability to track how pastoralist strategies emerged amidst often heterogeneous environmental and social contexts (Marshall and Hildebrand 2004).

THE ARCHAEOLOGY OF PASTORALISM

The study of prehistoric mobile pastoralism has suffered from the lack of an approach that targets the condition of variability and the formative role of interaction on the economic and social strategies of pastoralists. Rather, one of the primary interests for archaeologists engaged with the study of pastoralists is the emergence or origins of nomadism, an endeavor that illustrates the use of categorical definitions of "nomads" and ignores the likelihood that mobile pastoral adaptations were part of a varied and iterated process of development.

In their now classic model for the origins of nomadism in the Near East, Lees and Bates (Lees and Bates 1974) suggest that nomadic pastoralism emerged as a specialized economy from a context of mixed domestication (farming and localized herding) when irrigation technology allowed agriculturalists to exploit arid zones located farther away from the rain-fed areas that supported dry farming in Mesopotamia. Logically, these new lands would also be farther away from rich pastures, so those segments of the society engaged in herding would be forced to travel greater distances in order to adequately feed their herds. These amplified scales of mobility would demand increased specialization both in terms of human and animal ecology and would separate pastoralist segments of society from those engaged in planting. As a result, dislocated social groups would develop their own social institutions, relevant to their increasingly mobile lifestyle.

Lees and Bates's model of the transition from agriculture to more specialized pastoralism has been persuasive in the Near Eastern context (cf. Kohler-Rollefson 1992; (Zarins 1990; Danti 2000), and others have provided variations of this model for some regions of Iran and Central Asia (Adams 1974; Hole 1978; Hiebert 1994). But in all these scenarios, pastoralists represented a marginalized element of settled agricultural society who were correspondingly pressured into specializing their occupation in marginal environments as "nomads" (Cribb 1991). Lees and Bates are explicit about not using an "ideal typical" definition of nomadism (1974, 188), and their model recognizes that there was likely a gradual procession from settled agro-pastoralism to nomadic pastoralism. As they primarily focus on discerning the systemic relationship between "different" productive modes (i.e., irrigated agriculture and specialized pastoralism), they nevertheless cite a point of no return when a "nomadic" way of life becomes so specialized that it is rendered intelligible as a distinct social form.

Soviet archaeologists and ethnologists, working within a Marxist historical paradigm, have also suggested that Eurasian pastoralists were first represented by a segment of agriculturally based societies, which were slowly separated due to population pressure and increasing aridity in the Eurasian steppes at the start of the first millennium BCE (Gryaznov 1955; Masanov 1995). Khazanov (1994, 91) argues that the problem in equating earlier evidence for mobile pastoralism in prehistory with the emergence of "nomadism" in Eurasia is that "There are no grounds for thinking that pastoralists of the third and even the second millennia BCE were *real nomads*" (emphasis mine). For Khazanov, the key limitation to the identification of nomadic pastoralism as an emerging mode of life in Inner Asia is that earlier prehistoric groups do not match with a historically derived definition of "nomads" per se.

Khazanov suggests that "pure nomadism" (vs. semi-nomadism, distant-pastures husbandry, or seasonal transhumance) is characterized by the "total absence of agriculture, even in a supplementary capacity" (Khazanov 1994, 19). This, he argues, did not become a predominant mode of life until the mid first millennium BCE, among Iron Age groups such as the Scythians, Cimmerians and Saka (Khazanov 1994, 94). Yet, Miller-Rosen and Chang's evidence for the production of domesticated crops in Semirech'ye around 750 BCE problematize the claim for "pure nomadism" among the Iron Age Saka (Chang et al. 2003), while data I present in this volume illustrate the development of mobile herding strategies without substantial agricultural production as early as the mid third millennium BCE (also Frachetti and Mar'yashev 2007).

The archaeological record of the western Eurasian steppe does suggest that domesticated sheep/goats and cattle first emerged in relation to mixed agro-pastoral subsistence strategies of the Neolithic. Settled agricultural practices of Neolithic societies associated with late Sredny Stog and Tripolye cultural materials are well dated to Neolithic phases (c. 5000–4000 BCE) in the territory north of the Black Sea and in southern Russia (Rassamakin 1999). Predominantly pastoralist societies are not documented in the western steppe region until the start of the third millennium BCE, when they emerge in relation to the Yamnaya cultural horizon. Given their geographic proximity as well as their ties in material culture, it seems likely that specialized pastoralism amongst the Yamnaya may illustrate one of the first distinctions between agricultural and herding communities in the north-Caspian region around 3000 BCE—but the motivations for this departure are not clearly enumerated.

In the western steppe we may confidently look to agricultural societies for the earliest regional evidence of animal domestication, but the extent to which pastoralists were at all marginalized or directly derivative from agricultural socioeconomic systems is unclear. In fact, recent work in the central steppe at Botai seems to suggest that pastoralist strategies emerged there as an independent innovation that had little to do with agricultural societies in its early stages (chapter 2). Current research in the western steppe is also beginning to illustrate that early pastoralist populations were diverse in their economic strategies. Archaeological studies by David Anthony in the Samara valley illustrate the use of wild plants with domestic animals around 2100 BCE (Anthony et al. 2005). Furthermore, his excavations at Krasnosamarskoe have not revealed any evidence of domesticated plants in Middle Bronze Age contexts, even though a comprehensive flotation strategy was employed (Popova 2006). Natalia Shishlina (2004) also notes this trend at Early/Middle Bronze Age sites in the north Caucasus, where her paleobotanical study sites were also devoid of domesticated plants.

Whereas early pastoral economies in the western steppe were likely derived in part from neighboring Neolithic agricultural societies, ties between agricultural economies and early forms of specialized mobile pastoralism are without evidence in the central and eastern Eurasian steppes.[3] For example, Eneolithic groups related to the Atbasar and Botai assemblages of the central steppes reveal no evidence for a developed agricultural economy in the third millennium BCE (Kislenko and Tatarintseva 1999). Early third millennium BCE groups of southwest Siberia such as the Afanas'evo in the Minusinsk basin were primarily hunter/fishers, with only incipient forms of cattle and goat herding (Khlobystina 1973; Shilov 1975; Vadetskaya 1986). Faunal evidence in these eastern steppe regions indicates that pastoral exploitation of cattle, sheep/goats, and horses predominanted by the middle part of the third millennium BCE (Tsalkin 1964), well before the introduction of agriculture in Eastern Eurasia.

If we invest in the idea that Bronze Age steppe populations were largely mobile pastoralists (Kosarev 1984, 60), a rough and ready synthesis of the available archaeological data concerning the long-term exploitation of the Eastern Eurasian steppe suggests that pastoralism emerged from a hunter/fisher lifestyle of the Eneolithic (c. 3500 BCE), was formalized during the Early Bronze Age (c. 2500 BCE) and only later during the early Iron Age was integrated with agricultural activities. This position is supported by Vainshtein, who argues that models of agricultural transition to more mobile forms of pastoralism are archaeologically untenable in the eastern steppe, and "Ruling out the immediate transition to nomadic pastoralism by hunter tribes of the steppe . . . is hardly grounded . . ." (Vainshtein 1978, 129). From this introductory overview we may conclude that the "agriculture to pastoralism" developmental model is dubious for the eastern Eurasian steppes, because the current archaeology seems to support a direct transition from mobile hunting/fishing economies to mobile pastoralism.

Future research may also illustrate that the diffusion of domestication practices is more intricately linked with the intensification of formative pastoralist networks across Inner Asia, rather than being the result of migratory waves of marginalized agriculturalists. Bronze Age pastoralists promoted a network of interconnections between local and regional groups by redefining the extents of their landscape; the landscape was regulated by the routinized spatial and temporal patterns of their seasonal migrations and was extended or manipulated in concert with periodic changes in those routines. Beyond the local landscape, periodic variation in migratory distances and communication between regional groups may have generated interactions between groups across wider regional boundaries, potentially linking societies in a chain of contact that was irregular and punctuated in temporal and geographic senses.

Early archaeological parallels between pastoral systems of Bronze Age steppe societies and those of ethno-historically known nomads were generally based on one-dimensional evidence, such as the presence of domesticated animals in archaeological contexts (Gryaznov 1955; Shilov 1975; Kosarev 1981; Tsalkin 1964). This type of evidence does not, in itself, clarify the potential variation in migration distances, settlement patterns, seasonal mobility, or corollary social and economic practices that may have characterized early pastoral ways of life (Vainshtein 1980, 59). As a result, the reconstruction of such practices in Bronze Age societies (Sal'nikov 1967, 245; Kosarev 1981, 208) has been limited to a normalized understanding of what Eurasian steppe nomads "do," derived from essentialized interpretations of ethno-historical and ethnographic descriptions (Rudenko 1927; Levin and Cheboksarov 1955; Khazanov 1978, 44–45), rather than from reconstructions of pastoral strategies based on independent assessments of archaeological evidence.

A ready assessment of the evidence for emerging pastoralism across the Eurasian steppe reflects a geographically differentiated process. The prevalent use of domesticated animals in the steppe zone in the Eneolithic and Bronze Age is not clearly related to the emergence of agricultural societies, unlike the situations in Mesopotamia, the Yellow River Basin, or even Neolithic Europe. In fact, in many regions of the steppe, like those east of the Urals, domestication may be more closely paired with the emergence of mobile herding without significant dependence on domestic plants. Just as agriculture was revolutionary for Neolithic societies in Mesopotamia, Europe, and China, the development of mobile pastoralism was equally transformative to the boundaries and scale of social interactions, political organization, and economic growth across Eurasia at the start of the Bronze Age.

If the essential character of mobile pastoralism is indexed by a dynamic geo-temporal distribution of social and economic interactions, we may account for both the structure and the variation of pastoralist communities through the landscapes they produce. Pastoralist landscapes physically embody the local continuities and fluctuations of nomadic strategies through time and provide a recoverable context through which archaeologists can trace the wider-scale trajectories of interrelationships among prehistoric and later societies of Central Eurasia.

PASTORALIST LANDSCAPES

Landscape, as a general concept, has been variously defined by geographers, anthropologists, archaeologists, and others (Ashmore and Knapp 1999; Johnson 2007, Ansheutz et al. 2001). Here, a *pastoralist landscape* is defined as the socially and naturally (co-) created contexts that frame the perceived and physical extents of practices and experiences of pastoral societies. The perceived extent of a society's landscape is a product of the spatial and temporal patterns of that society's behavior, which is contiguous with the actual distribution of particular locations coupled with the historical memory and stochastic accumulation of socially meaningful locales in the collective cultural geography of interrelated agents and groups (Hägerstrand 1975). From this view, the landscape is a socially perceived construction that reflects the active layering of ritual, political, economic, and natural relationships as they are mutually distributed across a territory and co-generated through time (Stoddart 2000, 3–4; Ingold 2000, 189).

Pastoralist landscapes are defined by the scalar flexibility of both the perceived and physical boundaries of interaction and regional exploitation. The physical extent of pastoralist landscapes is dictated partly by environmental conditions such as topography, hydrology, vegetation, and climate. This is not a claim for environmental determinism but rather for environmental pragmatism. Pastoralist mobility, for example, is first and foremost a strategic response to the environmental conditions used to grow pastoralists' primary subsistence resource: their herds. Mobility orbits are strategically changed in reaction to short-term fluctuations in the natural environment such as extremely wet or cold summers in alpine meadows, for example. These pragmatic choices impact the environment in both intended and unintended ways. For example, in years of unusually high rainfall in mountain steppe contexts, upland meadows may not be grazed as usual because of the inclement conditions at higher altitudes and the greater abundance of adequate pasture at lower elevations. The effects of this altered plan are then passed back to the environment as midland pastures become overused and alpine meadows become overgrown. Thus, for each series of reciprocal reactions, there is an anthropogenic ripple effect that lasts longer than the immediate condition. Physical constraints of the environment are not insurmountable but demand strategic practices for particular outcomes (Stone 1996). Ultimately, the environment contributes to the structure of pastoralist landscapes because it presents conditions that are experienced in actual ways at the most local practical scale by pastoral groups, even though the environment itself is affected by forces within and outside the immediately perceived experiences of populations.[4]

The analytical scale of pastoral landscapes (and others) is defined across four dimensions, three of space and one of time, which are scaled in response to both social and natural constraints and evolve in form according to the manipulation and impact by humans on the boundaries of their social geography, natural environment, and sociopolitical interactions (Ingold 2000, 189; Smith 2003, 5–7). As an analogy, we find within ethnographic studies that mobile pastoral societies exploit and define a territory that is socially significant on a variety of scales and according to a variety of motivations. These may include feeding their animals, negotiating economic and political relationships, meeting social obligations, and opportunistically reacting to the changing conditions of their environmental and social habitat (McGlade 1995).

Pastoralist landscapes reflect both enduring and changeable contexts and illustrate variations in patterns of human activity over time and territory. Thus, the pastoralist landscape, writ large, cannot be presented as a synchronic snapshot of the geography or spatial layout of nomadic life but rather must be characterized by the constant renegotiation and re-iteration between the conceptual reality and practical experiences of the societies which define it. For example, the pastoralist landscape of the Koksu valley exemplifies scalar change consistent with its dynamic history as much as it illustrates a structured pastoral ecology dictated by annual variances in pasture resources and climate. To understand pastoralist societies diachronically, we must trace the factors that impose structure on the shape of their landscapes and give attention to the variability, contingency, and opportunities within that structure which enable extensions of interactive contexts beyond synchronic boundaries. The geography of interaction and communication for mobile pastoral societies is approached in this study through a conception of societies and individuals within constantly changing temporal and spatial currents, rather than geographically or chronologically framing them vis-à-vis social or cultural categories (such as the Andronovo or the Mongols).

This book defines the conceptual scale of particular pastoralist landscapes from the archaeological remains and imprints of the social geographies of pastoral people. Seasonal settlement camps, burial grounds, pasture zones, and rock-art represent the result of human investment and occupation of particular locations and practical patterns of movement and land use in and around those locales. Pastoralists often conceptually define their social territory to encompass a wide geographic space, but their practical lives exist within a physical habitat bound between permanent and temporary locations (such as summer pastures which may vary from year to year). Through repeated practices, their perceived landscape becomes physically tangible, and many of these periodically activated locations are recoverable through archaeology. Human constructions are footprints across the landscape that speak to a wider social arena of occupation. In pastoralist landscapes, these footprints reveal a web of migratory patterns and social interactions underwriting the dynamic picture of pastoralist life over the *longue durée*.

SOCIAL INTERACTION AND LANDSCAPE

Rather than stopping points along a geographic highway, the reality and historical significance of particular places: a burial ground, a pasture, a spring, a rock face, have been embedded in the landscape by the local experiences and perceptions of Eurasian mobile pastoralists for more than four thousand years. Mobile pastoralists construct their social geographies through the practical employment of, and investment in, historically meaningful places that accumulate significance through a palimpsest of interactions. The time depth and Cartesian distribution of regional pastoralist landscapes, the periodic interfaces between "place" and "experience," are recoverable geographically as well as archaeologically (Smith 2003).

Key to the concept of interaction is the routinized geography of human experience in the landscape (Giddens 1984, 119). Specifically, this study relies on the observation that people interact across four dimensions. Thus, interaction in the landscape occurs at "nodes" in the landscape as well as at the "spaces between" those nodes, while spatial patterns set in time dictate when people come into contact and the nature their contact (Bender 2002; Upham 1992, 139).

In the case of the Bronze Age steppe cultures, variation in the strategies of regional groups underlies the extension and renegotiation of the landscape over time. Even slight fluctuations in practice, such as traveling an extra ten kilometers for better pasture or relocating a winter settlement due to unfavorable social conditions, structurally fosters the development of new networks of interaction between social groups and individuals and can have significant effects on the distribution and diffusion of material culture, ideas, and technology across wider geographic arenas. Like all landscapes, pastoralist landscapes mutate in concert with the scale and nature of the social interactions of regional populations.

The social landscape of mobile pastoralism reflects both a physically extant and culturally perceived phenomenon, so that contexts of interaction may be a result of changing perceptions of the geography of active nodes and empty space within one's practical experience. For Bronze Age pastoralists of the Koksu River valley, for example, the geography of interaction is tied to the variable patterns of their annual mobility as well as the opportunities presented to them through social venues such as ritual and domestic contexts. Together, these factors situate interactive opportunities temporally and spatially throughout the entire landscape and contribute to different outcomes for predictable and opportunistic encounters, such as accession of valuable goods, new social alliances, or conflicts.

Although a theoretically broad concept, interaction can be documented practically through tangible contexts or materials, such as archaeological evidence of ritual practices at burial and ceremonial centers, social and economic interactions at shared environmental niches such as pastures, or trade, marriage, or conflict around domestic arenas. Although the overarching landscape of interaction associated with the societies discussed was likely more dynamic than these places alone can illustrate, communication and contact can more plausibly be recreated using these tangible cases.

The motivation for interaction is a difficult aspect of social dynamics to interpret from archaeological materials. Schortman and Urban (1987, 1992) have traced the way interaction has been theorized throughout the history of archaeology and suggest that early archaeologists viewed the mechanisms of interaction as an engine for either cultural diffusion or technological progress and placed the motivations for cultural interaction in basic "survival" fitness (Schortman and Urban 1992, 8). Schortman (1989) has forwarded the alternative idea that interaction is tied to social identity, whereby factors beyond evolutionary selection for improved technology or energy preservation, such as status, group affinity, wealth, social mobility, power, and other forms of "social capital," figure into the rationale and motivation for interaction.

> Various identities have advantages and disadvantages under different circumstances of interaction with social actors who themselves possess particular identities. Individuals employ their identities strategically to accomplish their own goals vis-à-vis other social actors. From this perspective, interaction is a series of encounters in which people adjust their publicly proclaimed identities to maximize their own advantage.
>
> Schortman 1989, 54

Although this study does not explicitly explore the nature of identity creation among Bronze Age pastoralists per se, the concept underlies the issue of interaction. Promotion of identity can be seen as a general class of motivations for interaction; one that in its own right may manifest itself in a variety of ways such as desire for power, interest in better property, or the negotiation of social roles. Thus, in considering the role of pastoralists in the social history of the Eurasian steppe, interaction is seen as a constant factor in the development of social roles and identity boundaries, which contribute to the nested scales of its landscape. Although every motivation or explanation for interactions cannot be gleaned from archaeological material, this view of interaction as a means for negotiating identities presents a broad and encompassing paradigm that is useful for modeling macro-regional relationships of Bronze Age societies in Eurasia.

The purpose of recreating the ways steppe societies encoded and employed their landscape is to develop an understanding of the spatial and temporal dynamics of human communication and interaction, especially as it relates to the nature and impact of mobile pastoralism in the history of the Eurasian steppe. Communication and interaction are presented as fundamental processes for the negotiation of political and social identities, economic exchanges, stylistic diffusion and technological transfer, which have been noted as key attributes of Bronze Age pastoralist societies of Eurasia and subsequent cultural developments of the steppe.

In much of the literature on the Andronovo period, interaction (*vzaimodeistvie*) or connection (*svyaz'*) is presented as a result of population displacement between different regions of the steppe and is documented through historical linguistic and material associations between regional "culture groups" (Kuz'mina 1994, 248). For example, Potemkina (1995b, 14) writes that "contact and interaction of ancient cultures is one of the most important factors for historical progression [of Bronze Age societies]. Specifically, connections shown in various [material] forms illustrate differentiable cultural syntheses and cultural transformations—both important factors for the genesis of new cultures."

Culture, in Soviet terminology, is a distinct material manifestation of social identity (Dragadze 1980). Thus, models of interaction and connection that rely on direct relationships between material cultural forms and a social entity equate the boundaries between material cultural distributions and the mutability of social identity, conflating the process of social contact between regionally distinct populations with the progressive formation of macro-scale cultural entities. Under such a paradigm, material hybridity or replacement carries an assumed correlation with demographic drift from different territories, such that one regional group's material culture and ethno-linguistic characteristics (and sometimes genetics as well) are transferred to another region or group by physical displacement, material diffusion, or regional colonization. Migration and population displacement result in the subsequent formation of a new culture and either the spread or displacement of distinguishable populations (Kuz'mina 1998). In her revision of interaction among Bronze Age steppe populations, Koryakova (1998, 211) suggests that

> Any culture corresponding to an ethnic or social structure develops from the interaction between internal and external factors. The dynamics of cultural genesis can be revealed in the interrelation between tradition and innovation, which 'work' differently in different spheres. A culture passes through several stages: formation, progressivity, stabilization and transformation or disintegration. Stable stages are reflected better in archaeological material, usually represented by a number of similar sites within a given area. All the factors of social development act in balance, although this can be easily disturbed if even one basic component is changed for any reason.

The reconstruction of Bronze Age social interaction developed within this study stems from the view that societies are indeed the agents and recipients of diffused cultural forms but that social identities are more directly related to the practical manner in which individuals and groups exploit their environment and utilize material culture in socially activated contexts. This perspective is especially relevant to mobile pastoral societies, because they commonly influence diffuse geographic and social arenas of interaction and consequently manipulate the extents of their experienced geography to accommodate changing identity boundaries at local and global scales.

LOCAL AND GLOBAL STRUCTURE OF PASTORALIST LANDSCAPES

This book renders the form and variability of pastoralist landscapes newly visible through the fluctuating mobility of herd management and through the mutual interactions, trade networks, and political relations of civilizations of differing scales[5] from prehistoric to historic times. The social geography of Eurasia has had various shapes throughout history, defined by human activity set within a dynamic local environmental and social milieu and articulated at wider scales through the tendrils of stochastically connected networks and regional interrelations (Lattimore 1940, 21; Sinor 1969, 2). The nature of interactions among steppe populations are rarely investigated from the perspective of the pastoralists themselves, thus the characterization of various strategic systems may seem to be categorically and historically discontinuous, rather than indexing the flexibility in the local and normal development of regional populations.

Historical and ethnographic data indicate that pastoralists of Semirech'ye, for example, migrated as much as one hundred kilometers on a yearly basis, living in the highlands in the summer and in the desert lowlands in the winter. Yet this appears not to always have been the case. Bronze Age settlements in the Koksu valley are typically located from ten to fifty kilometers from rich upland pastures, and the longer distances likely represented the upper limits of pastoral mobility. Therefore, this study conceptualizes the "normal" extent to a local pastoral landscape gingerly because variation in the economic and social strategies of Bronze Age pastoralists precludes a set definition of the local landscape. I argue that variation was the very impulse that positioned pastoralists of the Bronze Age as agents to promote a network of interaction that bridged local and "global" landscapes over time. The synergy between local and global landscapes is presented as a process by which we can understand the spread of material culture across and between different social geographies.

"Local" refers to the geographic extents of practices and experiences of pastoral populations at a scale documented through recoverable contexts of interaction as well as those elements of the perceived landscape that can be documented archaeologically (or ethnographically). The Bronze Age definition of local cultural territory may have been inherently variable, but particular locations demonstrate significant spatio-temporal continuity with an embedded sense of importance for structuring the ecology of herd exploitation and the negotiation of ritual and political relationships. This archaeologically defined "heart" of the prehistoric landscape emerges from the geographic distribution of the most commonly exploited settlement contexts (based on their size and frequency), by prevalent locations of large Bronze Age cemeteries, and by the locus of thousands of rock-art panels.

The viable heart of a pastoralist landscape forms through constant reiteration of experiences that provide a fundamental sustainability of human populations across space and time. This reorients our focus on nomads from existing on the outer limits of civilized landscapes toward seeing their critical role in weaving local phenomena across a global fabric of social relationships. In light of the proposed variable patterns of mobility associated with pastoralist strategies, even archaeological contexts documented at a distance from pastoralist contexts of deep investment may still articulate within "local" extents of variation, provided there is sufficient practical and material evidence to suggest an active social link between these nodes and others that illustrate significant spatial and temporal durability.

This definition of the local context highlights an epistemological problem concerning the criteria we use to categorize clinal phenomenon or to define when one "thing" starts and another ends. The widest analytical scale of a pastoralist landscape, as a whole, is difficult to delineate, in that it is derived from the geographic extents of the archaeological and environmental contexts that form it, which themselves reflect fluctuations that were part of the dynamic nature of prehistoric mobile lifestyles. Thus the analysis of the local landscape may not account for all of the variability represented in past practices, but illustrates those nodes that were formative in shaping the spatial and temporal scales of social interaction.

The dynamic structure of local-scale networks of interaction has a major impact on the shape of epi-local phenomenon. The extent of the macro-landscape is therefore respectively dynamic, meaning that from a teleological perspective it can range from anything outside the perceived and experienced local landscape (the epi-local) to the "absolutely" global. Locally reproduced pastoralist landscapes resonate with and dialectically instruct globally recoverable meta-phenomena, and thus may inform contemporary debates of globalization from a new perspective.

To be clear, "globalization" as such is a contemporary process by which the economic and social activity of agents (individuals or groups) has expanded to encompass a literally global arena, ultimately linked through discursive and non-discursive mechanisms and often seemingly unrelated social trajectories. In the context of contemporary global markets, for example, this process relies on the renegotiation of political relationships, economic networks, and social boundaries between individuals, groups, societies, or nation-states. Globalization describes the scalar reformation of the conceptual geography and social arenas for discourse inherent in social, economic, and political interactions (Woods 2000). Yet globalization provides a rich theoretical paradigm to reconcile local, regional, and supra-regional interaction and communication and is useful for exploring the complex political and economic dynamics of past societies whose interactive institutions closely resemble geographically and temporally iterated networks (Frachetti in press).

We may consider that the reformulation of local landscapes through expanding and contracting strategies of mobility, communication, and interaction among pastoralists are generated from the local perceptions of phenomena that incur wider-scale input (e.g., environmental or political change). We may recognize that throughout history and prehistory, iterative changes in the geography and timing of interaction resulted in the spread of innovation and technology as well as the formation of novel social and political structures at scales that can be relatively defined as "global." In the Bronze Age and in later periods of Eurasian history, "globalizing" conditions can be traced to the interstices of interaction across pastoralist landscapes.

The most basic scalar element of globalization is "globality." Beck (2000, 10) discusses globality in terms of the interconnectedness of societies around the world, where "Various economic, cultural and political forms . . . collide with one another." For the twenty-first century, the perceived world spans the entire globe (ergo globe-ality), but the perception of the "whole world" is a historically contingent concept, which must be scaled according to the technological and geographic perspective of particular times and societies in the past. For example, as late as the fifteenth century, the "perceived world" of western Europeans was substantially smaller than the "globe" we know today, which is only to say that the widest global picture would not have entailed an analogous geographic area, but nonetheless would have entailed a comparable ontological distance from oneself or one's society. Thus, globality could be more generally defined as the interconnectedness or juxtaposition of oneself or one's society with the most extensive scale of one's perceived existing world.

Globalizing is a state of practice rather than a particular process (i.e., globalization is one process of globalizing). The requisite contextual conditions for globalizing to occur are common to many political-economic arenas and include both a recognition of organizational boundaries (both geographic and econo-political) and the formulation of strategies to build around or outside of them. Thus, globalizing can occur through a variety of concurrent processes that allow for complex re-formulations of power relationships, even without an established, rigid hierarchy or centralized power structure (contra world-systems or peer-polity models). As such, globalizing as a theoretical model is helpful in the examination of "complex non-state" social organizations, which may best describe the structure of mobile pastoralists of Central Eurasia for much of their (pre) history.

This provides a basis for the definition of "globalizing" as the state of practice whereby interactive connectivity is achieved between oneself and the historically relevant global extreme, and in which the "conceptual global geography" of a society is expanded through strategic interaction, be it economic, political, social, or ideological. Accordingly, countless globalizing processes have occurred throughout history, each with its own unique underpinnings and contextual pressures, and each filtered through the perceived structural lenses of individuals in local landscapes.

Prehistoric globalizing is a concept that fruitfully frames the economic and social conditions of Bronze Age Eurasia. This process describes how the boundaries of sociopolitical landscapes were transfixed by the development of a network of interaction rooted in localized patterns of land use, in the communication of semiotic forms, in the extension of interactive contexts across territories, and in the non-uniformity of power structures over time (Frachetti *in press*). Of course, there are substantial differences between twenty-first century globalization and the processes underlying Bronze Age political and economic regionalization.

On the basis of archaeological remains, this study asserts that the majority of pastoral groups across Central Eurasia were committed to local migrations and established controlled and bounded political and economic landscapes through their pastoral movements and ritual, political, and social investments in historically durable locales. This structure was also periodically altered according to variations in their range of mobility and contexts of settlement and interaction. For instance, pastoral groups might have pressed the boundaries of their migratory orbits to account for a variety of impulses at differing scales such as environmental factors, social conflict, or simple curiosity. The implementation of choices and strategies in light of these everyday and periodic occurrences could, processually and periodically, extend the links of the local communication network, without a "prime mover" or monolithic cause such as climate change or population movement.

Chapter 2 explores in detail the archaeological geography of Bronze Age pastoral societies and provides an analytical point of departure for understanding the shape of pastoralist landscapes and interaction of Central Eurasia in prehistory and later periods. The Bronze Age archaeology of the Eurasian steppe represents the critical archive for understanding the earliest forms of pastoral economy and the emergence of wide-scale networks of interaction. The archaeological corpus of material culture, settlement types, burial forms, and technological innovations is the product of more than eighty years of research, primarily by Russian and (former) Soviet scholars. To date, the most comprehensive work in this region is published in Russian and is still largely inaccessible to western scholars. The details of this archaeology are significant to the way we understand the trajectory of pastoralist lifeways in the region, and the academic history of their recovery and interpretation is equally important to understand.

Thus, the following chapter provides a current reading of the archaeological evidence and interpretation of the earliest pastoralist populations in Central Eurasia. What emerges is an elemental view of the regional archaeological assemblages. I make an effort to contextualize my own reading of the data with a synthesis of the Soviet academic paradigms that underwrite most discussions of the archaeological archive, in order to reassess the scale and homogeneity of Bronze Age economies, material traditions, technologies, and regional relationships. Previous scholars have argued that Bronze Age pastoralists played a major role in the transfer of language and culture throughout the second millennium BCE. If this is the case, then what was the mechanism by which these materials were transferred, and how can we productively justify the current understanding of the Eurasian archaeological record with the long term and dynamic formation of pastoralist landscapes proposed here?

2

AN ARCHAEOLOGY OF
BRONZE AGE EURASIA

Not only does prehistory extend written history backward,
it carries on natural history forward.

V. G. CHILDE 1951, 15

A BRIEF HISTORY OF BRONZE AGE SCHOLARSHIP IN EURASIA

In 1913 S. A. Teploukhov excavated the first of a series of burials in the Andronovo valley of southern Siberia (Minusinsk region). The burials and the materials found therein were sufficiently different in form from the those of the Afanas'evo and Okunev cultures which had been previously documented in the region and so were considered by Soviet cultural historians at that time to be a distinct archaeological culture group. In 1927, after more than a decade of excavations and study of these burials in the tributary valleys along the Yenisei River, Teploukhov proposed "the Andronovo Culture" to define the corpus of material recovered from Bronze Age sites in the region (Teploukhov 1927).

In Soviet academic parlance, an "archaeological culture" was defined as "an aggregate of archaeological features, similar to each other with a coherent repetition of styles and characteristics (*priznaky*) and differentiated from other aggregates of archaeological features" (Sorokin and Gryaznov 1966, 5). When Teploukhov published a description of the characteristic ceramic forms, burial style, and metallurgy of the Andronovo Culture in 1927, Soviet archaeologists working across the steppe zone were quick to align material analogues from sites in Kazakhstan, the trans-Urals, and south Russia with those from southern Siberia; recognizing significant similarities in regional handmade ceramic beakers with fluted necks, incised decorations, and flat bottoms. By the 1940s most Soviet archaeologists had adopted the Andronovo Culture as the moniker for a broadly comparable archaeological assemblage of ceramics, burial styles, and metallurgy collected from the Ural Mountains across southern Siberia to the Altai, and south to the deserts of Uzbekistan and Tajikistan (Vinogradov et al. 1986).

Like their contemporary culture historians in Europe and the USA (e.g., Clark 1952), early Soviet archaeologists developed a cultural geography that corresponded to a typological chronology: the staged evolution of steppe societies documented by stylistically derived categories of archaeological material. Thus, the defining artifacts and forms of the Andronovo typology were clearly enumerated as:

1. Graves delineated by stone fences, or as kurgan mounds, sometimes also with stone arrangements around them.

2. Burials with rectangular cists or pits, covered with a capstone or wooden lid.

3. A burial ceremony consisting of inhumation or cremation; in the case of inhumation the interred skeleton is (typically) lying on its left side, with the head usually to the west, hands positioned near the face and legs bent at the knees: this burial pose is not to be seen as "writhing" but rather is associated with a pose of a peacefully sleeping person.

4. Male skeletons (as a rule) do not have many grave goods except handmade ceramics; female skeletons usually have grave goods, such as beads on their feet (from shoes); often in children's graves games are found, such as sheep bones.[1]

5. Among bronze grave goods in the graves of females, the most characteristic are bracelets made of thin convex-concave plates with divergent or convergent ends; bracelets with divergent spiral finials; temporal spiral pendants; cockling of thin bronze-leaf on organic bases; also earrings with bell mouths on one end and a sharp point on the other, and sometimes covered in gold foil; [and] "barrel shaped" beads.

6. Clay pots in the burials, as a rule, are set near the head, on the western part of the burial, and are themselves vessels with open tops, straight or slightly angled sides without bulging or any kind of intricacy of profile, decorated with flowing or small stepped patterns around the shoulders, soft round sides, sometimes with an indent at the transition from the shoulder to the base; the upper diameter of the jars, as a rule, is close to the height of the vessel; the surface is sometimes "washed", and not-infrequently polished with brown, grey-brown, and black colors, independent of the surface color, [the fabric] is black or grey, seen in the cross section of broken vessels. Other types include jar forms, differentiated primarily by vertical elongation and slight bulging of the walls, lacking rounded shoulders and curves toward the bottom.

7. Ornamentation of [Andronovo] clay vessels is rich and is characterized by the following traits: decorations define the edges [of the vessels], incised with thin lamination, flat or rippled, and small as a rule, i.e., plain or rippled stamps, if one uses convenient archaeological terminology; also angled

incisions or straight lines. Decorations are placed in a "zonal" manner in the upper part [of the vessel], the middle, and rarely on the lower part of the vessel; continuous coverage of designs on the surface is rarely encountered. The ornaments exhibit a "geometric" character; decorations are derived from incised straight lines, angles, zigzags, triangles, rhombuses, meanders, and various [shapes] similar to meandering figures carved into parallel stripes, which end in bold corner angles—which we call meandering figures.[2]

8. Andronovo settlements consist of large rectangular houses (200–300 m^2 and larger), with a type of semi-dugout, i.e., the lower part is set into the earth approximately one meter. The walls of the structure are made of wooden logs or stones.

9. As archaeological sites, Andronovo settlements exhibit a large number of domesticated animal bones: horses, cattle, and sheep; rarely dogs are also encountered, though pigs are never found. Wild animal bones are also rare.

10. Tools are also characteristically found at Andronovo settlements: stone hoes, stone grinders or pestles, clay vessels with hangers, children's games and bone awls.

11. In Andronovo graves and burials, one infrequently finds objects considered to be of greater value (because of their rarity and the quality of their form). These include extraordinary bronze axes, celts, arrowheads or spearheads of the Seima-Turbino type, and bronze knives or daggers of the Srubnaya type. (This list was paraphrased from Sorokin and Gryaznov 1966, 5–7.)

By the 1950s the Andronovo Culture was synonymous with the Bronze Age of the Eurasian steppe and defined the historical paradigm of the region for both Soviet and Western scholars alike (Gimbutas 1958). Yet debates surrounding the conceptual utility of the Andronovo Cultural category began shortly after it was proposed, primarily because regional variations in material assemblages precluded a consistent definition, either temporal or material, across the entirety of the steppe zone (Formozov 1951; Zdanovich 1984). Some Soviet archaeologists preferred to see the Andronovo as a cultural "territory" or "community" related through common material and technology, wherein coherent regional subgroups evolved over time (Zdanovich and Zdanovich 2002).

By the late 1960s the basic archaeological elements of the Andronovo Cultural Community were collated both regionally and chronologically so that variations of the elements listed above supported a cultural-historical sequence of Bronze Age groups broadly organized as an evolution of social and ethnic populations: the Alakul in the western steppe and Fedorovo culture in the east. Archaeological cultures described material assemblages but were quickly seen as indices for social, ethnic, and linguistic relationships between regionally specific and chronological sequential Bronze Age populations.

The typologically derived chronology of the Andronovo culture has been fundamental to arguments concerning regional displacement of Bronze Age populations

(Sal'nikov 1948; Margulan et al. 1966; Kuz'mina 1964b; Kuz'mina 1986). Before the availability of a regionally comparative base of radiocarbon dates, the typological sequence relating regional Andronovo subcultures rested on associations between decorative elements and dimensions of handmade ceramic forms, as well as regional nuances of metallurgical and burial styles. Yet, even as a chronological typology, archaeological studies exposed inconsistencies within the Andronovo cultural-regional progression.

As excavation produced a wider corpus of data from burials and settlements across the steppe, more examples of regional material variation and increasingly frequent overlaps in decorative styles forced archaeologists to rethink the general chronology of the Andronovo, especially the bipartite division of western culture groups (the Alakul) and eastern culture groups (the Fedorovo) (Fedorova-Davydova 1973). Furthermore, settlement sites from the Tobol region, such as Alekseevka, showed stylistically mixed ceramic forms with elements from various regions within a singular chronological horizon (Fedorova-Davydova 1973). Regional overlap and stylistic similarities rendered the Fedorovo and Alakul cultures broadly contemporary and regionally parallel culture groups (Potemkina 1983, 13–14; Potemkina 1995a).

Material studies at sites such as Sintashta, Petrovka, Alekseevka, and Tasty-Butak in the western steppe region led archaeologists to add the Petrovka culture as a pre-Alakul stage in the western steppe and to separate the later Bronze Age phases of the Fedorovo and Alakul into regionally conscribed variants such as the Cherkaskul, Narinksy-Atasu, Begazy-Dandybaevsky, Sargarinsk-Alekseevka, Karasuk and Dongal cultures (Loman 1987; Margulan 1979; Kadirbaev and Kurmankulov 1992). Many archaeologists saw the material similarities among these myriad cultural assemblages as a proxy for ethnolinguistic diffusion, resulting from the process of regional migration and population expansion across the steppe throughout the Bronze Age (Potemkina 1995a; Parpola 1998; Kuz'mina 1994, 57–61).

THE INTELLECTUAL BASIS OF ARCHAEOLOGICAL "CULTURES"

At the core of Soviet archaeological classification was a Marxist-historicist approach to social evolution (Bromlei 1976; Semenov 1980). Marxist-historicist evolution was framed explicitly in terms of the dialectic between the productive forces of the economy and the cultural-ideological expressions of social consciousness (Petrova-Averkieva 1980). According to this paradigm, societies are categorized in terms of historically situated socioeconomic formations, which follow a developmental trajectory associated with Marx's five economic modes of production: primitive (pre-class society), ancient (Asiatic/slave holding), feudal bourgeois (capitalist), and classless (communist) (Marx and Engels 1967; Semenov 1980). Specific social groups or societies were delimited in terms of their internally productive relations, which were used to correlate the diversity of distinguishing cultural traits among them. The academic transposition of the material similarities of the Andronovo cultural assemblage into an evolutionary history of steppe communities and their ethnic and linguistic character occurred in parallel with the growing refinement of the Soviet-Marxist concept of "ethnos".

The Soviet concept of ethnos formed the basis for ethnography and archaeology in the USSR (Bromlei 1976; Bromlei 1974a; Bromlei 1974b) and has carried through to the post-Soviet era as well. The Soviet academic paradigm[3] framed discrete groups of peoples (*narody*) into distinctive social units, or ethnoses, according to their mode of production, sophistication of material culture, or associated degree of sociopolitical complexity (Dragadze 1980; Bromlei 1983). Yulian Bromlei (1976, 12) defines ethnos as a micro and macro phenomenon, "ethnos in the narrow [micro] meaning of the word and in the most general form can be defined as a historically formed community of people possessing common, relatively stable specific features of culture, as well as being aware of their unity and difference from other similar communities." Ethnos in the narrow sense might be "used to define an ethno-social organism" (Bromlei 1976) that can change its form (Semenov 1980) through time based on the historically situated conditions of economic and political-ideological processes (Dragadze 1980; Bromlei 1983).

Paradoxically, an ethnos (in the broad sense) can be a combination of many ethnoses (in the narrow sense). "Americans" can be considered an ethnos, while "Italian Americans", "Jewish Americans", "African Americans", and "Cuban Americans" would each be a distinct ethnos as well. In this sense, Soviet archaeologists struggled with precisely the same complications as western anthropologists when trying to define archaeological "cultures:" namely that they are neither static nor monolithic (Arutiunov and Bromlie 1989; Watson 1995; Swell 1999). Specifically, the dialectical relationship between the macro-scale "social organism" and ethnos is analogous to the structure/agency (or culture/community) dialectic that has underpinned western anthropological debates since the 1970s (Foucault 1973; Giddens 1984; Bourdieu 1977). In the Soviet inflection of Marxist dialectics, the material proxies of economic modes of production—regional cultural assemblages—were employed to trace the historical distribution of ethnic and political bodies across territory and through time through a discourse of ethnogenesis.

As early as the 1930s, ethnogenetic theories emerged from the basis of Marxist historicism and social typology (Shnirelman 1995). Ethnogenesis, from the Soviet viewpoint, refers to the development of new ethnic "groups" (*plemya*; literally, "tribes"), arising from changes in the productive relations of society (Arutiunov 1994). Thus, a key relationship exists between ethnogenesis and the Soviet adherence to an historical and progressive model of social evolution (Petrova-Averkieva 1980; Gellner 1980). Parallel developments in the concept of ethnos and archaeological cultures ultimately served to underwrite the Soviet approach to ethnography and archaeology. For Soviet archaeologists, the proxy for social grouping (ethnos) was economic production whereas the proxy for economic production was material culture—thus similarities or transformations observed in material cultural were used as indexes to trace the historical trajectory of discrete societies and their regional interrelatedness. The archaeology of the steppe in 2007 is no longer dominated by Marxist historical materialism; yet the archaeological sequence of the Bronze Age is still largely arranged according to the idea that "cultural" entities progressively evolve into new cultures through the process of ethnogenesis and thereby produce new material aggregates in distinctive regions (Koryakova 1998).

The primary published models for explaining this process include migration models and contact/expansion models. Although many scholars over the past century have had a hand in generating and contributing to these models for steppe interaction, Elena Kuz'mina and Tamila Potemkina have distilled them with the most clarity in relation to Bronze Age steppe materials.

Since the late 1950s, Elena Kuz'mina's studies of the Eurasian steppe, especially her excavations in the Elenovskaya region of the Southern Urals (e.g., Ushkatty, Baitu, and Atken-Sai), have been instrumental in codifying the periodization of ceramic and structural forms relating the Alakul and Fedorovo material classifications (Kuz'mina 1964b). In 1986, Kuz'mina published a synthesis of the Andronovo Cultural material from the Caspian Sea to the Tian Shan Mountains and, using a combination of material studies as well as readings of Vedic texts, outlined the variation of culture groups in the steppe region presented above and their ethnic and social character.

Kuz'mina suggested that populations from the southern Urals and southwestern Siberia migrated into the central steppe region at the beginning of the second millennium BCE and moved south to Semirech'ye and the arid steppes and mountains of

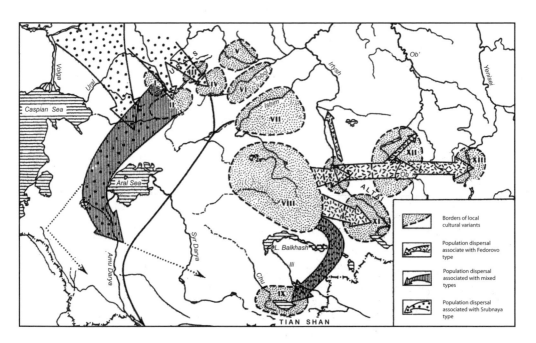

FIGURE 3

Proposed migrations of Andronovo subculture groups 1500–1300 BCE. After Kuz'mina 1994, 394.

Kyrgyzstan and Tajikistan by 1300 BCE (fig. 3). In a recent discussion of the prehistoric spread of bronze metallurgy to China, Kuz'mina reiterated her theory of Bronze Age migration between regional variants of the Andronovo culture and the Seima-Turbino metallurgical phenomenon (Kuz'mina 2004).

> During the second half of the second millennium BCE, Andronovo tribes populated the whole territory of the Asian steppe between the Yenesei and Ural Rivers. In the west, the archaeological type called Alakul was formed on the basis of Petrovka period sites. Related Fedorovo type-sites developed in eastern Kazakhstan and southern Siberia. In Semirechie, which includes a part of Kazakhstan and Kirgizia, a unique type emerged. Cattle breeding, as well as that of horses, and sheep, dominated the complex economy of the Andronovo tribes with supplemental agriculture. Metallurgy and metalworking, however, also played a very significant role, operating through local resources, and leaving traces in almost every settlement.
>
> Kuz'mina 2004, 59

Kuz'mina links the proposed migration of Andronovo (Fedorovo) pastoralists into Semirech'ye with the diffusion of metallurgy into Xinjiang, around 1500 BCE (see also Goryachev 2004). These developments, she argues, were coincident with the spread of the chariot and specialized horse riding, which enabled the Late Bronze Age tribes to spread rapidly across the steppe (Kuz'mina 1998, 73). She further suggests that "the rapid drop of temperature at the end of the second millennium BCE caused part of the population to adopt a new, mobile form of cattle breeding lifestyle" (Kuz'mina 2004, 76).

Tamila M. Potemkina provides an alternative synthesis of "interaction" between Andronovo populations during the Bronze Age. Potemkina (1995a; 1995b) argues that the development of an increasingly "productive" agro-pastoral economy from the late Eneolithic to the Bronze Age, along with technological developments in metallurgy and population growth, spurred interactions of populations living in the Tobol, Ural, and Ishim River Basins. Potemkina draws on detailed analysis of archaeological materials, specifically ceramic styles, to delineate periods of cultural concentration (the forming of cultural communities), then expansion and overlap (regional extension), followed by movement to a new area (regional separation), and finally the re-concentration of a new cultural community.

Potemkina's synthesis also relies heavily on general assessments of environmental "prime movers" to explain the northward and eastward expansions of populations during the early Alakul period, as well as later southerly and easterly population displacements. She suggests that this shift in cultural geography was sparked by the demand for new pastures for populations with an increasingly mobile pastoral economic base (Potemkina 1995b, 23–24). Potemkina's contact model, although more regionally focused than the overarching explanation offered by Kuz'mina, also eschews the durability of pastoral systems over time.

In that Potemkina's model describes movements and interactions as responses to calculable demands (economic demands primarily), it disallows the notion of contact or interaction as a process without an evolutionary direction, or one that reiterates itself in a nonlinear way. This point becomes particularly salient when we consider that both Kuz'mina and Potemkina also rely on the ethnic identification of Andronovo groups as either Indo-Iranian or Ugric (especially in the northern border with the forest-steppe zone). They both suggest that the proliferation of the Andronovo culture—be it through migration or regional contact and expansion—represents a prehistoric phase of ethno-linguistic evolution fundamentally tied the paradigm of ethnogenesis (Koryakova 1998).

To summarize, the formative archaeological studies of the Eurasian steppe in the Soviet tradition served to produce a deeply entrenched historical-geographic paradigm for understanding social identity and economic change during the Bronze Age. The basis for this paradigm was clearly based on a link between material culture and socioeconomic entities. Changes in material culture across regions indexed direct diffusions of the forces of production, and thus the emergence of "new" culture groups provided the essential rubric for understanding social evolution across Eurasia through time.

This book alternatively suggests that material and social change—though related processes—may be more accurately modeled vis-à-vis generative mechanisms produced from interactions that balance environmental and institutional structures within the contextual geography of local landscapes. During the middle of the second millennium BCE, short-lived oscillations toward aridity are reflected in the paleoclimatic record (ch. 3). These changes were not catastrophic and, at most, we might expect only a minor deviation in pastoral strategies given the impact of these paleoclimatic changes.[4] For example, pastoralists of the Koksu River valley have maintained social and economic investments in particular locations in the landscape from at least the middle third millennium BCE and have accommodated environmental oscillations, social and political shifts, and many other variables within locally reiterative social and economic strategies. This proposal has significant implications for our understanding of the structural reality of culture historical processes across Eurasia.

POST-SOVIET BRONZE AGE STUDIES

Archaeo-botanical, archaeo-faunal, geo-archaeological, paleoecological, and radiometric methods are rapidly challenging the established understanding of prehistoric steppe communities, a goal common to American and European scholars (both Eastern and Western alike). In the post-Soviet era, the primary thrust of Bronze Age research has been to use these archaeometric methods to produce an absolute chronology of Bronze Age assemblages and to remap the associated regional trajectories of domestic economies, technology transfer, and social entities of the steppe.

Perhaps the most fundamental methodological progress in steppe archaeology is reflected in the growing corpus of radiocarbon dated sites attributed to Bronze Age pastoralists.[5] Specifically, the calibration of radiocarbon dates rewrites[6] the chronological relationships of Bronze Age archaeological assemblages and draws into question the sequenced evolution of regional populations, their respective socioeconomic organization, and the processes of regional diffusion of their technological innovations (Shishlina et al. 2000).

According to traditional typological chronologies, the Early Bronze Age is associated with pre-Andronovo populations across the steppe. These include the Abashevo culture in the forest-steppes near the Volga, the Surtandy culture in the trans-Urals, and the Okunev in the Yenesei Basin and eastern steppe zone. All of these assemblages were dated typologically from roughly 2000–1700 BCE. The Middle Bronze Age referred to the period from about 1700 BCE to 1400 BCE and included the Sintashta-Petrovka cultures, the Alakul culture, and Fedorovo culture (Vinogradov 1995). The Late Bronze Age was generally considered from 1350 until 1000 BCE and included the Atasu culture, late Alakul, and some related groups such as the Elovskaya culture, sometimes categorized as "Andronoid" cultures (Kuz'mina 1986; Zdanovich 1988). The "final" Bronze Age represented the transitional period from 1000–800 BCE, after which the Iron Age began.

A concerted effort in the past decade to produce absolute, calibrated chronologies on a regional scale has significantly pushed the Bronze Age cultural schema further into antiquity and in some cases has forced even more fundamental revisions of regional cultural histories (Görsdorf et al. 2001, 2004; Hanks et al. 2007; Frachetti and Mar'yashev 2007; Chernykh et al. 1997, 2000). On the basis of calibrated radiocarbon dates, the transition from late Eneolithic to the Early Bronze Age is now documented variously across the steppe zone, but generally dates from 3500–3000 BCE (Telegin and Mallory 1986; Rassamakin 1999), and correlates with a general shift toward pastoralist organization around the start of the third millennium BCE.

In the western steppe zone, Rassamakin (1999, 157–174) has compiled calibrated radiocarbon dates for assemblages ranging from the Eneolithic to the Early Bronze Age. Rassamakin dates the Early Bronze Age in the western steppe region from around 3000 BCE in association with the emergence of the "Yamnaya culture" (or pit culture), centered in the territory from the north Caucasus and the steppe territory north of the Caspian Sea to the Ural River near Orenburg (fig. 4). Shishlina's calibrated chronology of the Catacomb culture dates related pastoral populations in the trans-Caucasus as early as 2600 BCE (Shishlina et al. 2000). Further east, the Late Eneolithic/Early Bronze Age of the steppe zone around the Tobol and Irtysh River basin (trans-Urals) is attributed to the Botai and Tersek cultures (c. 3500–2500 BCE) (Kalieva and Logvin 1997; Kislenko and Tatarintseva 1999; Brown and Anthony 1998).

A concerted program of radiocarbon analysis by German and Russian archaeologists has produced a comparable recalibration of the Early and Middle Bronze Age chronology for southwest Siberia and the eastern steppe zone (Görsdorf et al. 2001; 2004). Radiocarbon dates from Afanas'evo burial monuments in the Minusinsk Basin are

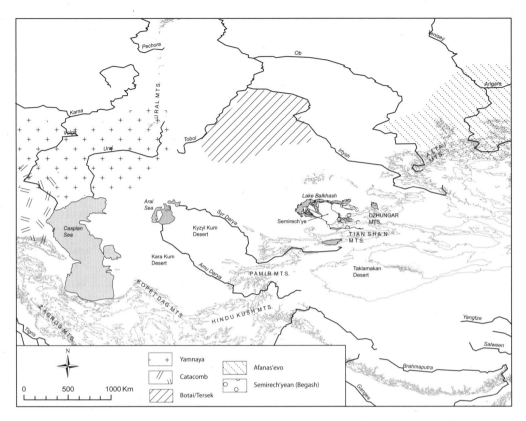

FIGURE 4

Geography of Eneolithic and Early Bronze Age culture groups across the Eurasian steppe zone (3500–2200 BCE). Map data source: Environmental Systems Research Institute 1994.

(conservatively) calibrated between 3200–2500 BCE. This early date range provides compelling chronological justification for the independent emergence of pastoral economies in that region (below). Radiocarbon dating also illustrates the continuity of pastoralist populations in the eastern steppe region. Görsdorf's report documents a locally continuous sequence of materials and burial styles from Afanas'evo to Okunev (2500–1715 BCE) to Andronovo types (1715–1425 BCE) in southwest Siberia, lending support to the idea that steppe pastoralists may exhibit greater regional stability than previous models suggested.

The Middle (2500–1900 BCE) and Late (1900–1300 BCE) Bronze Ages are the periods in steppe culture history primarily associated with the emergence of more specialized pastoral economies, as well as the expansion in the distribution of broadly comparable regional material assemblages (fig. 5). The Srubnaya culture (1900–1200 BCE) of the Russian forest steppe also shows material affinities with Middle and Late Bronze Age populations of the western steppe, furthing debates for interactions between differently structured groups in the western steppe region (Anthony et al. 2005).

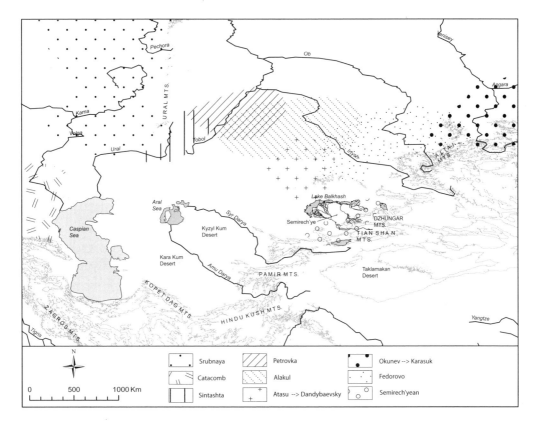

FIGURE 5

Geography of Middle and Late Bronze Age culture groups across the Eurasian steppe (2200–1000 BCE). Map data source: Environmental Systems Research Institute 1994.

E. V. Cherynyk's work at the site of Kargaly, located at the interface of the steppe and forest-steppe zones, has also provided radiocarbon dates for early metallurgy in the Ural mountain region. Kargaly illustrates a continuity of mining and smelting starting in the Early Bronze Age and intensifying at the start of the second millennium BCE. Radiocarbon dates from the nearby settlement of Gorny date the mining and production settlement as early as 1740 BCE. Metal production at Gorny appears to have been fueled by the emergence of wider arenas of economic interaction that began in the Middle Bronze Age and flowered throughout the second millennium BCE (Chernykh 2004).

Recent excavations of Middle Bronze Age settlements and burials at the site of Begash in Semirech'ye illustrate that pastoralists maintained durable landscapes in the eastern steppe as early as 2500 BCE (Frachetti and Mar'yashev 2007). Fedorovo-type ceramics have been recovered in layers dating between 1950–1700 BCE, while continuous seasonal reuse of the settlement illustrates that pastoralists were actively engaged in exploiting local territories throughout the second millennium BCE.

Comparing chronologies across the eastern steppe, the chronology and continuity documented at Begash situates pastoral groups in mountain zones of Semirech'ye a few centuries before the prevalence of Okunev material forms around the Yenisei River and more than five hundred years before the purported southeastern expansion of Fedorovo (Andronovo) pastoralists from the northeastern steppe. These systematic calibrations of the chronological details of steppe archaeology prompt a reconsideration of the proposed inter-regional relationships used to explain the evolution and spread of pastoralists throughout the second millennium BCE and perhaps before. In addition, the discovery of local continuity of pastoral adaptations in a number of regions further problematizes the practical evidence for large scale demic diffusion throughout the second millennium BCE.

In the trans-Urals, Sintashta and Petrovka culture groups had been typologically dated to the seventeenth through sixteenth centuries BCE, whereas most scholars currently accept a calibrated radiocarbon chronology dating these assemblages to the start of the second millennium BCE (2100–1800 BCE) (Hanks et al. 2007). Subsequent material phases, such as the Alakul and Fedorovo, are typically attributed to the Late Bronze Age in the trans-Urals, with the traditional chronology of 1300–1000 BCE shifted by calibrated absolute chronology to 1800–1400 BCE.

The Final Bronze Age is datable between 1500–1000 BCE, at least in the western steppe zone (Hanks et al. 2007). This period in the central and eastern steppe corresponds with post-Alakul/Fedorovo assemblages such as the Atasu, Begazy-Dandibaevsky, Sargary, Karasuk, and Cherkaskul cultures (Görsdorf et al. 2001; Frachetti and Mar'yashev 2007), although there are comparably fewer radiocarbon sequences to discuss.

At the core of the Andronovo regional chronology and culture history rests the question: How do the chronological and archaeological trends of different regions index the social and economic practices and relationships of steppe societies? How homogeneous or interrelated are Eurasian pastoralist landscapes throughout history, and to what degree do pastoralist landscapes reflect in situ developments of economic and social systems? Understanding the overlapping traits in the cultural geographies and material histories of different populations is fundamental to characterizing the evolution of pastoralist landscapes in Eurasia. However, as "Andronovo" materials are currently presented in the literature, it is difficult to understand them as proxies for wider-scale economic developments without tacitly reproducing the historical-evolutionary paradigm of ethnogenesis, which stands at odds with the conception of local continuity in Eurasian pastoralist landscapes forwarded in this study.

In fact, despite the greater antiquity of calibrated chronologies (fig. 6) the geographic distribution of Bronze Age materials and their association with regional culture groups and explanatory models of second millennium BCE social dynamics show little revision in the past fifty years. Admittedly, it is difficult to summarize the steppe Bronze Age without reference to this sequenced "cultural" paradigm of steppe societies. The categorical classification of the Andronovo culture shapes nearly all the work done to date and

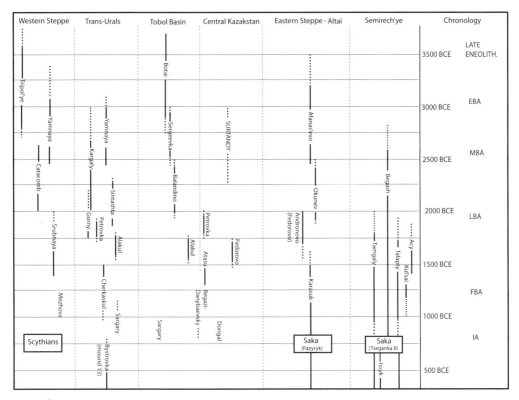

FIGURE 6

Comparative regional chronology of archaeological assemblages and sites across the Eurasian Steppe throughout the Bronze Age.

still functions to provide a common terminology among scholars. As David Anthony remarks about related theories, it makes little sense to "throw the baby out with the bathwater" without analytical justification (Anthony 1990). However, if used as more than a codex for broad material and chronological provenience, regional cultural categories mask the complexity and potential flexibility of social identity among Bronze Age steppe societies. To understand how pastoralist landscapes of the steppe result from locally embedded cultural factors and through meta-local processes, we must start by unpacking archaeological facts from their paradigmatic casings.

Recent facts concerning the chronological and material inconsistencies within the Andronovo cultural sequence force us to look more critically at the defining elements of the culture history of the steppe. Reexamining the data helps, first, to justify our basic understanding of regional Bronze Age economies and social organization through time, and second, helps to clarify which elements of this record represent inter-regional diffusions and which reflect more embedded practices in localized settings. Here we will address three key elements of the broader Bronze Age archaeological landscape: economy, social organization (through architecture and burial), and material culture.

MOBILE PASTORALISM IN THE LATE ENEOLITHIC/EARLY BRONZE AGE (3500–2500 BCE)

The economy of Eurasian steppe societies is not monolithic nor static and never has been. As a rule, the vast majority of steppe territory is best exploited as natural pasture—thus pastoralism seems ubiquitous as a general adaptation across the steppe ecotone. However, notable variations in economic strategies across the steppe throughout the Bronze Age highlight significant differences in regional ecologies and the alternative geographies of social contact and interaction among regional pastoral populations. Thus to understand the emergence and metamorphasis of preshistoric pastoralism in the steppe zone we must start by comparing regional processes of domestication and variation in the development of specialized pastoral systems across Eurasia.

The emergence of mobile pastoralism as a specialized adaptation occurred in both the western and eastern steppe regions around the end of the fourth millennium BCE. Mobile pastoralism, as defined in chapter 1, should not be conflated with evidence for animal domestication or the exploitation of domesticated animals as a supplement to either hunting/fishing or agriculture. In regions such as the north Pontic and south Russian forest steppe, domesticated animals had been part of mixed subsistence economies since the Neolithic, or since at least 5000 BCE. This fact is reflected in the mixture of wild and domestic fauna from Neothlithic forest-steppe sites such as Khvalynsk, and from sedentary agricultural villages of societies associated with Tripol'ye, Maikop, and other archaeological assemblages in the Caucasus and Ukrainian steppes (Shishlina 2004; Benecke and von den Dreisch 2003). The archaeology of the western steppe and circum-Pontic documents that agriculture and herding were diffused aspects of the Neolithic subsistence strategy of Eastern Europe (Rassamakin 1999) but few would characterize these Neolithic populations as specialized mobile pastoralists.

In the western steppe region, it was not until the final centuries of the fourth millennium BCE (c. 3100 BCE) that archaeological remains document a substantial shift in socioeconomic strategy toward specialized pastoralism. The emergence of mobile pastoral strategies in the western steppe is associated with societies living north of the Caspian Sea and in the Caucasus, traditionally categorized within the Yamnaya culture. In this case, the predominance of domestic cattle, sheep, goats, and horses interred in Yamnaya burials alludes to a shift toward more intense pastoralism and the occurrence of wheeled wagons or carts within burial kurgans index a more intensely mobile lifestyle (e.g., Vinogradnoe [Rassamakin 1999]). These artifacts contribute to an argument that Yamnaya groups exploited the open steppe at a wider range than their contemporary agro-pastoral neighbors, such as the Tripol'ye culture to the west (Rassamakin 1999; Whittle 1996; Brown and Anthony 1998). In addition, the general scarcity of settlement sites with Yamnaya type materials has led to the argument that these societies were nomadic in nature (Chernykh 2004, 231).

Given their regional proximity and use of similar domesticates, the Yamnaya economy likely developed out of earlier Neolithic stockbreeding in the north-Pontic, Caucasus and the southern fringe of the forest-steppe region. Economic endeavors in this region also entailed exploitation of local copper ore sources at Kargaly, which may suggest that regional populations which engaged in ecologically specific strategies also generated diverse pastoralist economies (Chernykh 2004). Shishlina's work on Early Bronze Age pastoralists of the Catacomb culture in the north Caucasus illustrates that micro-regional distribution and seasonal variation of pasture resources may have dictated local patterns of pastoral mobility among communities (Shishlina 2001). Her studies of the paleoecology of the northern pontic zone at the start of the third millennium BCE further suggest that the transition to more mobile forms of pastoralism coincided with a climatic optimum (Shishlina 2004). The seasonal distribution of pastures facilitated the formation of pastoralist landscapes in that region, as populations cyclically exploited local rangelands between river zones and the more open steppe.

For decades the prevailing consensus has been that Yamnaya populations were responsible for the initial spread of mobile pastoralism eastward across the steppe at the start of the third millennium BCE. Similarities between the ceramic styles of the Yamnaya and Afanas'evo cultures—localized in southwestern Siberia—initially led scholars to relate the two cultural traditions through proposed eastward migrations of mobile Yamnaya pastoralists (Kuz'mina 1998). In addition to exihibiting similar material culture with the Yamnaya, Afanas'evo groups are typically believed to be of "Caucasiod" cranial morphology (Mallory and Mair 2000), which has been another longstanding cornerstone in the argument that they were related to Caucasian Yamnaya groups (Kuz'mina 1998). Craniometrics have also been used to differentiate Afanas'evo individuals from Eneolithic populations of Xinjiang as well as later "Okunev" societies, whose cranial phenotype has been describe as Asiatic (Hemphill and Mallory 2004). It should be noted that the variability of cranial traits among fourth millennium steppe populations is not well documented *within* the small dataset available, such that traits attributed as "Caucasian" do not demonstrate discrete geographic focus *a priori*. Furthermore, the biological traits that may liken these two skeletal assemblages may have been the result of earlier genetic drift not at all associated with the spread of pastoral economic strategies in the fourth millennium BCE. In other words, even if Afanas'evo crania and Yamnaya crania exhibit discrete metric similarities, this is not evidence that one derived from the other in the early Bronze Age. In fact, radiocarbon dates currently demonstrate that Yamanaya origins for the Afanas'evo culture are dubious. The calibrated C^{14} dates of Afanas'evo material are generally slightly earlier than those taken from Yamnaya contexts in the western steppe, which complicates a diffusionist explanation of the emergence of pastoralists in the eastern steppe (Görsdorf et al. 2004; Rassamakin 1999).

Although their origins may be obscure, communities associated with Afanas'evo materials still represent the earliest mobile pastoralists east of the Ural Mountains (Okladnikov 1959; Vainshtein 1980; Khazanov 1994, 91). Vadetskaya documented bones of sheep, cattle, horses, and wild game in Afanas'evo burials (Shilov 1975) illustrating an incipient strategy of cattle and sheep/goat herding, supplemented by hunting and fishing. The Afanas'evo subsistence economy might best be characterized as a mixed or transitional form between hunting/fishing and localized pastoralism, arising from local antecedents[7] or combining native strategies with diffused domestic innovations among local populations. Thus, the earliest forms of Bronze Age herding entailed the semi-domestic exploitation of animals in the Minusinsk Basin and Altai region, more than 1000 kilometers east of the Yamnaya culture zone. Perhaps the strongest evidence that divides the Yamnaya and Afanas'evo pastoralists in the mid-fourth millennium BCE is the discontinuity of pastoral economic strategies among societies living between these territories.

Between the regions of the Yamnaya and the Afanas'evo archaeological assemblages, Eneolithic and Early Bronze Age steppe societies of the northcentral steppe were engaged in the processes of animal domestication, but their development is characteristically distinguishable from their slightly later eastern and western neighbors. Living around the confluence of the Tobol and Ishim Rivers, "Botai" culture groups reflect a subsistence strategy clearly focused on the horse—a fact that has brought the sites of Botai, Krasnyi Yar, and Vasilkovka IV to the forefront of debates concerning the earliest horse domestication in Eurasia (Olsen, Litauer et al. 2006). As early as 3600 BCE faunal and archaeological evidence from these sites demonstrate that the diet of Botai populations relied heavily on horse meat (Kalieva and Logvin 1997; Brown and Anthony 1998; Dudd et al. 2003). Horse bones represent a remarkable 99 percent of the fauna from Botai, and the age structure of these specimens illustrates a prevalence of adult animals, which is typically associated with hunting strategies rather than pastoral management of domestic herds (Benecke and von den Dreisch 2003; Levine 2003). Olsen has astutely noted, however, that a direct link between high pecentages of adult specimens and hunting strategies may be overstated, citing varied uses of adult animals for secondary products such as milk, as well as selective culling of foals due to range capacity as causes for varied age-sets within archaeofaunal datasets (Olsen 2006). She suggests that the mortality pattern among the Botai horses is inconclusive in assigning them as wild or domestic animals, and that hunting with the help of some domesticated, ridden horses is a more logical interpretation of the Botai horse economy.

The archaeology of Botai-culture sites offers some key evidence to support the idea that this late Eneolithic society relied minimally on a small percentage of domestic horses to assist in driving wild herds, transporting kills, and mitigating uncertainty in the northcentral steppe zone. Artifacts such as bone thong-smoothers, used to produce strong leather straps, document a prominent industry at Botai. Olsen (2003) argues that leather thongs and straps were instrumental for taming and controling select horses for riding in the hunt and subsequently for transporting horse kills. She also reports the recovery of horse dung remains in the house structures at sites like Krasnyi Yar, likely reflecting its use as roof insulation throughout the cold winters of Inner Eurasia (Olsen 2003; Bradley et al. 2006). The concerted collection of horse dung also suggests corralling of at least some of the horses within the faunal assemblages of Botai-type sites. The debate concerning the correlation between horse taming, riding, managing and domestication is ongoing and new data are regularly shifting our confidence in various interpretations of the archaeological evidence (Brown and Anthony 1998; Levine 1999a; Kislenko and Tatarintseva 1999).Whether the populations of Botai were horse managers, simply hunters, or used some combination of these strategies, there is little reason to liken the Botai economy to that of Eneolithic and Early Bronze Age groups from the Urals, southern central steppe, or eastern steppe.

Material similarities in the ceramics associated with Eneolithic/Early Bronze Age groups across the steppe zone do suggest a wider arena of interactions at this time, though at this stage it is difficult to link material-cultural similarities with the subsistence strategies of regional pastoralists. The antecedent elements of a more connected economic geography were taking shape in the late fourth millennium BCE, but the subsistence economies of the Eurasian steppe reflected greater diversity than coherence throughout the Early Bronze Age. The predominance of horse remains at Botai distinguishes the Eneolithic populations of the north central steppe from the predominately cattle and sheep/goat economies that emerged in the eastern and western steppe at the end of the fourth millennium BCE. This fact, coupled with differences in settlement ecology (below), further supports the argument for locally adapted economic strategies across the steppe in the Early Bronze Age.

PASTORAL ECONOMIES OF THE MIDDLE AND LATE BRONZE AGES (2500–1000 BCE)

Although regional domestic economies of the Early Bronze Age likely developed along different trajectories, the mid-third millennium BCE marks a significant steppe-wide transition to mobile pastoralism among central Eurasian communities (Akhinzhanov et al. 1992). Benecke and von den Driesch (2003) illustrate that steppe societies dependent upon horse meat in the fourth and early third millennia, such as those at Botai, made a rapid transition to the exploitation of cattle, sheep and goats around 2500 BCE. The composition of archaeofaunal assemblages at sites in the north central steppe, such as Baladino and Sergeevka, also indexes a significant shift in herding strategies, since cattle and sheep demand greater seasonal mobility and regular range rotation for successful herd growth. In the eastern and western steppe, domestic economies changed through varying degrees of intensification of the incipient pastoralist economies discussed above, with a noteworthy reduction in exploitation of wild animals and increase in domestic herd animals, especially sheep and goats.

The economic intensification of mobile herding at the start of the middle Bronze Age reflects one of the first and most dramatic transitions of economic strategy across the Eurasian steppe, which alludes to an early development of interconnections, perhaps through incipient regional networks of interaction. The geography of early pastoralist networks could be no better than "patchy" given the unique environmental and social settings of various regional groups at this time, which may have contributed to different trajectories of transition and diversity in the makeup of regional pastoralist economies from the Middle to Late Bronze Age.

Middle Bronze Age sites from the trans-Urals to the Tian Shan Mountains illustrate the predominance of a mixed herd composition of cattle, sheep/goat, and horse, which incidentally is the herd structure that came to characterize steppe pastoralism for the next 4000 years. Yet, despite similarities in the domestic species exploited by western, central and eastern steppe pastoralists, locally adapted forms of herding economies in each zone mark the formation of regionally distinguishable pastoralist landscapes throughout the Middle Bronze Age. For example, Antipina shows that cattle remains at Middle Bronze Age sites in the western steppe zone (circum-Pontic and north Caspian) typically represent more than 70 percent of represented species, while at some sites cattle represent nearly 90 percent of the total domestic fauna. In these cases, sheep and goats average about 15 percent with only a few cases as high as 36.5 percent (Antipina 1997, 26). Compositional heterogeneity among these faunal assemblages is geographically patterned, which suggests a link between regional micro-ecologies and economic strategies in the trans-Caucasus and north Caspian at end of the third millennium BCE (Shishlina 2001). Contemporary sites of the trans-Urals illustrate more balanced herd compositions, with cattle typically making up about 45 percent of the herd and sheep/goat making up roughly 30 percent (Tsalkin 1966). The slight variations in composition among these groups are more difficult to link to alternative pastoralist strategies and may be explained simply as internal diversity among different groups, or a methodological effect of non-standardized archaeological recovery of archaeofaunal assemblages over the past decades (Antipina 1997; Morales-Muniz and Antipina 2003).

The predominance of pastoral strategies in the eastern steppe, and perhaps even the initial introduction of domesticated animals, seems to be independent of the trajectory documented in western Eurasia. Middle Bronze Age pastoralism in the eastern steppe zone shows a proliferation of the incipient domestic aspects of the Afanas'evo economy, specifically an increase in exploitation of sheep/goat and cattle. Comprehensive studies of fauna from Semirech'yean sites are still underway, but preliminary studies at sites such as Begash in the Dzhungar Mountains show that the earliest pastoralists there relied more heavily on sheep and goat than did those from contemporary sites in the western steppe, where cattle tend to dominate in the mid third millennium BCE. The increasingly specialized sheep pastoralist economies in the eastern steppe in the first half of the third millennium may have served to bolster a corridor of mountain pastoralism which emerged from the incipient pastoralist strategies of Afanas'evo culture groups or, perhaps, diffused northward through the mountains from agropastoral economies in southern Central Asia earlier in the third millennium BCE (see also footnote 7). Nevertheless, from a comparative perspective Middle Bronze Age pastoralist economies across Eurasia reflect considerable regional variation in the dominant herd animals maintained through the end of the third and start of the second millennia BCE.

Pastoralist sites of the second millennium BCE reflect even greater intra- and interregional variability in herd composition than earlier periods. For example in the trans-Urals, cattle comprise from 25.6 percent to 80 percent of domestic fauna recovered from Late Bronze Age steppe settlements, whereas ungulates range widely from 2.6 percent to 39 percent. Faunal statistics from large, centralized settlements like Arkaim illustrate continuity with Middle Bronze Age herd compositions, as cattle were comparatively more predominant (60.4 percent) followed by sheep/goat (24.2 percent) and horse (15.4 percent) (Zdanovich 1997).

If we look to the economic implications of intensified pastoral systems of the western and eastern steppe, we see a variety of economic activities beyond what species statistics alone can illustrate. For example, Chernykh notes the likelihood that the Srubnaya settlement at Gorny (2000–1700 BCE) was an interface for exchange between metallurgists and pastoralists in the beginning of the Late Bronze Age (Chernykh 2004). Antipina further argues that the age structure of the faunal remains at Gorny illustrates that domestic cattle were used primarily for meat rather than milk (Antipina 1999). Comparative diversity in the faunal record in this context may reflect differentiated contexts of consumption and interaction rather than productive differences on the part of actual pastoralist groups. Thus, it would seem that the pastoral strategy west of the Urals at the start of the second millennium BCE is best described as a form of cattle ranching. Domestic herds reflect a specialized economic product raised either to support the specialized communities of metallurgists around Kargaly, or as key commodities for trade with economic arenas like the "country of towns" (Zdanovich and Zdanovich 2002). The development of specialized economic transactions may have fueled the emergence of social hierarchies among sedentary societies living in large fortified settlements in the Ural region at the beginning of the second millennium BCE, which illustrates a potentially long-term trajectory of economic relationships in the western steppe. In fact, radiocarbon dates from Kargaly demonstrate that mining was already underway by early third millennium BCE (the Yamnaya period) and thus the development of trade for metal and meat may have developed significantly earlier.

Late Bronze Age sites with evidence of metallurgical production in the central steppe such as Atasu and Myrzhik also illustrate mixed herd structures dominated by cattle, sheep/goats, and horses (Kadirbaev and Kurmankulov 1992). The intensification of pastoralism in neighboring regions such as Semirech'ye throughout the second millennium BCE may have contributed to the growth of these settlements and their productive metallurgical economy. Archaeological evidence from the Dzhungar Mountains demonstrates substantial investment in the construction of durable settlements and the control of local territories on the part of seasonally mobile populations whose primary economy was rooted in mobile pastoralism. These seasonal camps, located in the passes of the

Dzhungar Mountains, illustrate a periodic increase in mobility around 1600 BCE (Frachetti and Mar'yashev 2007), perhaps reflecting an extension of migratory ranges related to brokerage endeavors on the part of pastoralists living between ore sources and distant production centers (Frachetti 2002; Mei 2003).

The recovery of substantial, stone-constructed settlements across the steppe zone has traditionally encouraged scholars to think that Late Bronze Age populations were largely sedentary and integrated agriculture with their herding strategies. For example, the subsistence economy of the Sintashta culture is typically presented as agro-pastoral with large-scale settlements, such as Arkaim, suggesting a degree of permanent settlement—at least for segments of that society (Koryakova 2002, Zdanovich 2002a). Paradoxically, strong evidence for agricultural production at any time during the Bronze Age is nearly nonexistent across the steppe and is especially scarce in the eastern steppe region.[8] Nevertheless, a few noteworthy artifacts demand consideration.

Kuz'mina refers to concrete evidence of preserved grains and stalks of wheat found at Alekseevka, a Late Bronze Age site located in the south Urals (Kuz'mina 1994, 195). These stalks were found in the context of a ritual offering (*zhertva*), and no other examples were recovered from the settlement context (Krivtsova-Grakova 1948, 73). The most widely cited evidence for agricultural practices throughout the steppe is the existence of stone pestles, grinding stones, bronze "sickle"-shaped knives, stone adzes, and other tools presumably used for agriculture (Kuz'mina 1994, 196–199). These artifacts suggest that plant products played an important role in the diet of steppe pastoralists; however, explanations of the way agricultural production may have been integrated with regional pastoralist strategies is still left largely to ethnographic analogy and speculation (Pashkevich 2003).

Recent excavations in the Samara valley by Anthony et al. (2005) illustrate that non-agricultural pastoralist economies can be associated with year round settlements. Detailed botanical and faunal research from the site of Krasnosamarskoe illustrate that groups living at the ecological transition between the steppe and forest-steppe were pastoral generalists, who took full advantage of a diversity of wild plants as they controlled seasonally diverse pasture areas across local biomes (Popova 2006).

The evidence of Bronze Age pastoralist economies from across the steppe illustrates a highly iterated development of specialized adaptations to localized ecological and social conditions in the Middle and Late Bronze Age. The origins of domestication for a number of key species such as horses are still hotly debated, and the spread, transmission, or assimilation of herding systems based in cattle, sheep, and goats is still a largely an under-documented process across the steppe zone. However, from the available faunal evidence and the associated ecological settings across Eurasia, we may better understand the development of pastoral ways of life from the perspective of local trajectories of change, facilitated by an expanding scale of interaction from 3000–1500 BCE, which facilitated the diffusion·of domestic innovations, technology, and material culture among neighboring steppe populations.

METALLURGY

From the 1960s, the work of Evgenii Chernykh and his students represents the most extensive studies of steppe metallurgy. Chernykh (1992, 18–25) rightly notes that the use of metallurgical studies for the recreation of social interaction is not without methodological problems. However, because copper and tin deposits are discretely distributed across the steppe zone and metal production sites are neither evenly nor frequently recovered in the region, copper and bronze metallurgy represent a social technology that demanded conscious planning and geographic negotiation to produce and distribute (Chernykh 1992, 6). The proliferation of copper and bronze artifacts, from the small personal decorations found in Afanas'evo burials to the elaborate assemblage of arsenical and tin bronze items attributed to the Seima-Turbino phenomenon of the Late Bronze Age, suggests that the importance of metal objects—both functionally and symbolically—spurred the evolution of metallurgical technology during the later part of the second millennium BCE amongst pastoralists of the steppe.

METAL SOURCES

Though the particulars of Chernykh's proposed framework for regionally distinct "metallurgical provinces" have been debated and refined, his discussion of both the technological and the formal relationships between metal artifacts of the Bronze Age is still current. Chernykh identifies two large "provinces" of metallurgy during the Bronze Age, namely the Circumpontic Metallurgical Province (CMP) and the Eurasian Metallurgical Province (EAMP). The CMP stretches from the western steppe region to the Urals and is dated by calibrated radiocarbon from the Early Bronze Age to the early Late Bronze Age (3300–1900 BCE) (Chernykh et. al 2000; Chernykh et. al 2002). The EAMP covers the central and eastern steppe zones, and likely represents a diffusion of metallurgical technology developed in the CMP across the steppe at the start of the Late Bronze Age (c. 2000 BCE) (Chernykh 1992, 190; Chernykh et. al 2002). Chernykh defines these regional systems of ore extraction, metal production, and artifact circulation based on spectrographic analysis of alloyed components in the metal itself. Ancient copper mines of the CMP are predominately located in the mountainous regions of the Ural and Carpathian mountains. Recent studies at sites such as Kargaly in the Orenburg region illustrate that the technology for mining and detecting ore sources was already well developed by the third millennium BCE in the steppe region, if not much earlier (Chernykh 1997; Chernykh 2002).

In the EAMP, substantial copper and tin deposits are localized in the Altai mountains and Minusinsk basin, as well as along the Ili River and in the Dzhungar Basin of Xinjiang (western China) (Mei and Shell 1998; Mei 2000). Additionally, isolated copper deposits exist north of Lake Balkhash in Kazakhstan. Presumably, regional groups used these ores at least by the early third millennium BCE, although it is difficult to provenience Early Bronze Age alloyed artifacts to specific ore sources in this region (Chernykh

1992). By end of the second millennium BCE the EAMP as a whole extended across most of the Eurasian steppe zone.

The earlier stages of the EAMP are associated with the Andronovo Cultural Community (specifically the Sintashta-Petrovka and Alakul cultural groups) as well as neighboring culture groups in the forest steppe and Volga region such as the Abashevo and Srubnaya cultures. The middle of the second millennium BCE (Late Bronze Age) reflects increasing distribution of metallurgy across the EAMP, primarily associated with the long distance distribution of tin-bronze artifacts known as the Seima-Turbino phenomenon. Tin-bronzes of the Seima-Turbino type (as opposed to earlier arsenical bronze) are provenienced to Altaic sources of tin, which adds to the argument that the Late Bronze Age was a period of greater interaction between eastern and western steppe populations.

REGIONAL METAL FORMS AND PRODUCTION CENTERS

Metallurgy in the eastern steppe can best be understood, stylistically at least, as changing from simple to more complex throughout the Bronze Age. The metallurgical consumption of Afanas'evo groups, for example, was limited to small decorative copper objects of simple form (Chernykh 1992, 183). The range of objects attributed to the subsequent Okunev phase is slightly wider and more elaborate; including knives, awls, nails, and bracelets. The chemical composition of most metal artifacts from Okunev burials is essentially pure copper, with only trace elements such as antimony, arsenic, lead, and silver (Kavrin 1997, 162). Okunev artifacts, which date to the chronological horizon with the Middle Bronze Age (c. 2500 BCE), are also more stylized, and a few bronze artifacts have been found, for example the bronze spearhead found at the site of Moiseikha (Chernykh 1992, 184). This trajectory of change reflects progressive metallurgical exploitation in the areas of the Altai and Yenisei River Basin through the end of the third millennium BCE.

Among the most enigmatic metallurgical developments across the steppe zone is the widespread distribution of metal artifacts known as the Seima-Turbino phenomenon. Seima-Turbino bronzes illustrate that knives and axes with component compositions consistent with tin sources provenienced in the Altai Mountains were transmitted far into the western steppe region (Chernykh 1992, 226). Chronologically the Seima-Turbino phenomenon dates to the Late Bronze Age (c. 1900–1700 BCE) within the greater Eurasian Metallurgical Province. Seima-Turbino metals include tin-bronze sickle-knives (fig. 7), socketed spearheads, ceremonial axes, and personal effects. These forms are best known from five steppe burial sites: Satygha and Rostovka on the Irtysh River and Seima, Reshnoe and Turbino along the Volga River (Chernykh 1992, 216). Notable other collections of Seima-Turbino metals are found with the "Borodino treasure," recovered far to the west in Moldavia. This elaborate horde of materials illustrates that ceremonial tin-bronze axes, as well as flint and nephrite-jade axe heads, were displaced at great distances across the steppe zone.

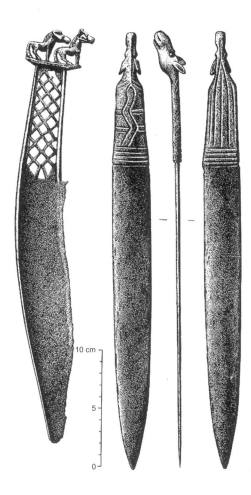

10 cm

5

0

FIGURE 7
Bronze knives of the Seima-Turbino type
from the Seima burial ground. After
Chernykh 1992, 223.

Chernykh suggests that the Seima-Turbino ores and styles that are found among mixed metallurgical assemblages in steppe contexts illustrate events of population displacement from the Altai region, because spectral analysis of the artifacts show that the ore sources for Seima-Turbino metals and stone objects have a decisive provenience there (Chernykh 1992, 226).

By the middle second millennium BCE, copper and bronze artifacts were more prevalent in the EAMP, both in terms of stylistic variation and geographic range (Chernykh 1992; Kuz'mina 1986, 35) (fig. 8). Highly stylized casts and technically well made metal artifacts are common in burial and settlement contexts of the middle second millennium BCE, and evidence for regionally specialized production of metal is apparent in Central Kazakhstan and further east (Mei 2003). Studies by Kadirbaev and Kurmankulov (1992) at the sites of Atasu, Mirzhik, and Ak-Mustafa illustrate that Central Kazakhstan was also a production center for casting and smelting copper and bronze during the late second millennium BCE. At the end of the Seima-Turbino period, a proliferation of

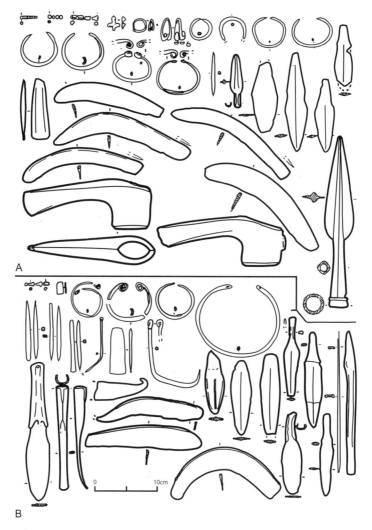

FIGURE 8
Metallurgy of the Middle and Late Bronze Age (a) Southern Ural mountains;
(b) North and central Kazakhstan. After Chernykh 1992, 190.

tin-bronze production characterizes metallurgical centers throughout central and eastern Kazakhstan (Kadirbaev and Kurmankulov 1992). Late/Final Bronze Age sites illustrate the development of complex metallurgical production centers representing an economic progression from the Atasu culture to the Begazy-Dandybaevsky and Karasuk
cultures of the Final Bronze Age (Margulan et al. 1966, 237).

The network model presented in this study is useful in reinterpreting the metallurgical distribution documented throughout the second millennium BCE. The articulation
of regional pastoralist landscapes may have fostered interactive processes that allowed

for the widespread distribution of the Seima-Turbino-type metals, as well as more wide-spread metallurgical distribution in the post-Seima-Turbino period of the Final Bronze Age. Perhaps a system of ore transport or ingot trade formed in the later half of the second millennium BCE from the Altai region to the west, potentially monitored by pastoral populations living in corridor regions such as the Dzhungar Mountains (above). In the concluding section of the book I present in greater detail a new model of interaction that revisits the nature of Bronze Age metallurgical distribution across the steppe in the second millennium BCE.

SOCIAL ORGANIZATION AND SCALE: ARCHITECTURE
AND BURIAL EVIDENCE

The steady increase in the discovery and excavation of settlements and burials in Eurasia provides ample comparisons of architecture and burial construction across the steppe zone and offers insights into the variation of social organization and demographic scale of Bronze Age steppe populations, even within a given cultural-historical period. Kuz'mina (1994) presents a comprehensive survey of Bronze Age settlements and burials across the steppe region. Here I focus on the comparative scale and structure of these domestic constructions. I aim to illustrate two points: first, settlement forms and technologies are differentiated regionally and ecologically, and second, domestic constructions reflect local traditions rather than diffused technologies. Concerning burials, there is a great degree of diversity, but burials do reflect a meta-local condition of shared ideology across the steppe. Taken together, the data illustrate locally derived adaptations employed by populations participating in varied and extensive networks of communication.

Few Early Bronze Age settlements have produced material consistent with either Yamnaya or Afanas'evo archaeological assemblages. Those that are known, such as Mikhailovka (Masson and Merpert 1982), yield Yamnaya material forms, but other artifacts such as domestic faunal assemblages correspond poorly with assemblages recovered in Yamnaya type burial sites. In the eastern steppe, there is a comparable dearth of Early Bronze Age settlement evidence, although new research excites the possibility that third millennium BCE settlements can be recovered in greater numbers throughout the region.

Well documented evidence for Eneolithic/Early Bronze Age settlements of the Botai and Tersek cultures is available for the northcentral regions of the steppe. Botai settlements reflect hamlets or villages with one hundred or more pit-type houses grouped along river ways, with superstructures of logs and earth (Kislenko and Tatarintseva 1999). Archaeologists have classically reconstructed the pit-houses at Botai as round dwellings approximately 5–6 meters in diameter, with log and sod construction (e.g., Kislenko 1993, fig. 3). However, recent studies of Botai-type settlements at sites such as Krasnyi Yar and Vasilkovsky IV show that the structures were likely rectilinear in form,

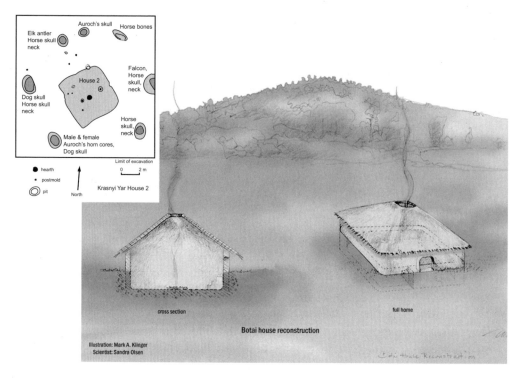

Inset labels:
Auroch's skull
Horse bones
Elk antler
Horse skull
neck
Falcon,
Horse
skull,
neck
House 2
Dog skull
Horse skull
neck
Horse
skull,
neck
Male & female
Auroch's horn cores,
Dog skull
Limit of excavation
0   2 m
● hearth
• postmold
◎ pit
North
Krasnyi Yar House 2

cross section
full home
Botai house reconstruction
Illustration: Mark A. Klinger
Scientist: Sandra Olsen

FIGURE 9

Botai culture settlement reconstruction. Inset: Excavation plan of Botai-culture house at Krasnyi Yar.
Source: Marc Klinger and S. Olsen, with permission.

with rows of houses forming dense areas of settlement covering 4–6 hectares (Olsen
et al. 2006; fig. 9). These settlements are rich in horse remains and reflect material cultural analogies ranging from the Surtandy culture of the southern Urals to the
Afanas'evo culture in the Altai (Zaibert 1993). Olsen cites the size and organization of
the Botai-type settlements, as well as the annual diversity of subsistence resources, as
evidence for a broadly sedentary way of life for the Botai people. An estimated population of 130–400 individuals in these villages further implies the formation of domestically productive communities around the middle of the fourth millennium BCE in the
northern steppe zone (Olsen 2006).

Significantly, a dénouement in the occurrence of Botai type settlements is recorded
at about 2500 BCE in the Tobol region, with only two sites, Sergeevka and Balandino illustrating in situ transition from prevalent horse hunting/management (which defined
the Botai culture) to mixed cattle and sheep breeding (typical of the Middle Bronze Age)
(Kislenko and Tatarintseva 1999, 215–216). The shift around 2500–2000 BCE in
domestic economy toward more intensive cattle and sheep herding corresponds with
the prevalence of more highly seasonal settlements such as Petrovka-2. Thus, the departure in form and scale of these sites corresponds with economic evidence to link these

transitional sites with early Middle Bronze Age cultural assemblages of the Petrovka type. However, at this same time we also see the innovation of large scale fortified settlements of the Sintashta type in the trans-Urals, marking the start of the Middle Bronze Age in that region.

The settlements of the Sintashta-Petrovka period reflect a considerable degree of variation. Sintashta and Arkaim represent the archetypes of the "country of towns" settlement form, with thick circular defensive walls and cellular housing units forming a cohesive structure (fig. 10). These settlements were large, fortified, and centralized; the outer fortifications at Sintashta enclose roughly 6.2 ha (Gening et al. 1992, 390). The settlements were supported primarily by herding groups, taking advantage of the rich ecological niche along the many rivers and tributaries in the Ural region. Taken alone, Sintashta type settlements are regular in their form, with concentric circular passages and tiered structures within. Broadly contemporary with these large settlements are settlements of the Petrovka type, which are typically located along the banks of tributary

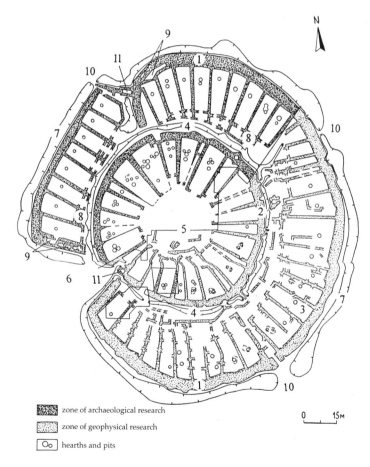

FIGURE 10
Plan of excavations at Arkaim. After Zdanovich and Zdanovich 2002, 256.

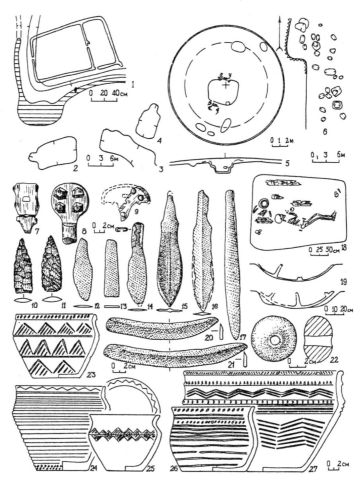

FIGURE 11

Archaeological materials of the Petrovka culture. After Zdanovich 1988, 168.

rivers or nearby springs, across the region of the south Urals and north Kazakhstan (Hanks et al. 2007) (fig. 11). Houses of the Petrovka type are typically smaller and rectangular, with a total area ranging from 25–100 m² with sandy/clay floors, log-beam walls and roofs, and shallow foundations from 15–20 cm below the surface.

Ludmila Koryakova suggests that uneven economic and technological relations between centralized populations at fortified sites like Sintashta and tribal groups living in surrounding territories led to the establishment of a variety of scales of core-periphery exchanges (Koryakova 2002, 103). Koryakova argues that around 2200 BCE the structure of regional interaction was reflective of a complex chiefdom, though she also notes that the trajectory of social complexity in the trans-Urals at this time did not reflect progressive evolution to an arbitrarily greater level of complexity—at least not until the start of the first millennium BCE.

Late Bronze Age settlements show a comparable degree of regional diversity. Alakul houses are commonly semi-subterranean, with rectangular foundations 0.6 to 1.3 meters deep, numerous fireplaces, and, sometimes, stone walls and foundations (e.g., Shandasha, Elenovka-I and II [Kuz'mina 1994, 69]). Alakul-type settlements are similar to Petrovka settlements in their location along rivers,[9] although they are frequently larger, with house areas from 100–200 m². For example, the settlement site of Shandasha, located in the Orenburg region exhibits stone foundations (around 80 m²) with shallow footings (Kuz'mina 1964a). However, notable deviations from this construction style at sites like Tasty-Butak, illustrate that pit houses were also used in this period (Sorokin and Gryaznov 1962). Tasty-Butak is located on the banks of the Tasty-Butak tributary of the Ural River in northern Kazakhstan and is characterized by small groups of rectilinear structures, approximately 100 m², without stone or wooden foundations (fig. 12). In spite of its humble construction, Tasty-Butak reveals a commitment to permanent habitation, based on the fact that as many as eleven wells were found associated with the four houses, each with a depth of four to five meters (Sorokin and Gryaznov 1966, 61). A few of the wells'

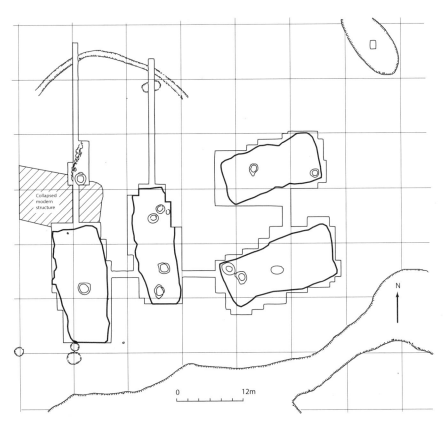

FIGURE 12

Plan of Bronze Age settlement at Tasty-Butak. After Sorokin and Gryaznov 1966.

shafts were fortified by a lattice of saxaul, a steppe hardwood tree (*Haloxylon* sp.) Zdanovich argues that such investment in water resources is indicative of year round maintenance of the settlement (Zdanovich 1988, 140).

By distinction, Fedorovo settlements such as Alekseevka, Yazevo, and Yavlenka are believed to represent a number of settlement events, because of the their mixed stratigraphy (Kuz'mina 1994, 70). Structurally, Fedorovo settlements are similar to Alakul; however Kuz'mina writes that "a large number [of Fedorovo settlements] have mixed cultural horizons which suggest they were *settled more than once*" (Kuz'mina 1994, 70; emphasis mine). Although it is not completely clear in the text, I interpret Kuz'mina's use of the phrase "*neodnokratnaya zaseleniya*" to mean settled and resettled with substantial breaks in habitation, instead of a reference to seasonal patterns of settlement.

The relationship between stratigraphic deposition and settlement practices is complex at sites of mobile pastoralists. Late Bronze Age levels at the site of Begash reflect mixed stratigraphic contexts, which I argue are the result of revisitation as part of a regular pattern of seasonal reuse of the settlement (Frachetti and Mar'yashev 2007). Seasonal leveling and cleaning of settlements produces mixed cultural and stratigraphic contexts, and can confuse chronological associations between material forms and site occupation. In light of this, the variable settlement geography and mixed stratigraphy that characterize Fedorovo sites in the more arid regions of central Kazakhstan such as Ikpen'-I may be reflective of a seasonal landuse pattern, rather than stochastic use and disuse of the site. In other areas such as northern Kazakhstan, where the environment is more diverse (Biyashev et. al 1975; Lavrenko and Karamysheva 1993), the coexistence of seemingly permanent settlements and those with mixed stratigraphy may reflect a diversification of the population's settlement ecology. In these regions, some groups may have lived in settlements on a seasonal basis, while other groups exhibited a more highly sedentary or permanent habitation strategy.

The settlements of the Late and Final Bronze Age (e.g., Atasu) include an industrial aspect, with smelting and casting workshops as part of the overall layout of sites (Kadirbaev and Kurmankulov 1992). Late Bronze Age settlements of Semirech'ye reflect a similar stone construction to those noted for the Fedorovo culture, as well as those of central Kazakhstan. However, no metallurgical production sites are known in the Semirech'ye region.

BURIALS

Burials are the most widely studied Bronze Age site-type in the steppe zone. In fact, commonalities in the mounded (kurgan) form of steppe burials contributed to the early generalization of the Andronovo Complex (Gaul 1943; Sal'nikov 1948; Kuz'mina 1964a; Sorokin and Gryaznov 1966) and to broader cultural classifications such as the "Kurgan culture" (Gimbutas 1958; Gimbutas 1965). However, steppe burial forms throughout the second millennium BCE also exhibit considerable regional variation.

Steppe burials of the Sintashta-Petrovka type in the western steppe zone are recognizable as low kurgans (~0.5 m) with a diameter ranging from 12 to 16 m (e.g., Sintashta, Berlik, Ulyubai, Bol'shekaragan). Beneath the earthen mound there is usually a burial chamber (approximately 4 × 2.5 m) delineated by wooden framework (*ograda*) with a pit burial (1–1.5 m deep) in the center (e.g., Bol'shekaragan-grave 13 [Zdanovich 2002b]). At sites in northern and central Kazakhstan, the burial chamber is often laid out in stone, presumably because wood resources are scarcer (Zdanovich 1988). In these cases, the burial chamber is commonly topped with a capstone or wooden lid. Within the chamber, bodies are typically laid flexed on their left side, with the head oriented to the west or northwest.

Alakul period burial forms are more variable than are those attributed to the Petrovka culture. Alakul burial construction types include earth and stone kurgans (e.g., Alakul, (Sal'nikov 1952), as well as rectangular stone structures without kurgans (e.g., Tasty-Butak (Sorokin and Gryaznov 1962). There is also considerable variability in the ritual interment of the body. Most commonly, bodies are laid on their left side in a flexed position, with the head oriented to the west. However, at Alekseevka, the bodies were oriented to the east (Kuz'mina 1994). Furthermore, cremation ritual is found at Alakul sites such as Kulevchi-IV, associated with the transition to the final Bronze Age (Vinogradov 1984) and cremation has been suggested for Final Bronze Age sites in the Tian Shan mountains such as Kul'sai (Goryachev 2001). Recent studies in Semirech'ye by the author have also revealed Bronze Age cremation burials at Begash, associated stratigraphically with cultural contexts dated as early as the late third millennium BCE (Frachetti and Mar'yashev 2007).

The high degree of variability within the Alakul cemeteries makes it difficult to formulate a firm typological framework. Zdanovich (1988, 142) remarks that "within one burial field, as a rule, [there is] a concentration of construction types of different periods of the Bronze Age, so that short of completely opening the whole area it is often impossible to comment about the chronology and cultural associations. Today we may only determine general tendencies concerning the development of burial construction of the Alakul culture."

Fedorovo burials also reflect considerable variation between sites in the Minusinsk Basin, the Tobol region, and central and eastern Kazakhstan. The burial form east of the Irtysh River is most commonly a low kurgan constructed over a rectangular or oval wooden or burial chamber (e.g., Fedorovka [Sal'nikov 1948]). On the western and southern extents of the Fedorovo culture, burials regularly are a low stone arrangement with central box or cist made of flagstones (e.g., Burluk-I [Zdanovich 1970]). In both structural types, the orientation of the burial pit is generally east to west, and the burials are shallow, often less than one meter deep.

Bronze Age burial forms reflect a broadly comparable "grammar" across the steppe region, with many common forms such as kurgans or stone frames, stone cists, and lined burial chambers. However, within regions it is difficult to attribute specific characteristics

as archetypical, given that cemeteries commonly reflect a variety of burial forms. Archaeologists working in the steppe have noted this difficulty as well. Kuz'mina avoids overem-
phasizing burial form as a discriminatory factor in understanding the geography and
chronology of regional Andronovo cultures (Kuz'mina 1994; also Zdanovich 1988).

This study conceives of burial forms as significant ways by which smaller regional
groups differentiate themselves internally. This may explain the internal variability in
burial form for the Alakul and Fedorovo cemeteries, for example. Most archaeologists
working on the steppe have placed an emphasis on finding commonalities in the burial
record between regions, but I suggest that a more informative approach may be to focus
on the differences that occur within regions, in order to explain how variability in burials and other socio-ritual contexts may be seen as indicators of differential access and
articulation within unbalanced social, political, or economic spheres.

BRONZE AGE CERAMICS

Archaeological material culture—ceramics, metallurgy, and stone implements—
represents the primary evidence used to support models of regional expansion and cultural diffusion of steppe pastoralists. Prior to the use of archaeometric techniques to distinguish in detail the nature of material homology, archaeologists relied on stylistic
categories to relate various regional populations and their ways of life. As with economic
studies, material studies—especially concerning metallurgy—have benefited from scientific techniques such as elemental analysis, residue studies, and petrographic analysis
to shed more light on steppe cultural sequences. Nevertheless, ceramic form and decoration remain the dominant indexes for material provenience and chronology in a
steppe context.

The Andronovo ceramic seriation is intricate and is based on more than eighty years
of combined research by many archaeologists (Krivtsova-Grakova 1948; Kuz'mina
1964b; Kosarev 1981; Fedorova-Davydova 1973; Zdanovich 1984; Gryaznov 1969). Andronovo ceramics are generally divided according to decorative style, form (shape and
size), and more recently by fabrication. Stylistic and formal variations are still by far the
most widespread and commonly used seriation criteria. Classifications of material variability and its use as proxies for social groups are deeply entrenched in steppe archaeology. Material groupings influence nearly all of the conclusions and interpretations of
the geographic and chronological relationships between Bronze Age societies of the
Eurasian steppe zone.

To the non-expert, the features that differentiate Petrovka ceramic vessels from
Alakul ceramics are slight, Alakul from Fedorovo even less, and Alakul/Fedorovo from
Nurinsky-Atasu almost undetectable (Kuz'mina 1986, 66–68). However, to those who
have devoted their careers to this material, identifiable differences are found in the technology of fabrication, as well as in the shape of the vessels and the location of their decorations (Loman 1990; Kuz'mina 1986). The details of these differences are outlined

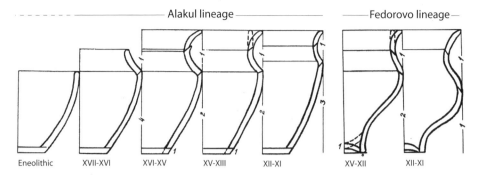

FIGURE 13

Evolution of Andronova Ceramic Forms. After Kuzmina 1994, 407.

more completely in the works of these authors, and therefore I will not devote pages to translate their work here. However, since much of this work is inaccessible to most western scholars, a brief overview of key factors and their typological relationship aids in our examination of the comparative elements of steppe societies in the Bronze Age.[10] The primary components used to differentiate Andronovo ceramic types are form, decoration, and fabric.

FORM

The form of Andronovo ceramics falls generally into three categories: straight walled jars, straight walled jars with everted or "fluted" necks, and round-walled jars with fluted necks (fig. 13; Kuz'mina 1986, fig. 12). Straight walls and some fluted and non-fluted necks characterize the ceramics of the earliest Andronovo variant, the Sintashta-Petrovka type; these overlap stylistically with early Alakul ceramics.

Late Alakul and Fedorovo ceramics exhibit rounded shoulders (referred to as bulges), as well as sharp sloping around the base and foot of the vessel (figs. 14 and 15). This formal transition is documented in the western steppe at sites such as Tasty-Butak-I (Sorokin and Gryaznov 1962) and at late Fedorovo sites in eastern and central Kazakhstan, such as Atasu-I and Bylkyldak-II (Margulan et al. 1966, 115, table X-#2, #3). Atasu ceramic forms reflect a transition to the rounder body forms of the ceramics of the Late or Final Bronze Age culture groups such as the Begazy-Dandybaevsky and Karasuk cultures. Ceramics from sites such as Malye Koreny-3 in the Minusinsk Basin (Ziablin 1977, 105, drawing 3), and Buguly-II and III in Central Kazakhstan reflect a rounded, globular jar form, with a vertical rim (Margulan et al. 1966, 192, table XX; 1979, 118). This change in shape represents the evolution from the straight body with "bulging" shoulders of the late Fedorovo, Nurinksy and Atasu ceramics.

Vessel shape alone is not enough to categorize the majority of Andronovo jar types, because the simpler hand-made vessel forms (such as the straight sided, undecorated,

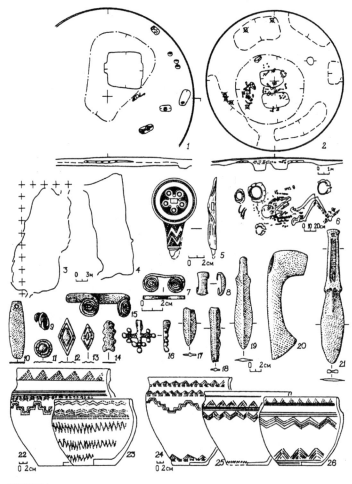

FIGURE 14
Archaeological materials of the Alakul culture. After Zdanovich 1988, 169.

and non-fluted jars) are ubiquitous in archaeological contexts of all periods across the steppe region. Moreover, the degree of overlap in shape between Alakul and Fedorovo jars blurs the categorization. Therefore, cultural affiliations are often assigned according to the regional location of the site, rather than on a purely formal basis, especially in the case of Fedorovo and Alakul materials (Zdanovich 1988).

DECORATION

The types of incised and stamped decorations on Andronovo vessels are more regionally differentiable than is vessel shape, and motif styles have been used as the justification for new "cultural" variants, as well as evidence for regional population movements. The incised motifs of Andronovo vessels are in fact rather simplistic, largely represented by geometric shapes (e.g., triangles, rhombuses, and meandering lines). In fact, ceramic

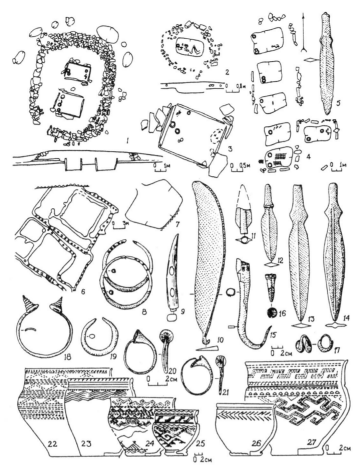

FIGURE 15

Archaeological material of the Fedorovo culture. After Zdanovich 1988, 170.

types are differentiated more by the placement and coverage of decorations over the vessel, rather than by the actual motifs themselves (fig. 16).

For example, Petrovka and early Alakul ceramic styles share similar patterns of incised and impressed geometric decorations and meandering linear incisions around the neck of the vessel. However, the earlier Petrovka ceramics are typically decorated on the neck and shoulders and tend to be undecorated on the main body of the jar. Alakul decorations are often distributed over the entire vessel, including the neck, shoulders, and body (Kuz'mina 1986, 67). Fedorovo ceramics are also typically decorated around the neck and shoulders of the vessel, but reflect a greater density of meandering lines and larger geometric stamps. Later ceramic types, such as Nurinsky, Atasu, Begazy-Dandybaevsky, Karasuk and others, each reflect a mixing of a relatively unlimited potential selection of hand-incised motifs, dots, lines, and stamps. Nurinsky ceramics reflect small incisions of triangular forms, often with linear rings separating decorations

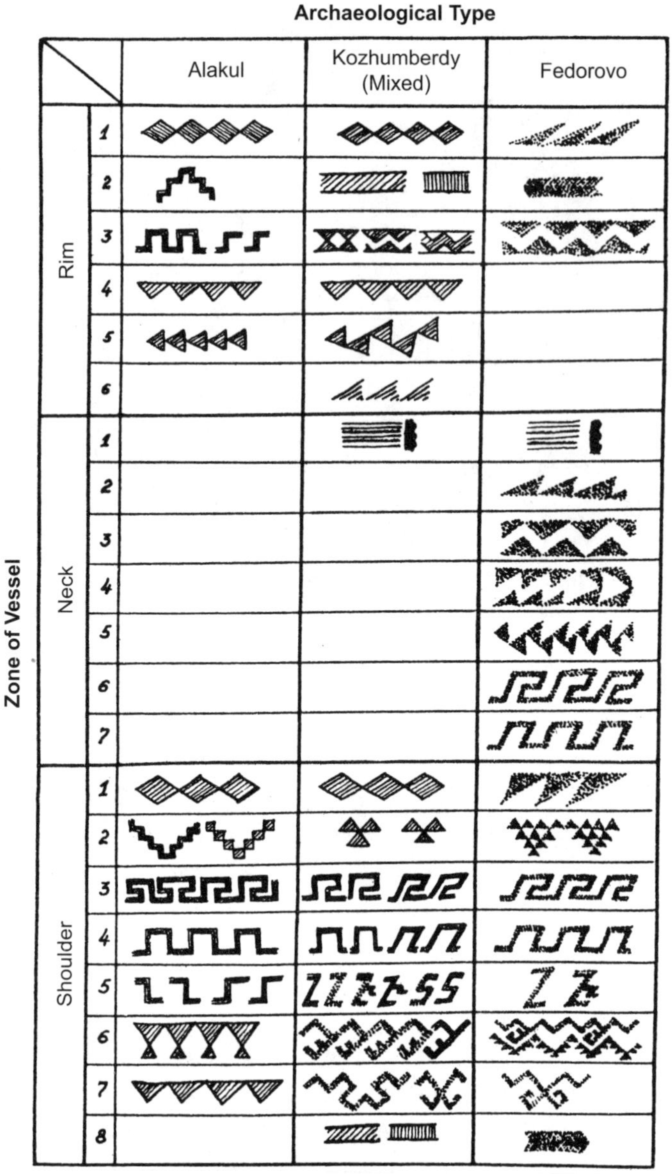

Archaeological Type

Zone of Vessel		Alakul	Kozhumberdy (Mixed)	Fedorovo
Rim	1			
	2			
	3			
	4			
	5			
	6			
Neck	1			
	2			
	3			
	4			
	5			
	6			
	7			
Shoulder	1			
	2			
	3			
	4			
	5			
	6			
	7			
	8			

FIGURE 16

Alakul and Fedorovo ceramic motifs. After Kuz'mina 1994, 409.

around the neck from those of the shoulders and body of the vessels (fig. 17) (Margulan et al. 1966, table II, 64). Ceramic styles of the Nurinsky and Atasu phases are differentiated mainly from the placement of designs on the vessel; Nurinksy pots have decorations on the neck and shoulders whereas Atasu ceramics have decorations on the rim, shoulders, and base (Margulan et al. 1966, 67). Atasu ceramics reflect a more sparse coverage of rectangular and triangular stamped and incised lines. Begazy-Dandybaevsky

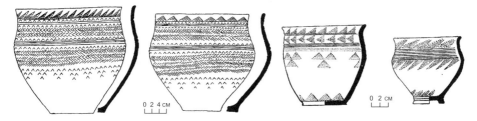

FIGURE 17
Nurinsky ceramics. After Margulan et al. 1966, 62–64.

ceramics reflect larger decorations, with a greater variety of incised and stamped designs sparingly placed across the rims and shoulders of the vessels (Margulan 1979, 118, 127, 129). Karasuk ceramics are similar to Dandybaevsky forms in both shape and decoration (Ziablin 1977, 108–109; fig. 18).

Mixed ceramic styles at sites such as Atasu (Kadirbaev and Kurmankulov 1992) and Ust-Narym (Chernikov 1960) are used to argue that the Fedorovo culture expanded south to the central steppes of Kazakhstan in the later half of the second millennium BCE. The appearance of Fedorovo-type materials is also noted in Semirech'ye, both in the Late Bronze Age levels at Begash (excavated by the author) and from other Late Bronze Age sites such as Kuigan, Talapty, Oi-Dzhailyau, and others (Mar'yashev and Goryachev 1993; Karabaspakova 1989; Mar'yashev and Goryachev 1999). On the basis of these materials, central and southeastern Kazakhstan is considered a peripheral inter-action zone for the Fedorovo culture, reflecting displaced populations from the heart-land of Fedorovo sites concentrated north around the Irtysh and Yenisei Rivers. As noted above, sites like Begash pose a contradiction to this theory, showing instead a local evo-lution of ceramic forms starting in the third millennium BCE with the earliest mobile pastoralists in Semirech'ye (Frachetti and Mar'yashev 2007).

Based on past models, the spread of the Fedorovo culture into central and eastern Kazakhstan, and to a lesser extent the Alakul culture, marks the transition to the Final Bronze Age. The Nurinsky and Atasu cultures of central Kazakhstan are also attributed to the Late Bronze Age, 1500–1200 BCE (Margulan et. al 1966; Kadirbaev and Kurmankulov 1992). Specifically, the Nurinsky culture is considered generally synchro-nous with the Late Fedorovo, as the two groups are differentiated only by minimal variations in their material culture.

Like differences in form, the consignment of stylistic traits to various culture-groups reflects a somewhat circular argument. Namely, regional archaeological assemblages that reflect combinations of ceramic styles known from initial classification schemes[11] are explained as cultural mixes and used as evidence for regional connections. However, the direction of the proposed connections is apparently based on the history of archae-ological typologies themselves, rather than on an independent argument for the mixture of various ceramic types in certain contexts. Furthermore, stylistic variations

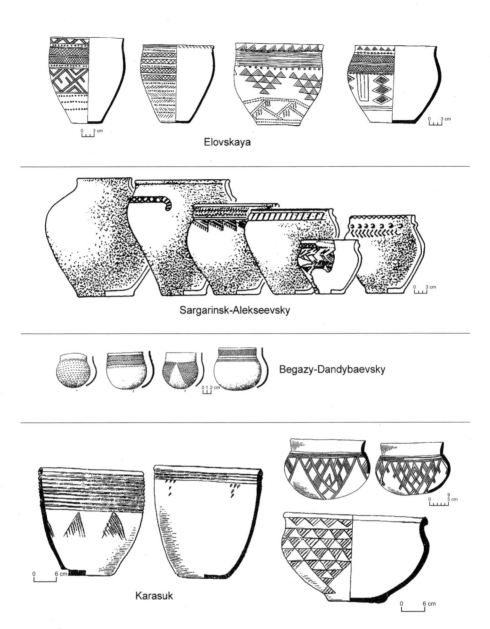

Elovskaya

Sargarinsk-Alekseevsky

Begazy-Dandybaevsky

Karasuk

FIGURE 18

Ceramic forms of various culture areas during the Final Bronze Age (1300–1000 cal BCE). Sources cited in text.

are considered by some archaeologists as a pseudo-genetic proxy traceable from generation to generation and are used to define social groups as indexes of ethnic difference (Kuz'mina 1994). The primary debate concerning steppe ceramic styles is not how different or similar they are, but whether these stylistic affinities represent a transfer of semiotics and cultural styles through person-to-person contact or regional migration, whether the materials themselves are being exchanged across regions through regional networks, or if some other system of diffusion is at work.

One cannot ignore that a close reading of the variability of decorative styles on Andronovo ceramics reveals localized typological trends (Kuz'mina 1994), and that some of the elements within these typologies are found a considerable distance from the locus of their greatest regularity. Nevertheless, since Andronovo ceramic decorations are handmade (rather than systematically produced), the geographic distribution of certain motifs is at best an inaccurate indication of an overarching system of symbolic or material transfer. Detailed analysis of ceramic decoration does illustrate that some form of stylistic dissemination occurred, but it is not helpful in elucidating the interactive process between the local populations that created the variability of designs or the ways the designs were distributed across the steppe.

FABRIC

Recent studies of the ceramic fabric of Andronovo vessels of the Late Bronze Age of central Kazakhstan suggest that the technology, techniques, and materials of ceramic production were locally derived and differentiated among regional populations. Loman's petrographic analysis of the constituent components of ceramics of the Sargarinsk-Alekseevka type at settlements of Dongal, Kopa I, and Upais illustrates that the temper of Late Bronze Age ceramics was highly variable between different settlements (Loman 1990; Loman 1993). His petrographic analysis shows that the clays and sands primarily reflected soils of local provenience and that the technology of using crushed fired clay and dung in the ceramic fabric was significantly variable, even within a relatively confined region. These studies suggest that the production of ceramics was a local phenomenon and that although the decoration of these handmade pots may have been similar, the populations that produced them did not practice similar craft techniques. Alternatively, these analyses may illustrate that various groups among local populations had access to different channels of trade or interaction, which may account for the degree of variation in their material assemblages. At this stage, studies of ceramic fabric raise significant questions concerning the nature of regional interaction, and cast doubt on the introduction of materials through long distance ethnic ties of Bronze Age regional populations (given the locality of clay sources).

The economic, structural, and material record of Bronze Age steppe societies illustrate that the elements of the Andronovo cultural category do not document a smooth spread of technology or homogeneity of pastoralist lifeways. Chronological inconsistencies and actual formal differences illustrate instead that populations of the western, central, and eastern steppe more likely contributed to the formation of shared, macroscale arenas of material culture and economic innovation by strategically negotiating the contextual conditions of their local landscapes. As the following chapters illustrate in detail, variations in pastoralist strategies contributed to aspects of their material and social worlds being assimilated or extracted from their neighbors. Perhaps occasionally there were larger-scale displacements—bursts of wider regional migration—resulting in more rapid diffusions. However, the archaeology of the steppe suggests a highly complex structure of interactions through the periodic alignment of landscapes rather than a smooth spread of either material or population. Decoding the formation of such landscapes in Semirech'ye is the task of the following chapters.

BRONZE AGE INTERACTION

Thus far, I have been concerned with laying out the details of the archaeology of the Bronze Age and reviewing some of the ways the culture-historical framework of the Andronovo period has led to interpretations and assumptions about the economic organization and material relationships between populations across the steppe through time. It is important to have this background, because archaeologists are still presented with the problem of explaining the similarities and differences in these data across geography and time. To date, archaeologists generally agree that some form of communication, diffusion, or interaction took place between regional populations of the steppe throughout the second millennium BCE to produce the overlap and extensive distribution of material culture presented above (Hiebert 2002; Chen and Hiebert 1995; Lamberg-Karlovsky 2002). The models used to explain the distribution of "Andronovo culture" carry with them implications for parallel processes, such as the spread of technologies, language, and ideology between Asia and Europe (Anthony 2007).

In a critique of the archaeological evidence underlying theories of Indo-Iranian and Indo-European language transfer across the steppe region during the third and second millennia, C. C. Lamberg-Karlovsky (2002) highlights the porous basis for current interaction models as reflected in material culture, regional ethnicity, and language (Lamberg-Karlovsky 2002). He cautiously remarks that current models may not best characterize the social dynamics of Bronze Age Eurasia, judiciously referring to the "untenable" and "elusive" nature of many of the material correlates for ethnic and linguistic definitions that underpin the models presented above. His rejection of current archaeolinguistic correlations is boldly expressed however, stating that "there is currently no compelling archaeological evidence for (or for that matter against) the notion that [steppe or oasis populations] are Indo-Iranian [speakers]" (Lamberg-Karlovsky 2002, 65–66). He further proposes that the spatial and interactive extents of regional populations should be elucidated by other means than stylistics *in order to* explain complex and dynamic processes such as language transfer, and not the other way around. Lamberg-Karlovsky's position, although directed at the issue of ethnic affinity and linguistic relationships, may be taken as a litmus for other debates that hinge on regional migration and ideas of population relocation or inter-ethnic contact during the Bronze Age, for example the spread of Seima-Turbino metallurgical technology or the diffusion of ceramic and burial styles.

To summarize, there is a compelling question about the nature of Bronze Age inter-action in the Eurasian steppe zone, which is made provocative by the apparent broad homology of styles and material forms ranging from ceramics to architecture and from what appears to be an emerging network of trade or transfer of metals. This chapter has traced the basis for the creation of the Andronovo culture and casts doubt on its utility as a paradigm for understanding living processes in steppe prehistory by emphasizing diversity among regional economies and material forms. I have proposed that the prob-lems with modeling regional relationships during the Bronze Age across the Eurasian steppe revolve around two basic discordances between the archaeology and proposed social reconstructions of the Bronze Age. First, the definition of regional "cultures" based on archaeologically assigned stylistic affinities is not a proxy for "culture" or "eth-nicity" in a living sense, and although they were conceived originally as material categories, cultural categories have distorted our view of complex interactive processes. Second, regional styles of material are a documented fact on the steppe, but how these styles blend, transfer, relocate, or otherwise morph cannot be clearly illustrated from ma-terial typologies. There is currently no proposed theory that offers specific details as to the reiterated contexts of trade or political-economic interaction consistent with actual practices of prehistoric pastoralist populations, or that takes into consideration the diverse spatial and temporal currents of interaction that contributed to the concentric scales of Bronze Age social landscapes across the Eurasian steppe.

The remaining chapters are devoted to the examination of one regional pastoralist landscape from the Bronze Age. This case study from the Koksu River valley illustrates the variation of regional and local pastoralist practices through a close reading of the environmental context, ethnographic background, and archaeological record. In this case, mobile pastoral practices are conceived within the boundaries of a social landscape whose extents are constantly reshaped according to strategies for negotiating dynamic constellations of political, material, and ecological conditions.

3

CONTINUITY, VARIATION, AND
CHANGE OF THE EURASIAN
STEPPE ENVIRONMENT

Its round-headed bluffs of dark shale, slashed with snow-drifts, rise from rolling
downlands covered with a luxurious growth of short, yellow-green grass, brightened
by brilliant patches of gentians, crocuses, edelweiss, and other Alpine flowers. Its
innocent-looking, but treacherous, bogs give birth to sparkling streams, which
form the numerous rivers that flow through barren foot-hills on to still more arid
plains, and terminate in large saline lakes. Groups of the dome-shaped tents of the
nomads are scattered over the plateaux [sic], and, wherever grass is plentiful, along
the edge of both river and lake; countless flocks and herds, the only wealth of their
wandering owners, dot this matchless pasture-land, and from a cloudless sky a
brilliant sun beats down upon plain and plateau.

J. H. MILLER (CARRUTHERS AND MILLER 1913, 319)

THE FORCE OF ENVIRONMENT

Ethnographers have long recognized that mobile pastoralism is largely an ecologically
strategic way of life (Bacon 1954; Barth 1964, Leslie and Little 1999). Decades ago
Douglas Johnson (1969, 4) wrote "It is the combination of seasonal and areal variability
in the location of pasture and water that makes the movements of pastoral nomads
necessary." Regardless of the other significant motivations that contribute to their social
and economic practices, pastoralists attentively monitor environmental conditions such
as seasonal rainfall and pasture and water resources and adjust their schedules of mobility, settlement, and socialization to accommodate these rhythms. As a result, pastoralist
landscapes are significantly shaped by the geographical and seasonal distribution of
environmental resources.

That said, the environment is not an inert backdrop; both nonhuman and anthropogenic forces and processes transform and shape it. Ecologists have long worked
against ideas of environmental determinism by demonstrating the reciprocal impact of
human strategies on the environment at immediate and protracted scales. Yet, the
perceived landscape defines the scale at which environmental conditions can be experi-
entially realized (Erickson 2000). Even though wider-scale environmental change is impacted by pastoralist behavior, local-scale variations in human strategy tend to fluctuate

in concert with the environment and thus may serve to mitigate a society's ability to re-
alize its role in environmental change. Consequently, the environment can appear as if
it is outside of human influence—a natural force—even though the history of human activity plays a fundamental role in its distribution and character.

Long-term environmental change is the focus of paleoclimatologists, wheras pastoral
ecology tends to describe geographically and temporally discrete relationships. Bronze
Age expansion and interaction supposedly correlate with climatic changes documented
for the early second millennium BCE. Few scholars, however, have related paleoclimatic
fluctuations in temperature and aridity to ecological assessments of the capacity of specific environments to support pastoral populations in prehistory (but see Kremenetski
et al. 1999). While paleoclimatic studies present macro-scale trends in changing aridity
and temperature, populations in prehistory would have experienced micro-scale changes
(such as periodic drought and warmer or colder spells). This chapter takes the first step
in rectifying these analytical scales by defining the current environmental context of the
study zone in comparison with its paleoclimatic record. The discussion of paleovegetation suggests that the past botanical constitution of the steppe is largely comparable to the
contemporary environment. Thus, a detailed assessment of the variability of the current
environment represents a critical first step toward understanding the ecological impact of
the perceived environment in structuring the pastoralist landscape over the long term.

Pastoral ecology characterizes the distribution and interrelationship of environmental conditions relevant to the perceived needs and behaviors of pastoralist societies as
well as the cumulative impact of pastoral systems in a given territory over time. Environmental resources may be directly exploitable, as in the case of natural water resources,
minerals and ores, wild plants and animals, and natural pasture. They may also be more
subtly negotiated or manipulated by tapping subterranean aquifers through *qanats*, im-
proving soil quality through slash and burn strategies, or pasturing animals on fallow
fields for symbiotic fertilization (Boserup 1965). As such, the Eurasian steppe provides a
diversity of ecosystems that condition an equally variable array of pastoralist strategies
through time and across territory.

The environmental geography of central Eurasia is presented here as a habitat with
considerable diversity in climatic trends and both intra- and inter-regional ecological
variation. Environmental variation is an essential key to the pastoral ecology of the
steppe since it reflects the distribution of various productive resources across a variety of
environmental contexts. Eurasian pastoralists commonly make ecologically sensitive
choices to change or exploit various resources of the steppe (Khazanov 1978). Their
strategies are shaped by the climate and biosphere and result in a history of ecological
knowledge of ways to be productively successful (Ingold 2000, 37). To understand the relationship between environmental distribution of resources and pastoralist strategies,
this chapter investigates the steppe environment as a contributing factor in the development and perpetuation of pastoral economies across Eurasia. This chapter also explores
in detail the geography and quantitative capacity of pasture contexts in the study zone of

the Koksu valley (Semirech'ye) to support domestic herds common to pastoralists of the region. I also compare the range assessments of the study region with other steppe contexts to illustrate the diversity of the steppe in terms of its productivity, which partially explains some aspects of regional diversity of pastoral strategies across Eurasia.

Ultimately, the environmental conditions and range productivity assessments presented in this chapter illustrate that seasonal and altitudinal variations are dominant forces in shaping pastoralist practices of the Koksu valley. Specifically, these variables condition the productivity of pastures across the local landscape and thus impact the social geography of one of the most valuable resources for mobile pastoralists: pastureland. I also suggest that, although environmentally conditioned changes in mobility and settlement pattern should be considered a regular influence in the lives of mobile pastoralists, they do not represent extenuating conditions to elicit drastic changes in subsistence strategies or significant population relocation. The calculated productive capacity of pastures in the Koksu valley, for example, is shown to be comparatively high across the region, which may partly explain the continuous record of pastoralist exploitation documented there since the earliest emergence of animal domestication in the region. By mapping the variation of micro-ecologies in the study zone and calculating the comparative productivity of various pasture zones, this chapter provides a detailed understanding of the nuanced force of the environment as a formative element in structuring pastoralist landscapes.

STEPPE ENVIRONMENTS AND PASTORAL STRATEGIES

At the most fundamental level, pastoralists rely on the availability of pastureland for the successful growth of their herds. This demand is only one among a complicated matrix of factors that affect when and how far pastoralists move, their degree of multi-resource exploitation, their preferred herd composition, social organization, and other aspects of their society. But as an ecological indicator, the geography, seasonality, and productive capacity of pasture is a useful starting point to understand the minimum range of mobility and the diversity of subsistence strategies necessary for successful pastoral existence in particular territory.

The "Eurasian steppe zone" in its broadest analytical sense spans from north of the Black Sea to Mongolia and from the forests of southern Russia and Siberia to the border of sandy deserts of present-day Kazakhstan, Uzbekistan, and Turkmenistan. These boundaries naturally correspond with the extents of the grassland and semiarid prairie environments of central Eurasia, which form the environmental backdrop of most of this expansive territory. However, the geopolitical situation of these territories within the (now independent) republics of the former Soviet Union also contributed to the ways they have been academically parsed and studied in the past. Specifically, the analytical borders of the Eurasian steppe zone are effectively contiguous with the political extent of the former USSR and the most intensive scientific research of this region was conducted by Soviet scholars. Thus, for many western scholars the steppe has remained a confusing and essentialized environment, presented as a vast and undifferentiated belt of grasslands. Soucek (2004) provides an excellent summary of the geo-history of Inner Asia, so here I focus on a few geographic and environmental parameters to contextualize the more detailed ecological investigation undertaken later in the chapter.

Environmentally the central Eurasian steppe zone variously spans five broad ecotones: forest steppe; steppe; semiarid steppe; arid steppe/desert; and mountain steppes. Russian geobotanists typically illustrate these environmental zones as a continuum from north to south, corresponding with increasing aridity, increasing temperature, and lengthening of the growing season (frost-free period) (Lavrenko and Karamysheva 1993, 5). The forest steppe zone is generally located north of 52° latitude, the "typical" steppe zone lies between 50°–52° latitude, semiarid steppe from 45°–50°, and desert steppe south of 45° latitude (Utesheva 1959) (fig. 19). Notably, Eurasian mountain steppe ecologies, such as those of the Ural, Tian Shan, Altai and Dzhungar Mountains, do not exhibit the degree of aridity or vegetation typical of their latitude. Mountain steppe zones exhibit a different environment because changes in elevation largely override the effects of climatic zones that are typically aligned north and south according to latitude. In areas of extreme elevation, altitude serves as a comparable index to latitude for changes in vegetation, temperature, and precipitation (see below).

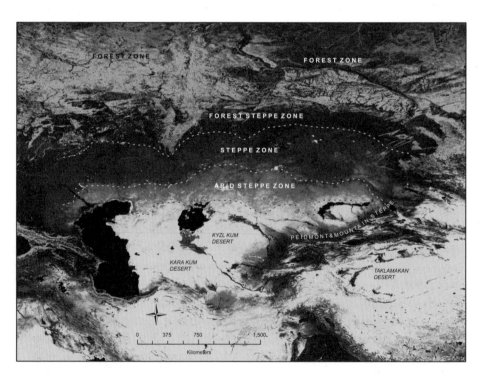

FIGURE 19

Environmental ecotones of Eurasia. Map data source: USGS Global Landcover.

All of the steppic regions of central Eurasia are affected by a continental climate, although to different extremes (Utesheva 1959; Ripley 1992). Continental climate is defined by substantial seasonal changes in temperature, precipitation and other meteorological conditions. For the ecotones listed above, the primary productivity of the biomass is related to the substantial variations in seasonal conditions, making seasonality particularly significant for assessing the different environmental potential for various zones and the way they are exploited (Stepanova 1961; Bykov 1974; Fedorin 1977). For example, in semiarid steppe contexts in the southern regions the growth period of the dominant vegetation types (*Stipa, Carex,* and *Artemisia*) is syncopated, meaning the different genera begin to flower at different times. So, while sedges (*Carex*) are flowering, feathergrasses (*Stipa*) are already beginning to dry and die (Lavrenko and Karamysheva 1993). For pastoralists living in these arid steppe zones the summer growth period is therefore relatively unproductive for pasturing when compared to northern steppe zones where the summer meadow vegetation flowers more consistently and the botanical composition of pastures is lusher. Not surprisingly pastoralist groups occupying the south in the winter must migrate north in favor of greener pastures.

The steppe zone also is differentiated into regional microniches according to climatic and geological variation of the central Eurasian landmass. The geography of small mountain ranges, rivers, and valleys contributes to the way humans have exploited this region by creating a diverse distribution of water sources, geology, vegetative niches, and microclimates across the central steppe zone. In terms of pastoral ecology, microecologies across the steppe are commonly shaped by the geography of major rivers, mountain chains, and plateaus, which serve to carve and differentiate the Eurasian steppe landmass. These features also provide convenient natural boundaries for heuristic sub-regions of Eurasia: the western steppe, northeastern steppe and Altai region, the central steppe, and the southeastern mountain steppes of Semirech'ye.

The western steppe zone stretches from the lower Volga and Samara basin, across the Ural Mountains, to the Tobol and Irtysh River Basin. The geographic features that have the greatest impact on pastoral strategies in this region are the Ural Mountains and the major river courses, which differentiate the vegetation, soils, and topography of the region. The three primary river systems in the region are the Volga, Ural, and Tobol/Irtysh. The Ural Mountains divide this territory into two halves. The western half includes the steppes and forests of the Volga/Samara river basin and is host to major Bronze Age settlement landscapes such as Sintashta and Arkaim in the rolling grasslands of the Ural River (Gening et. al 1992). To the east of the Ural range (or trans-Ural), the Tobol and Irtysh river valleys are characterized by forested steppes; they represent the easternmost boundary of the western steppe zone. These riverine ecosystems provide seasonally productive pasturelands, as well as ample fish and wild game, all significant elements of the pastoralist economy in the region (O'Connell et al. 2003).

The northeastern steppe is represented by well-watered drainage basins along the Minusinsk, Yenisei, and Ob Rivers, where rolling hills covered in typical steppe vegetation flatten to the western part of the region. The northeastern boundary of the Altai Mountains differentiates the western steppes of Mongolia from the forest steppes of southwestern Siberia. The variation in pasture productivity at different elevations is key to the pastoral ecology of this region as in other mountainous territory, where herding communities use vertical mobility to take advantage of richer highland pastures during the summer and drier, warmer lowland territories in the winter (Vainshtein 1991).

The central steppe region is synonymous with the central plateau of present-day Kazakhstan, represented by flat, windy, semiarid grasslands spanning from the north of Lake Balkhash across Kazakhstan, from the cities of Arqalyk to Karaganda. This region is carved into a jigsaw puzzle of valleys and plains by hundreds of small rivers and tributaries, which find their sources in lakes and low mountain ranges. These small rivers and valleys are important to the archaeological reconstruction of the region, as scholars have argued that stream waters were diverted for a simplified form of irrigation during the middle and Late Bronze Age (Margulan 1979). In addition, small river valleys form environmentally localized niches that serve to differentiate the steppe ecology and produce a variable topography.

Southeastern Kazakhstan, known as Semirech'ye (Zhetisu in Kazakh) or the "seven rivers" region, is geographically separated from central and northeastern Kazakhstan by Lake Balkhash. The seven rivers, which include the Lepsi, Aksu, Byan, Kapal, Karatal, Koksu, and Ili, flow from the Dzhungar and Tian Shan Mountains into Lake Balkhash. Geographically, Semirech'ye exhibits drastic changes in ecology from high, glacially capped mountains, to semiarid plains and dry, sandy deserts to the southeast of Lake Balkhash. This extreme climatic and topographic change occurs over a distance of less than four hundred kilometers from the mountaintops of the Dzhungar Mountains to the coast of Lake Balkhash. A similar environmental context can be found on the southern border of the Semirech'ye region, which is defined by the Zailisky Alatau and Tian Shan Mountains. Although higher and more extensive than the Dzhungar Mountains, the Tian Shan range represents an analogous environmental and socio-economic context to that known in the Dzhungar Mountains. The geographically condensed environmental transitions of mountains in Semirech'ye liken them to other high mountain systems of Central Asia, such as the Pamir and Tian Shan Mountains, and these ecologies are distinguishable from the flatland steppe regions of central Eurasia.

The river drainages of the Dzhungar Mountains represent an important geographic niche in the southeastern steppe zone because of their ecological and historical impact on the region. The wide upland passes and river valleys throughout the Dzhungar Mountains provided rich summer pastures for local mobile pastoralists. In addition to local pastoral economies, notable trade corridors lead through the mountain passes known as the Dzhungarian Gates, connecting Mongolia, western China and the steppes of Kazakhstan. Throughout history these corridors led caravans through Semirech'ye as primary pathways for both trade and military campaigns, most famously representing pathways of the Silk Route and campaigns of the Mongols in the thirteenth century (chapter 4).

PALEOCLIMATE OF EURASIA AND THE STUDY ZONE

As one would imagine, the climate of the Eurasian steppe zone, and of the Dzhungar Mountain region and Semirech'ye, has fluctuated throughout the Holocene (c. 10,000 BP–present (Velichko et al. 1984a). As in most regions across Eurasia, detailed reconstructions of climatic fluctuation in southeastern Kazakhstan are still in an early stage of research. However, comparative reconstructions of the Holocene climate from various locations across the steppe zone show that although general trends can be discussed at a macro-regional scale, there are significant differences between the eastern, western, and central steppe zones at the regional scale (Khotinskiy 1984a, Kremenetski 2003, 25).

Kremenetski (2003) provides an accessible summary of the major phases of climate change during the Holocene across the Eurasian steppe, synthesized from the most current paleoclimatic studies in the region (see also Khotinskiy 1984a; Khotinskiy 1984b). The western steppe zone experienced aridization during the period from 4800–2000 BCE, with a return of slightly wetter conditions from 2000–900 BCE. Kremenetski suggests that the climate in the western steppe north of the Caspian was similar to that of today by around 600 BCE. Northeastern Kazakhstan is separated climatically from the western steppe by the Ural Mountains, reflecting a more strictly continental climatic regime. On the basis of lake-level regressions and transgressions in Lake Balkhash a fluctuation toward regional aridity in the trans-Urals and northeastern territories is documented around 2300 BCE, followed by the return of wetter conditions around 1900 BCE (Kremenetski 2003, 23). For the interests of this study, the most important conclusion from Kremenetski's synthesis is that the second millennium BCE reflected a general return of wetter, cooler conditions from a period of aridization across the steppe zone around 2800–2000 BCE.

These oscillating phases of warming and aridity do not appear to have contributed to significant fluctuations in the geography or composition of steppe vegetation in northern and eastern Kazakhstan. Throughout the late Holocene, the mean temperature and annual precipitation fluctuated approximately 1–2 °C and 50–100 mm across the Eurasian forest-steppe and steppe regions. However, the general distribution of vegetation horizons (latitudinally from forest steppe to the desert-steppe) was fairly stable during the Atlantic and Sub-boreal periods (4000–500 BCE), and the vegetative composition of pastures zones is shown from palynological studies to have been broadly similar to that of today (Khotinskiy 1984b, 196–198).

The paleovegetation of grassy pastures, however, reflects less drastic difference from contemporary landcover when compared with other vegetation types of the region (see pollen diagrams in Kremenetski 2003, 20–22). Kremenetski remarks that paleovegetative change is more pronounced for forested areas of the northwestern steppe and in riparian micro-niches, where broadleaved tree species, Scots pine, and birch respond more markedly to fluctuations in rainfall and temperature. He further notes that "During the last 7000 years, dry steppe was the main vegetation type in the northern part of the Kalmukia region, as is also the case today. Climate shifts resulted in changes in the forested areas of the great river valleys and the ravine forests . . . which are reflected in the varying percentage pollen representation of [broadleaved trees]." (Kremenetski et al. 2004, 239).

Pollen studies from the Ozerki region in North Kazakhstan, for example, illustrate that percentages of steppe vegetation (e.g., *Artemisia* and Amaranthaceae (formerly known as Chenopodiaceae) of the past 4000 years reflect a generally consistent ratio, comparable to that of today (Kremenetski et al. 1997). Khotinsky (1984, 196) concurs with this assessment noting that

> These [steppe and arid] zones were established during the Atlantic period close to their present position and . . . have not shifted since that time. This does not mean, however, that the climatic conditions within these zones remained absolutely stable; in fact, data indicate that arid periods alternated with moist periods . . . precipitation during the Atlantic period was twice as great as at the present in this region, and the vast areas of Central Asia were covered with steppe. The pollen data from the steppe and forest-steppe zones of western Siberia . . . show an extensive spread of local mesophytic [steppe] vegetation but not in any radical zonal rearrangements.

The steppe's zonal consistency may be linked to the overriding impact of continentality on the adaptive characteristics of its endemic vegetation cohorts and to processes such as altitude and atmospheric anticyclones (Savina and Khotinskiy 1984). These processes mitigate the effects of climate change on steppe vegetation in particular settings across the Eurasian continent (Klimanov et al. 1994).

Paleo-climate studies of regional lake sediments in the southeastern steppe (e.g., Lake Manas [Chinese Dzhungaria]) illustrate the climatic trends of the Dzhungar region throughout the Holocene. These studies show that the beginning of the second millennium was slightly wetter than current conditions, followed by period of aridity across the region from approximately 1850–1550 BCE (Rhodes et al. 1996). This period, which corresponds to the Late Bronze Age in the study region, would have experienced a generally semiarid climate with marked seasonal fluctuations, similar to the climate found in the region today. Rhodes et al. (1996) provide a detailed vegetation reconstruction for the Dzhungar region showing the ratio between *Artemisia* and Chenopodiacae (Amaranthaceae), which is used as an index for the steppe vegetation throughout the late Holocene (fig. 20). This graphic illustrates that ratios around 1500 BCE are broadly equivalent to those of the contemporary vegetation.[1]

Recent paleo-environmental studies of the Dzhungar and Tian Shan Mountain regions also document changes in precipitation and temperature throughout the past 6500 years, using geo-morphological and paleo-botanical methods (Aubekerov et al. 2003) and paleo-sediment analyses of regional lakes and salt flats (Rhodes et al. 1996). However, these recent studies concur that the steppe vegetation of the region during the second millennium BCE was broadly comparable with that of today. Paleobotanical statistics from archaeological contexts at the Bronze Age settlement of Begash in the Dzhungar Mountains (table 1) also show that steppe grasses and flowering plants

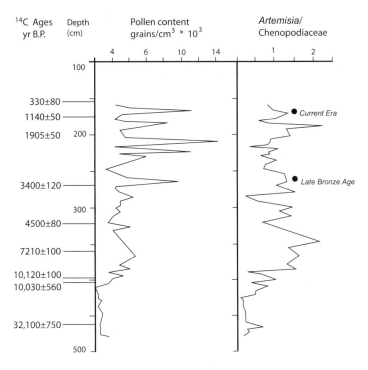

FIGURE 20

Paleobotanical trends in the Dzhungar region throughout the Holocene, showing the ratio of *Artemisia* to Chenopodiaceae. After Rhodes et al. 1996.

(Poacae [25 percent] and Amaranthaceae [45 percent]) dominated the vegetation of the area in the mid to late third millennium BCE,[2] reflecting a generally wetter climate when compared with that of today (Aubekerov et. al 2003). A relatively low percentage of *Artemisia* (17 percent) in this stratum also indicates that the mid-elevations of the Koksu river valleys of this region were not as arid as today, especially at lower elevations. In addition, localized pollen from pine trees (*Pinus* sp.) indicates a slightly cooler climate, and suggests that the tree line in the mountainous region may have extended to lower elevations during the late third millennium BCE.

Samples from Late Bronze Age strata at Begash suggest that throughout the second millennium there were intermittent changes in the region's climate. Climatological indicators, such as a rise in *Artemisia* pollen (to 30 percent), indicate increasing aridization after the generally wetter conditions of the late third millennium BCE. Although temperatures may still have been cooler at this time, the stabilizing effects of elevation and seasonality in the Dzhungar Mountains would have meant that upland steppe vegetation zones would have remained generally constant throughout the second millennium BCE and later. This is supported by the largely stable grass and sedge species populations of both the contemporary botany and paleobotany of Semirech'ye recorded in excavated archaeological contexts throughout southern Kazakhstan (Aubekerov et al. 2001).

TABLE I. Paleo-Palynology from the Prehistoric Settlement of Begash

Radiocarbon years BP	Botanical phase	Samples	Artemisia (%)	Chenopodiaceae (%)	Poaceae	Ranunculeae	Pinus	Ephedra	Artemisia/ Chenopodiaceae ratio
50	6	21–23	25	75	present	present	NP	present	0.333
1500	5	18–19	25	75	NP	NP	NP	NP	0.333
3800–2000	4	12–16	30	55	present	12	NP	present	0.545
4500–4000	3	6–10	17	45	25	NP	present	NP	0.377
5000	2	2–5	30	70	present	present	NP	NP	0.428
Undated	1	1	42	45	NP	9	NP	NP	0.933

NOTE: Summarized from Aubekerov et al. 2003. NP, not present.

In fact, the ratios for the Late Bronze Age around the Lake Manas region correlate with the *Artemisia*/Amaranthaceae ratios calculated from the pollen studies at Begash (Frachetti 2004, appendix 1). The climate in the Lake Manas region is expected to be comparatively drier than that in the Koksu valley, since Lake Manas is located to the east of the Dzhungar Mountain rain shield. Yet this point of inter-regional comparison does not reduce the significance of both studies illustrating that the paleo-environment of the later half of the second millennium BCE was broadly comparable with that of today.[3]

CURRENT ENVIRONMENT OF SEMIRECH'YE AND THE DZHUNGAR MOUNTAINS

The Dzhungar Mountains represent the northeastern part of the Semirech'ye region, located between 43°50′N and 46°50′N, and between 78°E and 82°50′E. These high mountains define part of the border between the present-day Republic of Kazakhstan and western China. The mountain range varies in elevation from the piedmont of less than 500 meters to glacier covered peaks over 4500 meters high (fig. 21). In fact, at these extremely high altitudes there are over 150 glaciers, with a surface area totaling more

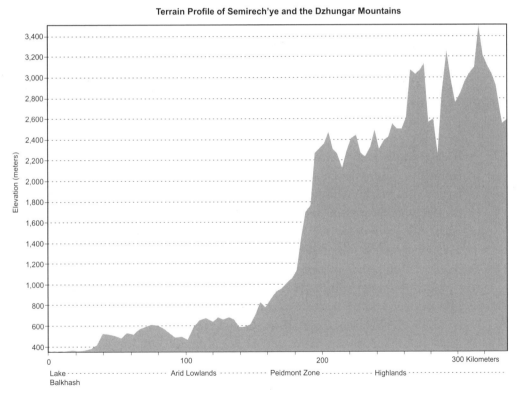

FIGURE 21

Profile of elevation change, west to east in Semirech'ye.

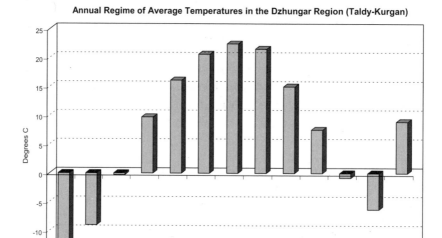

Annual Regime of Average Temperatures in the Dzhungar Region (Taldy-Kurgan)

FIGURE 22

Average annual temperature regime of the Dzhungar region. Source: Utesheva 1959.

than 1000 square kilometers (Goloskokov 1984, 8). These glaciers feed the seven rivers that flow northwest toward Lake Balkhash.

The contemporary climate is strictly continental, with drastic variation in temperature and precipitation between summer and winter periods (fig. 22). The altitude of the Dzhungar Mountains also has a major effect on the climatic geography, in that increases in elevation reflect greater precipitation, cooler temperatures, and drastic oscillations in the barometric pressure (Sokolov 1968).

Altitude dictates variability in seasonal temperature, soil zones, and growing season as well, all of which have a marked affect on the geographic distribution of vegetation in the Dzhungar Mountains. From the foothills to the peaks, every 100 m rise in elevation (above 600 m) accounts for a 0.5–1.0 °C decrease in mean temperature (Goloskokov 1984, 11). Dry hot summers are characteristic at lower elevations, whereas winter conditions in the highlands are cold and snowy. A relatively small accumulation of snow is typical at elevations less than 800 meters. Distinctly lower temperatures, a shorter growing season, and drastic fluctuations of temperature throughout the day are typical characteristics of the subalpine and alpine elevations (Utesheva 1959, 88). Middle altitudes (between 800 and 1200 m) have a more moderate climate, with a dry and warm autumn, a short and intensive spring and a cold winter (Goloskokov 1984, 10). These conditions dictate the vegetation of lowland ranges, which are characterized by arid steppe plants (*Artemisia* and scrubland), whereas highland pastures are characterized by rich fescue meadows.

The vegetative period at high elevations (>2000 m) in the Dzhungar Mountains is rather short (40–90 days), starting in mid June and ending in August. Yet the growing patterns of dominant steppe plants (fescues, needlegrasses, and bluegrasses) in the highland meadows of the Dzhungar Mountains are more homogeneous than those of lower elevations where the botanical composition is similar to arid steppe. Therefore, the "flowering" of the upland pastures is seasonally intense, producing a high density of biomass that is short-lived. This fact is highly significant in relation to the productivity and pastoral use of upland meadows.

In addition to seasonality and elevation, precipitation and slope aspect have a remarkable affect on the grassland composition in mountain steppe environments. The amount of rainfall in the Dzhungar Mountains is high, with cumulative annual averages ranging from 450–800 mm (to more than 1500 mm at high altitudes) (Utesheva 1959). The annual rainfall regime in the Dzhungar Mountain region shows considerable differences between warm and cold periods of the year. From April to October, the average amount of rainfall ranges from 200–500 mm, whereas in the cold months of October to March the average amount of precipitation ranges from 100–400 mm (Utesheva 1959, 263). The average amount of rainfall during cold and warm periods is misleading, because rain is not evenly distributed throughout the warmer months, with as much as 30 percent of the total annual precipitation falling in the months of March and April, followed by a drastic fall-off during June and July. Figure 23 illustrates the month-by-month regime of precipitation of the Semirech'ye region compared with other regions

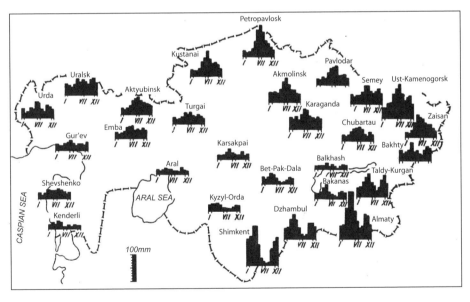

FIGURE 23
Average annual regime of rainfall across Kazakhstan. After Utesheva 1959, 271.

of Kazakhstan. From the graphs, one sees a sharp decline in rainfall after April in the southeastern region, whereas areas of central and northern Kazakhstan show an increase in precipitation throughout the summer months. The dry summers in the Semirech'ye region, especially in lowland zones, contribute to an arid-steppe and desert-like environment. It is only at higher elevations that summer rains remain consistent, and ranges remain green and productive for pasturing animals.

In the Dzhungar Mountains, substantial precipitation during the winter months is also notable, with nearly half (41 percent) of the total annual precipitation coming during the cold months (Utesheva 1959, 272). In the winter, it snows on average forty days of the year, while annual rain is recorded sixty days throughout months when temperatures are above freezing (Utesheva 1959, 280). Especially in the mountains this indicates that rainfall is often intense in the form of storms and is often concentrated, followed by periods of no rain or snow.

Elevation change in mountain environments has a remarkable impact on the way these general trends of rainfall are distributed. Utesheva notes that during the warmer months, an elevation rise of 100 m can yield an increase in precipitation of about 26 mm (1959, 270). Annually, the difference in precipitation between 500 m and 2000 m of elevation can range on the order of 400–500 mm. Thus although the month-to-month pattern is generally similar in both lowlands and highlands, the amplitude of rainfall is remarkably higher at highland elevations. This difference contributes to the diverse vegetation that characterizes different altitudes in the Dzhungar Mountains, as well as to the richness and rapid regeneration of highland pastures.

In addition to elevation, slope aspect has a remarkable effect on micro-regional differences in rainfall. Moist winds that strike northern slopes contribute to a cumulative annual precipitation between 500–600 (to 800) mm, whereas on southern slopes an average annual precipitation of less than 450 mm is recorded (Goloskokov 1984, 11). Temperature is also influenced by the aspect of slopes, primarily due to the exposure to sunshine. Southerly oriented slopes receive more intense sunshine, thus are notably warmer and drier. Also, the higher the elevation, the more drastic the divergence in temperature and moisture for northerly and southerly exposed slopes. These differences are ultimately important for understanding the productivity of rangelands and pasture composition in the Dzhungar Mountains because there is a correlation among temperature, moisture, and the types of vegetation that grow on slopes of different aspect.

Climatological drought and atmospheric drought both affect southeast Kazakhstan, although to varying degrees. Climatological drought may be defined as a prolonged decrease from the norm in the amount of precipitation in a region, causing adverse effects on vegetation, soils, animal ecology, and other environmental conditions. Climatological drought is not usually marked by abrupt change in southeastern Kazakhstan and is best understood as periodic fluctuation in the aridity and temperature that characterizes the climate generally. These fluctuations typically occur on cycles of ten to fifteen years (Gvozdetskii and Nikolaev 1971). Climatological drought is more difficult to assess in areas like the Dzhungar Mountains, as detailed records concerning the yield and bio-mass of natural ranges over long periods are not available.

Atmospheric drought is a quantitative concept and can be assessed meteorologi-cally from ratio changes in the atmospheric moisture and temperature in different regions (Utesheva 1959, 118). In Kazakhstan, warm period temperatures over 30 °C and moisture less than 25 percent are considered indicative of periods of atmospheric drought and commonly occur for periods of more than a week and perhaps even a month during the summer in the Dzhungar Mountains. As with precipitation, the effects of atmospheric drought are more pronounced in lowland arid areas where temperatures are commonly higher, and less pronounced in upland zones where atmos-pheric moisture is typically high and temperatures are considerably cooler year-round. This is significant in relation to rangeland productivity, in that regular aridity and drought are common in lowland areas but are not a major force in the ecology of up-land ranges in the Dzhungar Mountains. This fact contributes to the regular use of upland pastures during hotter months because they are generally predictable good sources of natural pasture. Extreme rain and moisture, rather than drought, tend to create limitations on the health of the vegetation in upland zones, sometimes creating localized swampy conditions that are uncomfortable for human and animal use (Chekeres 1973).

In summary, the contemporary climate of the Dzhungar Mountains is characteristic of other mountainous areas of the region, with abrupt changes in temperature and pre-cipitation both in a seasonal sense and between zones of different altitude. The low-lands of the Dzhungar Mountains are characterized by an arid climate and periodic drought, while upland areas are well watered by rain and runoff. Temperatures follow a rigidly continental pattern throughout the year, and the relative differences between summer heat and winter cold are comparable between various altitudes. In an absolute sense, however, summer heat is mitigated as one goes up in altitude, and winter cold and snow decrease as one goes down. The climate of the region and climatic differences at different altitudes contribute to a geographically non-uniform distribution of the re-sources that play an important role in pastoral strategies for living in the Dzhungar Mountains.

HYDROLOGY AND GEOLOGY OF SEMIRECH'YE AND THE STUDY ZONE

The Koksu River valley reflects a highly dynamic watershed with permanent and sea-sonal rivers, streams, and springs. Waterways are abundant throughout the Dzhungar Mountains, even in areas that exhibit arid-steppe conditions (lower elevations). The main body of water in the study zone is the Koksu River itself, although within the valley other permanent tributaries such as the Zhalgyzagash, Ashibulak, Bolshoi Terekty, and Mukri Rivers also represent sizable streams (see figure 29 in chapter 5).

In addition to permanent streams and rivers, the study zone is host to hundreds of spring sources at elevations above 1500 m. These springs contribute to the lush meadow vegetation of the upland pastures (Gvozdetskii and Nikolaev 1971). In addition, the erosive and alluvial effects of the hundreds of small tributary drainages throughout the study zone contribute to the varied topography of the Koksu River valley. The particularities of the geography of tributary ravines and river terraces are significant because most archaeological contexts recovered in the Koksu River valley are located near such contexts.

Another factor that has an impact on the human ecology of the region is the location of stone outcrops and the geomorphology of the valley. The geomorphology of the Koksu valley reflects the U-shaped basin typical of glacially formed mountain valleys, as well as moraines and other geological formations associated with glacial activity throughout the Pleistocene and Holocene (Pal'gov 1949). In addition to glacial morphology, tectonic activity throughout the geological prehistory of the Dzhungar range has contributed to many exposed basalt-rock outcrops (Aubekerov, pers. comm.). Rock outcrops are significant archaeologically because they are the primary surfaces for prehistoric rock engraving. The most prominent and extensive outcrops are located in the Eshkiolmes range and Terekty ravine, and smaller outcrops are commonly found along the slopes of other steep tributary ravines. The black stone outcrops, especially those with a southern aspect, transmit substantial solar radiation within their host ravines, thereby creating small micro-niches of warmer climate. The environmental and social contributions provided by rock outcrops are important considerations in the placement of settlements and other social contexts throughout the landscape.

Due to the dynamic relationship between the climate and mountain geography of the Dzhungar Mountains, the Koksu River valley should be considered a restrictive environment. From an economic perspective, restrictive environments may be defined as those environmental contexts where consumable resource productivity potential is geographically limited; where the availability of consumable resources is highly differentiated and/or drastically effected by natural periodization/variation of the biosphere (e.g., pronounced seasonality); and where consumable resources are highly heterogeneous (non-uniform). Environmental restriction should not be confused with marginality or unproductiveness, a point we now turn to in detail in assessing the pastoral productive of the Dzhungar Mountains and comparative cases across Inner Asia.

PASTORAL ECOLOGY AND RANGE PRODUCTIVITY IN EASTERN INNER ASIA

According to range scientists,[4] pasture grazing capacity (the number of grazing animals that can be supported on a pasture[5] of a given size that will produce an objective of animal performance without ecosystem deterioration over a long period of time (Heady and Child 1994, 156) is best understood as quantitatively variable. Some range scientists question the validity of the concept at all as a reliable approximation of pasture output. This is partly because the definition inherently entails a "value added" element related to acceptable animal returns for varying purposes and because ranges reflect a complicated matrix of yield determinants that are annually inconsistent and thus notoriously difficult to accurately assess (Roe 1997, 467). Consequently, when considering the pastoral ecology of particular contexts, calculations of grazing capacity will necessarily reflect a conditional calculation or "snapshot" measurement of the pasture conditions and grazing threshold of ranges in question. Given this conditional measurement, our reconstructions can at best provide a detailed but distilled representation of grazing capacity, not a dynamic view. However, the range grazing assessments calculated here achieve two key objectives that aid our ability to accurately assess the impact of environment on pastoralist strategies in the study zone. These objectives are to document and illustrate the considerable difference in pasture quality across various elevations in the mountain rangeland context, and to provide a quantitative index of the grazing capacity of different pasture zones, which can be used to accurately model various pastoral strategies in the study zone.

Setting aside theoretical limitations, there are four types of data needed to calculate the relationships between the geography of native ranges and grazing capacity: the composition, distribution and forage productivity of various range types; the area and seasonal changes of the rangeland; the forage requirements of the grazing animal; and the forage regime or duration of grazing (Tanner 1983; Workman and MacPherson 1973). The calculation of each of these factors is itself an intricate and complex endeavor, especially the forage productivity, which is conditioned by a number of contributing forces, not least among them botanical composition, climate, soil quality, altitude, and anthropogenic or zoogenic processes (Heady and Child 1994, 158; Du Toit 2000). The assessments here are based on a variety of published range science studies of the region, which provide detailed assessments of the botany of the region and working values for the forage productivity (i.e., herbage yield), animal requirements, and regime and duration of forage productivity in the study zone. Here we are concerned with generating a comparative picture of grazing capacity in the different vegetation zones of the Dzhungar Mountains as a guide for modeling pastoral strategies in both contemporary and prehistoric cases.

PASTURE RESOURCES OF THE DZHUNGAR MOUNTAINS

Due to mineral-poor soils and pronouced seasonality, the largest percentage (roughly 88 percent) of consumable vegetation resources in the Dzhungar Mountains is rangeland grass (i.e., natural grassland pasture) (Sokolov 1975, 592). The forage yield of various pasture zones is a function of their botanical makeup, geographic location, and exploitation by pastoralists. Within the composition of different classes of pastureland, nutritional productivity depends on the chemical composition and individual biological

TABLE 2. Pasture Characteristics in the Dzhungar Mountains

Pasture zone/Dominant pasture species	Growing season	Average forage yield per hectare	
		Green fodder	Dry fodder
Alpine (4400–2800 m)	20–30 days	600 kg	200 kg
Kobresia capilliformis, Dryandanthe tetrandra, Polygonum viviparum, Festuca kryloviana, Dichodon cerastoides, Pyrethrum karelini, Oxygraphis glacialis, Lagotis integrifolia, Schultzia albiflora, Potentilla gelida, Thalictrum alpinum, Festuca valesiaca, F. sulcata, Helictotrichon altaicum, H. tianschanicum, Poa stepposa, Carex Melanantha, C. orbicularis, Eriophornum schouchzeri, Saxifaga hirculus			
Subalpine (2800–2200 m)	30–70 days	900 kg	300 kg
Trollius dschungaricus, Polygonum nitens, Potentilla gelida, Myosotis suaveolens, Leontopodium fedtschenkoanum, Allium atrosanguineum, Festuca kryloviana, Alopercurus pratensis, Poa pratensis, Helictrotrichon pubenscens, H. asiaticum, Trisetum altaicum, Carex melanantha, C. stenocarpa, Festuca valesiaca, F. sulcata, Helictrichon altaicum, H. tianschanicum, Poa stepposa			
Mountain meadows (2300–1400 m)	50–80 days	1600 kg	530 kg
Festuca valesiaca, F. sulcata, Helictrichon altaicum, H. tianschanicum, Poa stepposa			
Steppe (1400–1000 m)	120 days	1000 kg	330 kg
Stipa capillata, Stipa lesingiana, Koeleria cristata, K. gracilis, Festuca valesiaca, Poa stepposa, Poa attenuate, Artemisia dracunculus, Medicago falcate, Nepeta pannonica, Phlomis practensis, Dactylis glomerata, Brachypodium pinnatum, Galium verum, Thalictrum minus			
Semidesert (800–650 m) desert <650 m	30–60 days	400 kg	130 kg
Stipa sareptana, S. capillata, Festuca sulcata, Artemisia sublessingiana, A. heptapotamica, A. terrae albae, Karagana kirghizorum			
Riparian	90–120 days	N/A	N/A
Populus talassica, Salix songarica, S. tenuijlis, S. wilhelmsiana, oleaster (shrubs or small trees with fruit resembling an olive), *Ulmus pumila* (elm)			

NOTE: Summarized from Goloskokov 1984.

schedules of various grasses, sedges, and flowering plants. At its most essential, the edible value of grass is increased by higher coefficients of albumen proteins and diminished by coefficients of cellulose (Larin 1937). Soil composition, temperature, length of growing season, precipitation, and other ecological factors also affect the productivity of grassland plants. In the Dzhungar Mountains, these factors are generally related to altitude and seasonality (Sobolev 1960).

The botanical composition of natural ranges in the Dzhungar Mountains has been most intensely studied by Goloskokov (1984). His thorough discussion of the botany demonstrates that grassland species represent nearly 65 percent of the rangeland vegetation in the Dzhungar Mountains (Goloskokov 1984, 126). A summary of his research concerning the composition of Dzhungar rangelands is the first stage in assessing the variable productivity of various zones of the region. Various cohorts of plant species can be delineated according to altitude, reflecting a distinctly vertical geography of resources within natural meadows and pastures in the Dzhungar Mountains that are edible for domesticated herds. Altitude (in conjunction with slope) is the primary index for available moisture, temperature, and soil type, which determine the botanical composition of various niches. Table 2 presents the botanical composition and forage productivity of pastures in the region. From a botanical perspective, mountain meadows are more than four times as productive as arid steppe regions.

The productivity of the Dzhungar Mountains is greatly differentiated according to seasonal fluctuations at various altitudes. Using the same botanical zones outlined in table 2, all pasture zones above approximately 1000 m must be considered inaccessible due to snow cover from late November to mid May, and those above 1500 m are closed from early September to mid June. Also, the growing season in the area is restricted by its high elevation and harsh continental climate. Thus, the prevalence of snow, coupled with the variable activity of the growing season at these altitudes, allows for a generalized seasonal calendar to be suggested (table 3).

TABLE 3.   Seasons and Months in the Dzhungar Mountains

	Alpine pastures	Subalpine	Steppe	Semidesert
Spring	June	May–June	May	Late March–early May
Summer	July–August	July–August	June–early September	May–early September
Autumn	September–October	September–early November	September–late November	Late September–November
Winter	November–May	November–May	December–April	December–March

In addition to the accessibility of various pasture zones, the seasonal change in rangeland productivity has been well documented by a variety of scientists working across the Eurasian steppe zone (Larin 1962a; Kharitonov 1980; Demin 1973; Kalinina 1974). These scholars have recorded the substantial falloff of productive yields of ranges after the conclusion of the growing season, as compared with the maximum yield at the height of productivity. In the Dzhungar mountain region, the seasonal conditions of various microclimates, as well as the normal growth patterns of pasture grasses, have major affects on the productivity of the ranges. Table 4 summarizes the percent use of pastures during different seasons as well as the dynamics of edible mass of fodder plants in each season across various pasture types. Table 5 summarizes the change in edible mass for a variety of different range types found in the study zone. Notable changes occur between the beginning of the growth period and the flowering period, when grasses increase edible yield by 30–35 percent. Usually, grasses retain approximately 80 percent of their edible mass for one month after flowering, but after two months they usually decline in mass by almost 50 percent. For the majority of steppe types in the Dzhungar region, the percent change in edible plant mass during the growth period (shown in table 5) is consistent with the percent change in edible mass during the growth period of steppe grasses in northerly areas with cold climates, such as Buryatia.

DATA SOURCES AND RESULTS OF PASTURE CAPACITY ANALYSIS IN THE STUDY ZONE

Productivity values for various pasture types were collected and summarized from a variety of sources to provide yield averages for various pasture types found in the Dzhungar region. These include alpine and subalpine meadows, mountain-meadow steppes, typical steppe, and semi-desert steppe (fig 24).[6] The values used here are taken from Larin's study of the pasture resources in Eastern Kazakhstan (Larin 1962b), cross-referenced with the edible mass values of the botanical cohorts which typify the Dzhungar Mountains, studied by Sobolev (Sobolev 1960, 234–35). Coefficients were calculated by averaging specific "fodder values" for these pasture types (Demin 1973, 166–172). The values were originally presented in the Russian unit "ц—tsentner": one tsentner equals 100 kg of plant matter; values have been converted to kilograms for the tables here. Demin also provided the values that used for the daily nutritional need for cows, horses, and sheep. The available area (in hectares) of pastures in each zone (e.g., alpine and subalpine) was calculated by totaling the number of pasture hectares within appropriate elevation boundaries within the study zone.

The consumable capacity of "alpine and subalpine pastures" (cryophytic meadows and motley grass meadows) ranges from 5–12 100 kg units/ha = 500–1200 kg/ha, with an average gross productivity less than 9 100 kg units/ha (Sobolev 1960, table 28, 235). In the study zone of the alpine regions within approximately sixty kilometers of the Koksu River, there are 1,728 hectares of "alpine and subalpine pasture." The carrying capacity for alpine

TABLE 4. Pasture Types of the Dzhungar Mountains and their Seasonal Dynamics

Type of pasture by plant cohort (after Sobolev 1960)	Spring		Summer		Autumn		Winter	
	Percent edible mass	Calculated edible mass (kg/ha)	Percent edible mass	Calculated edible mass (kg/ha)	Percent edible mass	Calculated edible mass (kg/ha)	Percent edible mass	Calculated edible mass (kg/ha)
Mixed grass/*Artemisia* desert steppe (type 61)	100	300	50	150	100	300	50	150
Motley grass/fescue sedge steppe (type 63)	100	900	70	630	60	540	—	—
Motley grass meadow steppe high altitude pastures (type 69)	100	840	80	670	60	500	—	—
Mountain high-grass meadows (type 71) (1000–2800 m)	100	1500	80	1200	60	900	—	—
Mountain steppe (type 75)	100	720	80	580	70	500	50	360
Subalpine meadows (type 77)	100	900	80	720	50	450	—	—
Alpine meadow (type 78)	—	—	100	600	—	—	—	—
Average for Dzhungar Mts. by season	100.00	737	77.14	650	57.14	456	14.29	73

NOTE: Calculations based on values from Sobolev (1960). Calculated edible mass = gross edible mass * plant density coefficient * percent mass, using the method described by Sobolev (1960).

TABLE 5. Comparative Seasonal Change in Edible Mass of Grass
in Mountain Steppe Regions

Phase of growth	Calendar date of sampling	Yield edible mass (100 kg/ha)	Percent of maximum yield
Productivity over the growing season for motley grass/fescue steppe pastures, Buryatia (Kharitonov 1980, 37)			
Budding	8–10 June	3.8	73
Flowering	18–22 June	5.2	100
Fruiting	15–18 July	4.3	83
Fall decline	8–15 August	3.1	59
Productivity over the growing season for bunchgrass/fescue steppe, Tian Shan (Kalinina 1974, 67)			
	18 May	3	35
	13 June	6	70
	10 July	8.5	100
	5 August	6.7	79
	20 September	4.9	58
Productivity over the growing season for cold forb and bunchgrass meadows, Tian Shan (Kalinina 1974, 93)			
	May	1.1	9
	June	5.1	37
	July	11	81
	August	13.6	100
	September	11.4	84
	October	7.5	55
	January	5.8	42
	March–April	4.1	30

NOTE: Phase of growth not reported for Tian Shan.

meadows within the study region is 0.71 cows per hectare, 0.69 horses per hectare, and 4.2 sheep per hectare. Thus, the total number of animals that can be supported within a ninety-day growing season is approximately 1,234 head of cattle, 1,200 horses or 7198 sheep or goats (table 6). The ratio of sheep to large stock is 3.6 sheep per cow or horse.

The consumable capacity of "mountain meadow steppes" is comparatively high, ranging from 110–300 kg/ha, with an average gross productivity of approximately 165 kg/ha. In the study zone, there are nearly 26,000 hectares of upland mountain pasture; and the mountain steppe meadows are twice as productive for cattle, horses, and sheep compared to subalpine and alpine contexts (table 6). In total, the high mountain meadows can sustain 37,317 cattle, 36,280 horses, or nearly 218,000 head of sheep.

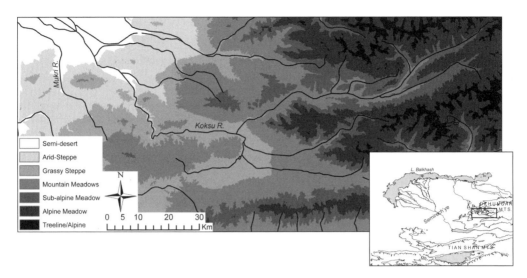

FIGURE 24
Qualified landcover classes according to NDVI value and altitude zones in the Dzhungar Mountains.

These numbers may seem extremely high, but if one considers that a rich nomadic family may own upwards of one thousand head of sheep (personal ethnographic observation), the actually population of the region would easily utilize the grass resources in this niche. In addition, these calculations are not adjusted for competition between species in mixed herds; rather, they represent the possible number of animals that could be supported if they were the lone species. Of course, the calculations are made more realistic by assuming, for example, that mixed herds including cattle, horses, and sheep will together exploit available pastures. This ratio of supportable animal numbers can be calculated by relating the coefficient of animal units per hectare. Applying such a calculation in the mountain meadows, roughly six sheep demand the equivalent meadow territory of one cow or one horse.

The "typical steppe zone" is less productive than the mountain meadows, with green mass yield ranging from 8–12 100 kg units/ha, with an average of 10 100 kg units/ha. Characterizing the shoulders and terraces of the river valley, the steppe environment occupies 17,530 hectares within the study zone. Since the altitude of this niche is lower, the growing season is longer, approximately 150 days (compared with 90 days for higher elevations). Throughout the summer grazing period, the steppe zone could support 7,513 cattle, 7,304 horses, or 43,825 sheep (table 6).

The "arid steppe/semi-desert" represents a smaller percentage of vegetated territory in the study zone (only 7.5 percent of total of summer green vegetation), with only 3655 hectares. In addition, the green vegetation that does exist is relatively low in yield, with an average value of about 4 100 kg units/ha. During the hot summer months this arid environment can support only 0.11 cattle (or horses) per hectare, and 0.78 sheep per hectare.

TABLE 6. Calculated Pasture Productivity for Cattle, Horses, and Sheep in the Dzhungar Mountains, Based on Hectares of Pasture in the Koksu River Valley (see Frachetti 2004 for method)

Pasture type	Alpine-subalpine	High-mountain meadow	Steppe	Arid semi-steppe	Totals/Averages
Area of available pasture (hectares)	1727	25,905	17,530	3655	48,818
Fodder value of 1 kg of plant material	0.50	0.55	0.45	0.30	0.45
Grazing period (days)	90	90	150	150	120
Yield of green mass per hectare (100 kg units)	9	16.5	10	4	9.87
Nutrient value in pasture (100 kg units)	7774	235,094	78,885	4386	216,937
Total available green feed in pasture (100 kg units)	15,548	427,444	175,300	14,620	482,084
Cows					
Daily nutritional need for animals (kg/day)	7	7	7	7	7
Possible number of animals over grazing period	1234	37,316	7512	417	25,825
Number of animals per hectare	0.714	1.440	0.428	0.114	0.529
Hectares required per animal	1.40	0.694	2.333	8.75	1.890
Horses					
Daily nutritional need for animals (kg/day)	7.2	7.2	7.2	7.2	7.2
Possible number of animals over grazing period	1199	36,280	7304	406	25,108
Number of animals per hectare	0.694	1.400	0.416	0.111	0.514
Hectares required per animal	1.44	0.714	2.4	9	1.944
Sheep					
Daily nutritional need for animals (kg/day)	1.2	1.2	1.2	1.2	1.2
Possible number of animals over grazing period	7198	217,680	43,825	2842	154,836
Number of animals per hectare	4.166	8.402	2.5	0.777	3.171
Hectares required per animal	0.24	0.119	0.4	1.285	0.315

Thus the maximum herd capacity for this niche is drastically smaller, only about one-tenth that of mountain meadows at the same time, with sustainable numbers of cattle and horses each around 400 head, and merely 2,842 sheep (table 6). This difference is one of the main reasons for vertical mobility patterns during summer months. The arid climate and desiccated vegetation below 800 m make these regions effectively useless for specialized pastoralism during the summer. However, as values during the spring and fall are twice that of summer, these dryer areas often represent pastures for use during colder seasons.

The varied productivity calculated in the study zone reflects a unique combination of environmental, meteorological, geographic and topographic conditions, which differentiates it from other steppe zones and even other mountain steppe niches in the region. In order to illustrate that mountain "steppe zones" should not be considered as equivalent environments across regions, brief summaries of some comparative studies of rangeland productivity in analogous contexts are provided here (fig. 25). The comparative regions were selected partly on the basis of their general similarity in botanical

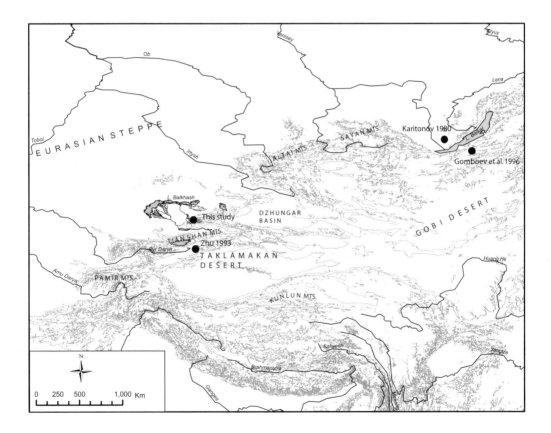

FIGURE 25

Location of comparative case studies. Map data source: Environmental Systems Research Institute 1994.

composition (although other factors such as climate distinguish them) and partly because they were investigated using the same method of calculating productivity. Detailed studies of calculated pasture capacities are not available for all regions of the steppe. Therefore, these comparisons are presented as case studies to highlight the variability of steppe rangelands and to further document some of the ecological conditions that underpin pastoral landscapes across Eurasia.

CASE STUDY ONE: NORTHERN CHINESE GRASSLANDS

In his summary of northern Chinese grasslands, Zhu (1993) provides general information on the composition, yield, and grazing capacity of various steppe types, as well as on their cumulative precipitation and temperature. These results are summarized in table 7. Compared with grassland ranges of the central steppes of Eurasia, "the Chinese steppe differs in structure . . . because [it] is located at higher elevations, on a plateau rather than a plain. In addition, the air is dryer, and a smaller proportion of the area is affected by the accumulation of salts. Another difference is the absence of synusiae of ephemeral species to constitute a vernal aspect,[7] the result of shorter, drier and windier weather in the spring" (Zhu 1993, p. 63)

Furthermore, Zhu presents a forage yield in these steppe conditions that is considerably lower than typical values in Alpine conditions.[8] As a result, Zhu's calculations for animals per hectare are approximately half of those calculated for alpine zones of the region (Larin 1962a), as well as those calculated above for the Koksu River valley.

Although the zonal characteristics of Chinese mountain vegetation are generally comparable to those of eastern Kazakhstan, productivity in China is restricted due to the effects of aridity. The horizon between typical steppe conditions and semi-desert steppe in Zhu's study region is 900 m, whereas in the Dzhungar Mountains the lower margin of the steppe is between 1000–1200 m. The important dominant species of the mountain

TABLE 7. Characteristics of Northwestern Chinese Steppe Ranges

Characteristic	Meadow steppe	Typical steppe	Desert steppe	Shrub steppe	Alpine steppe
Annual precipitation (mm)	350–500	280–400	250–310	380–460	450–700
Accumulated temperatures	1800–2500	1900–2400	2100–3200	2400–4000	<500
Foliage cover (percent of soil surface)	50–80	30–50	15–25	30–60	30–50
Forage yield (100 kg/ha)	1.5–2.5	0.8–1.0	0.2	0.5	0.2–0.35
Grazing capacity (sheep per hectare)	2.0–2.5	1.0–1.25	0.65	0.6	0.4

NOTE: After Zhu 1993.

TABLE 8.   Important Dominant Species of Northwestern Chinese Steppe Ranges

Steppe type	Plant species
Meadow steppe	
Steppe species	*Stipa baicalensis, Filifolium sibiricum, Leymus chinensis*
Meadow species	*Calamagrostis epigeios, Lathyrus quinquenervius, Hemerocallis minor*
Typical steppe	
Steppe species	*Stipa grandis, S. krylovii, S. breviflora*
Meadow species	*Caragana microphylla, Astragalus melitotoides, Trigonella ruthenica*
Desert steppe	
Steppe species	*Stipa glareosa, S. gobica, S. klemenzii*
Meadow species	*Reaumuria songorica, Calligonum mongolicum, Salsosa passerine*
Shrub steppe	
Steppe species	*Stipa bungeana, Andropogon ischaemum, Themeda triandra*
Meadow species	*Vitex negundo, Ziziphus spinosa*
Alpine steppe	
Steppe species	*Stipa purpurea, Festuca ovina, Poa alpine*
Meadow species	*Androsace tapete, Arenaria musciformis, Thylacospermum caespitosum*

NOTE: After Zhu 1993.

steppes in China include *Stipa* and *Festuca* species, and some species of *Artemisia* (table 8). The mountain ranges that define the border between Xinjiang (western China) and former Soviet Central Asia serve as a "rain shield" that traps moisture to the west, whereas the large deserts that surround the Altai and Tian Shan have a "drying influence" on the ranges of these mountains (Zhu 1993, 70). Thus, mountain steppe regions within the grassland latitudes of China (i.e., the region considered by Zhu to the east of these rain shields) exhibit generally lower mean annual precipitation levels than similar mountains in Mongolia, Kazakhstan and Russia.

CASE STUDY TWO: BARGUZIN VALLEY, BURYAT'YA (RUSSIA)

The Barguzin valley is located in a mountain forest zone, with extended steppe pastures situated between 53° and 56° north (Gomboev et al. 1996). The average summer temperatures are roughly between 15 °C and 20 °C, while winter averages are between minus 25 °C and minus 30 °C. Calculated productivity levels for pastures of the mountain forest zone of the Barguzin valley in Buryat'ya Russia show generally low productivity (table 9). There are a number of factors that account for such low productivity. First, the composition of the pastures is dominated by low-lying sedges (*Carex*) and sages

TABLE 9. Actual and Calculated Pasture Productivity, Livestock Carrying Capacity, Livestock Density and Pasture Area in Four Selsoviets of Barguzin Valley, Buryat'ya

	Argada	Baragkhan	Ulun	Bayangol
Pasture productivity				
Area of pastures (ha)	11200	12070	4992	15186
Yield of green mass (hundreds of kg/ha)	1.97	2.28	4.28	2.03
Total productivity of pastures (hundreds of kgs)	22,064	27,519	21,365	30,827
Calculated need in pasture productivity for actual animal numbers (hundreds of kgs)	104,927	83,611	56,066	100,973
Difference between actual and needed pasture productivity (hundreds of kg)	−82,863	−56,091	−34,700	−70,146
Ratio of actual to needed pasture productivity (percent)	21.0	32.9	38.1	30.5
Animal carrying capacity				
Calculated carrying capacity for SSU (heads)	8869	11,062	8589	12,392
Actual number of animals in SSU (heads)	46,007	35,805	24,147	44,370
Difference between actual and calculated numbers (heads)	37,137	24,742	15,557	31,977
Ratio of actual to calculated numbers (percent)	519	324	281	358
Animal density				
Normal density of animals in SSU (heads per ha)	0.79	0.92	1.72	0.82
Actual density of animals in SSU (heads per ha)	4.11	2.97	4.84	2.92
Difference between actual and normal density of animals in SSU (heads per ha)	3.32	2.05	3.12	2.10
Ratio of actual density to normal density (percent)	520	322	281	356
Pasture area				
Norm of pasture area for 1 SSU (ha)	1.26	1.09	0.58	1.23
Actual pasture area for 1 SSU (ha)	0.24	0.34	0.21	0.34
Difference between norm of pasture area and actual area for 1 SSU (ha)	1.02	0.75	0.37	0.89
Ratio of norm of pasture area to actual pasture area (percent)	518	323	281	359

NOTE: From Gomboev et al. 1996. SSU = standard stock unit (equivalent to Standard Livestock Unit, or a 454 kg (1000 lb) cow.

(*Artemisia*). The pastures are notably deficient in fescues (*Festuca*), which are character-istically among the most productive and versatile steppe grasses (Larin 1962b). The au-thors also attribute this low productivity both to deficient rainfall and repeated overgraz-ing of the pastures. The annual precipitation in the valley is low (<250 mm), which negates the usual climatic benefits of mountain pastures. The density of grass coverage is also notably skimpy, averaging between 15–30 percent. Compared with the mountain meadows of Dzhungaria, which exhibit rich grass coverage of between 70 and 80 per-cent (Sobolev 1960), the ranges of the Barguzin valley are sparsely vegetated. The au-thors compared the calculated productivity and pasture capacity with the actual use dy-namics and animal demographics in the region. The results of this comparison show a threefold excess of actual sheep per hectare over the calculated carrying capacity of the area. Thus, the region's pastures are quickly degrading due to overgrazing. These data may suggest that the pastoralists are not always quick to change their herd size, compo-sition, or pastoral orbits in response to climatic fluctuations or the subsequent effects on consumable range yields. Interestingly, the actual numbers of animals reported are sim-ilar to the calculated numbers for Koksu River valley. Chapter 4 adressess pastoral strat-egy and ecological manipulation in further detail through ethnographic studies.

CASE STUDY THREE: SOUTHWEST BAIKALYA (BURYAT'YA)

Kharitonov (1980) provides a general consideration of the pasture dynamics of Buryat'ya according to the botanical composition of various grassland types. These pasture types include motley grass/fescue steppe, Graminae–*Artemisia* steppe, and sedge and wild-rye steppe plant cohorts. Motley grass/fescue pastures occur at altitudes of approximately 800 m, whereas bunch grass/*Artemisia* steppe predominates at elevations below 700 m. The climate of Buryat'ya is harshly continental, with average annual temperatures between minus 0.5 °C and minus 2.5 °C, though summertime can be hot and dry, with daily temperatures regularly between 20 and 25 °C. The average January temperature is minus 25.6 °C. Kharitonov provides both green mass and dry mass values for the forage yield of these various pasture types, and from his calculations using "green edible mass" we find the expected threefold increase in pasture productivity of the region, when com-pared with Gomboev's more focused study. Kharitonov's calculations are summarized in table 10.

These comparative case studies illustrate that the steppe environment is generally di-verse and that its productivity relies on highly complex mixtures of ecological factors. Gomboev et al.'s (1996) study particularly suggests that in order to understand how pas-toral strategies relate to the complex environmental conditions of rangelands, we must also consider the fact that bad environments do not *necessarily* preclude the continuation of particular herding practices. However, over time, we may consider that slow changes to pastoral strategies, executed within the inherently malleable way of life of pastoral communities, might begin to reflect a shift in the geographic and social layout of their

TABLE 10. Calculated Pasture Capacity in Southwest Buryat'ya

Pasture type	Motley grass plus fescue steppe	Graminae plus *Artemisia* steppe	Sedge plus wildrye steppe
Dominant species	*Festuca lenesis, Arctogeron gramineum*	*Artemisia frigida, Poa botryoides*	*Carex duriuscula, Aneurolepidium pseudoagropyrum*
Yield of green mass (100 kg/ha)	5.2	6.6	4.95
Grazing period (days)	173	184	103
Potential heads of sheep per hectare [SSU]	1.2	1.2	.68
Necessary hectares per animal	.86	.81	1.45

NOTE: From Kharitanov 1980.

landscape. Gomboev's study further illustrates that pastoralists neither blindly repeat ineffective patterns of mobility when conditions are bad, nor do they completely disrupt their pastoral strategy in times of moderate environmental change. Instead they adapt their pratices through various technologies (social strategies, material technologies, etc.) to retain an acceptable return of success—in both an economic and social sense (Spooner 1973).

AGRICULTURAL POTENTIAL OF THE DZHUNGAR MOUNTAIN REGION

The discussion above has illustrated the rich potential of rangelands in the Dzhungar Mountains and the capacity of pastures of the upland meadows to support herds of various domesticated animals. The following section explores the potential of the Dzhungar Mountains for agricultural production, another proposed subsistence strategy for Bronze Age populations of the region. This section principally illustrates that agriculture was environmentally feasible in the region to a limited extent given the technology of Bronze Age populations. However, the limited arable niches in the mountain steppe meadows and valley basin of the Koksu River do not sustain large-scale agriculture without modern technologies (such as fertilizer, tractor tilling, and soil transplantation) (Jasny 1949; Stepanova 1961; Fedorin 1977). This fact suggests that the mountain environment was less than promising as a niche for substantial grain production and, much like today, likely played a relatively minimal role in the agricultural output of the region in prehistory. Thus far, no evidence of agricultural practices in the Koksu River valley during the Bronze Age has been found; therefore a less detailed reconstruction of the region's agricultural potential is provided here.

The following summary is derived from the studies of the soil and agricultural potential of the Dzhungar region by Sokolov (1968; 1975). Sokolov's study of agricultural potential considered a region of 12,334,400 hectares across the northeastern part of the Semirech'ye oblast, spanning environmental zones including high alpine and upland meadows, river floodplains, mountain steppes, and arid steppes and semi-deserts (Sokolov 1975). These studies offer detailed assessments of the agricultural potential of various territories in the Dzhungar Mountains and arid plains to the west of the alpine zone. After close assessment and classification of the soil types in these zones and their ability to sustain various types of agriculture and pastoral activity, Solokov (1975, 592) remarks that "agriculture is developed only in the mountain-steppe and partially in the desert zones of the oblasts [regions] where climatic conditions are favorable or there are possibilities of artificial irrigation". This trend is also reflected in the general land use of the region (table 11).

The majority of territories within the "plowed fields" category (which is only 8 percent of the usable territory) are in fact intensively irrigated agricultural lands located in the semi-desert and arid zones of the alluvial fan of the Koksu River (Sokolov 1975, table 208). These areas fall outside of the archaeological study zone considered in this study. Therefore, focus will be placed on agricultural assessment of the arid steppe zones of the upper Koksu River valley and the mountain-meadow steppes of the Dzhungar Mountains. The agricultural potential of the study zone is a product of climatic conditions, soil characteristics, and technology. The climate has already been summarized above, so a summary of the soils of the study region and their suitability for agricultural production given various technologies is provided here.

There are five main soil types that occur in the study zone. Sokolov uses number designations that correspond with his soil map (fig. 26; Sokolov 1968). These types include: type 28ab, Alpine and subalpine soils (including both chernozem and kaztanozems); type 33, mountain meadow chernozems; type 34 and 36, upland kastanozems; and type 12b, riparian light-grey soils (loess). In terms of agricultural productivity, these five

TABLE 11.   Agro-Pastoral Territory in the Dzhungar Mountains,
Piedmont, and Floodplain

Agricultural potential	Area (hectares)	Percent of arable land
Plowed land	705,900	8
Pasture (natural)	7,945,000	88
Hay cultivation	347,000	4
Total territory used for agro-pastoral production	8,997,900	100

NOTE: From Sokolov 1968, based on data collected in 1958.

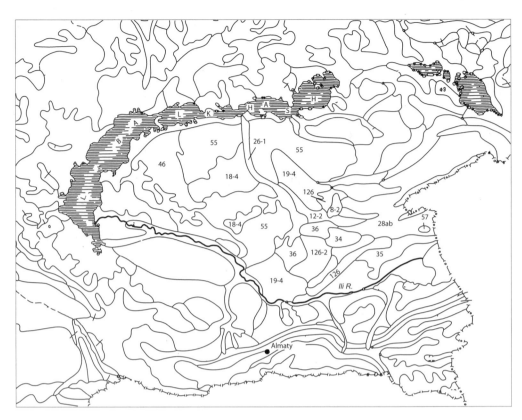

FIGURE 26

Soils of southeastern Kazakhstan and the study zone. After Sokolov 1968. Soil classes are found in table 12.

TABLE 12.   Soils of the Dzhungar Mountains and their Agricultural Propensities

Type	Propensity	Soil
28ab	Not agriculturally productive	Alpine and subalpine (includes chernozem and kaztanozems)
12b	Irrigated agriculture possible	Riparian grey (loess)
33, 34, 36	Dry farming possible	Mountain meadow (chernozems and upland kaztanozems)

NOTE: After Sokolov 1968.

categories fall into three groups of agricultural potential: not agriculturally productive, agriculturally productive given irrigation technology, and agriculturally productive using dry farming. The relationships are summarized in table 12, based on assessments of Sokolov (1968) and Sokolov (1975).

In the Dzhungar Mountain region, the upland areas with soils categorized by numbers 33, 34, and 36 represent the most promising agricultural zones for dry farming.

Sokolov's detailed assessment of the soils, climate, and geodynamics in these areas suggests that in the Dzhungar Mountains upland meadow chernozems can sustain grain agriculture through dry farming but are better suited for growing hay fodder (Sokolov 1968, appendix table 1). Sokolov adds the caveat that "mountain chernozems and kastonozems are among the best arable soils for dry farming, provided that there is acceptably flat relief" (1968, 117). The terrain of midland meadows (1000–1500 m) surrounding the Koksu valley is highly undulating, thus increasing the effect of leaching and erosion from runoff water in these areas. Thus, the topography of the areas with adequate soils for agriculture constrains their use. The best niches for agriculture in this region are the flat areas along small tributary rivers, where household gardens could be planted effectively in mineral-rich chernozems (Fedorin 1977).

Lowland zones in the Koksu River valley (650–800 m) exhibit carbonate loessic soils, which are highly prone to leaching and superficial humus composition, and are generally mineral poor (Sokolov 1968, 59). These soils are useful for agriculture only under conditions of artificial irrigation. Therefore one may conclude that while inter-montane river valleys, such as the Koksu River valley, can be productive agricultural zones given contemporary technology, during the Bronze Age it would have been difficult to manage any more than seasonal and small-scale household gardens.

This chapter has provided a general geographic perspective on the Eurasian steppe zone and has examined in detail the capacity of the environment of the Koksu River valley and surrounding ranges of the Dzhungar Mountains for pastoral exploitation and agricultural practices. These investigations illustrate that the pasture ranges in the study zone are geographically oriented according to elevation and that a seasonal schedule dictates their yield for herding activities. For optimal herd management (to sustain the maximum number of animals) upland pastures (1200–2000 m) are best exploited in the summer months of June, July and partly August, when ranges at lower elevations are dry and comparatively unproductive for herding activities. During the winter, snow and cold block upland pastures making them inacessible while lowland areas (600–850 m) present amenable conditions for winter camping and herding. These conditions include less snow, warmer temperatures, and dry grasses that can sustain herds during the coldest months of the year.

This chapter further demonstrates that the pastures within the study zone are highly productive for raising herd animals such as sheep, cattle, and horses, and that routinized usage of these pastures contributes to their regeneration and sustained productivity. Agriculturally, the study region can sustain only small-scale gardens with limited production, unless modern technologies of artificial irrigation and fertilization are available. Thus, the bulk of the territory in the study zone is best suited for use as pastureland.

4

BETWEEN ETHNOGRAPHY
AND HISTORY

*Pastoralism and Society in Semirech'ye and the
Dzhungar Mountains*

Chapter 3 suggested that the "restrictive" nature of the regional environment could be most effectively exploited through a mobile pastoralist strategy, but that variability in climate and resource geography across vertical zones in the mountains of Semirech'ye introduced a corollary degree of variation in the productive strategies of local societies. Moving beyond the complexity of steppe environmental conditions, this chapter delves deeper into the formative factors of pastoralist landscapes of southeastern Kazakhstan through a study of its ethnohistory and ethnography. Ethnography here is presented as comparative data against which archaeological data may be better understood. Ethnographic cases focus our interpretations of ancient landscapes according to known ways societies have adapted to the steppe environment and organized their social relationships throughout the more recent past. Close readings of select ethnographic and ethnohistoric sources provide a detailed view of the motivations and practices of mobile pastoralists in the Dzhungar Mountain area and Semirech'ye. More specifically, this chapter documents the spatial and temporal structure of seasonal migration, settlement geography, and sociopolitical geography that shaped the pastoralist landscape, while charting variability in the conditions of trade, political identity and hierarchy, and ritual and political interaction among groups.

This study uses ethnographic information as a source for ideas about how societies living in the Koksu valley, Dzhungar Mountains, and Semirech'ye during the Bronze Age may have experienced their environment and how their pastoral strategies were conditioned by social, ritual, and political interactions. This type of analogy is commonly known as formal analogy, which functions by comparing regional, economic, and social-scalar qualities between and among typically anachronistic groups (Binford 1968; Wylie 1985). In this case, analogical comparisons between movement patterns, settlement strategies, and environmental exploitation are supported by the fact that many of the prehistoric archaeological contexts investigated in this study, such as settlement sites, cemeteries, and rock-art loci, show continued use for millennia. This suggests that populations of different periods of prehistory and history invested in the same places with considerable functional and conceptual consistency throughout time. I do not suggest that pastoralist strategies were unchanging. Rather, closely identifying some arenas where pastoralists engaged with their environment and social landscape reveals a more lucid picture of possible prehistoric adaptations as well. Admittedly, this type of analogy is limited by the fact that throughout history different populations were under unique social and political pressures, which certainly affected their mobility strategies and social interactions. Nonetheless, this approach provides valuable insight into the experienced aspects of pastoralist life that likely contributed to the durable formation of pastoralist landscapes in Semirech'ye for millennia.

To address the potential discrepancy between the archaeological palimpsest of reiterated pastoralist practices over the long term and the historical specificity of social interactions as seen ethnographically, I situate formal analogies between the ethnographic and archaeological record in dialogue with historically particular ethno-narratives used as comparative models (Stahl 1993). Particular narratives recounted in the ethnographic and ethnohistoric record serve as models for understanding trade negotiations, interactive strategies, seasonal rituals, or individual sociopolitical considerations in the past. These anologies are made empirically relevant to the prehistoric case only when tested by available archaeological data, as middle range theories (Raab and Goodyear 1984).

Thus, this chapter looks to ethnographic studies that relate information concerning formal similarities attested by archaeological and historical continuity and also introduces ethnographic models of social and political organization, to which the archaeological data will be compared. Ethnography provides a vivid image of the way pastoral populations living in the study region have shaped their environmental, social, and ritual landscape throughout time. This ethnographic view also represents the starting point from which we will trace certain aspects of the pastoralist landscape further into antiquity.

THE ETHNOHISTORICAL SOURCES

No primary historical sources exist from ancient societies living in eastern Eurasia comparable to the sources of Egyptian, Sumerian, or Classical Greek or Roman periods. The most original documentary sources are firsthand accounts by travelers or historians from the late first millennium BCE to the twentieth century CE, which describe the peoples living in the eastern part of the Eurasian steppe zone. The earliest descriptions of

Dzhungaria and the region of Semirech'ye are from Chinese chroniclers who wrote of the populations living on the western frontier of the Han dynasty (206 BCE–220 CE). The most cited among these sources is the *Shi ji*, written by Sima Qian (c. 145–90 BCE), the *Han shu*, written by Ban Gu (c. 32–92 CE), and the *Hou han shu*, written by Fan Ye (c. 398–445 CE). Nikita Bichurin (the monk Iakinf) translated these documents and other early Chinese sources into Russian in the mid nineteenth century (Bichurin 1950), and Edouard Chavannes translated those documents into French at the end of the nineteenth century (Chavannes 1900). Subsequently, these translations have been used by a number of nineteenth and twentieth century culture historians who wrote and traveled throughout the eastern steppe regions and the mountainous border with China (e.g., Bartol'd 1963–1977; Aristov 1894).

Chinese chroniclers described the nomadic societies living throughout the Tian Shan and Dzhungar regions like the Wusun as "[neither] agriculturalists nor gardeners, [they] migrate with their herds from place to place in search of pasture and water" (from the *Shan han shu* in Bichurin 1950, II:190). Although the early Chinese sources are informative in that they speak to the long standing interrelationship between steppe nomadic communities and regional urban political bodies, the scope of such histories reveals a factually coarse and unnuanced cultural characterization of societies on the periphery of the Chinese (and later Persian) empires. In spite of their unuanced representation of nomadic society, early chroniclers did document significant demographic data and information concerning the wealth and military strength of steppe tribal groups (Bichurin 1950, II:190). The histories from this period primarily expose the view of nomadic societies held by the Qin and later Han state, whose interests in the nomadic Wusun and Hsiung-nu tribes was essentially political and economic (Golden 1992, 64)

In addition to the early Chinese sources, Turkish and Persian chronicles from the thirteenth to the fifteenth centuries, such as the *Tarikh-i jahan gusha* (c. 1252 by al-Juvayni (Juvayni et al. 1997) and the *Tarikh-i al-Rashidi* (late fifteenth century by Mirza Muhammed Haydar) (Haydar Mirza and Thackston 1996) contain brief discussions of the "Turkic" peoples living in southern Kazakhstan and Semirech'ye before and after the Mongol invasion (Abuseitova and Baranova 2001). Like the earlier Chinese chronicles, these histories presented chronologies of regional khans and the military geography of their territorial control, with only passing reference to their pastoral way of life. In his account of the *Gürkhan* of the Kara-khitai,[1] Juvayni notes relocating more than "40,000 households" across the territory of the Upper Yenisei River and Semirech'ye and "his people had prospered and their cattle [grew] fat, he brought the Qanqli under his sway and dispatching an army to Kashgar and Khotan conquered that region also" (Juvayni et al. 1997, 356). Although not a primary description of the pastoralist way of life in the region, one might infer that the decision to move the population to Semirech'ye was linked to both ecological and political concerns. Furthermore, the prosperity of the pastoral population in the region apparently enabled military campaigns that expanded the political landscape of the Kara-khitai throughout the twelvth century CE.

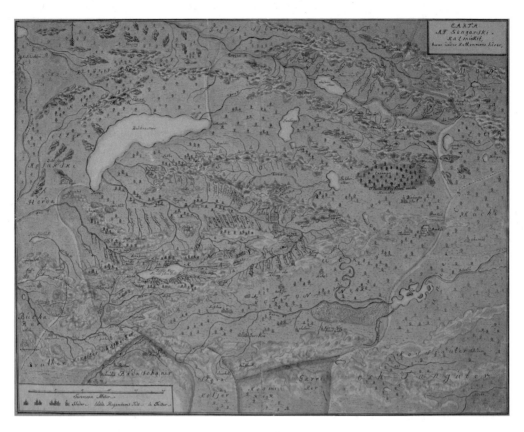

FIGURE 27

"Carte de la Dzoungarie," Johan Gustav Renat (1716–1733). Source: Alla Tiders Kartor: A Treasury of Maps. 1988.

More detailed history is provided in the works of the historian/chronicler to the Mongols, Rashīd al-Dīn, who wrote of steppe societies in relation to the Mongols in the Altai region and Dzhungaria in the beginning of the fourteenth century (c. 1307) (Rashīd al-Dīn Tabīb and Sayyad 2000). Noteworthy European travelers of later centuries, such as Marco Polo, Plano Carpini, Peter Pallas, and Johan Gustav Renat (among others) also likely passed through the well known passes of the Dzhungarian Gate on route to China and their annals contribute to the body of early documents about the region. Especially noteworthy is Johan Gustav Renat's map of the geography and tribal camping grounds in the Dzhungar Mountains (fig. 27). Renat was a Swedish prisoner of war who was captured by Kalmykhs in the early 18th century. His map is itself a scaled copy of a larger Kalmykh map that reflects in great detail the location of summer and winter settlements, and gives a fairly accurate geographic depiction of the region (described by Bartol'd 1962, 163).[2]

The first studies of the pastoral societies of the steppe territories that can be considered "ethnographic" in the academic sense were initiated in the late eighteenth and early nineteenth centuries. Many of the eighteenth century records are simple ethnographic notes nested within the pages of geographic and cartographic studies commissioned by the Russian Geographic Society (e.g., Pallas et. al 1794). Later, Tsar Nicholas I (1825–1855) commissioned "statistical reports" of the populations living in the eastern frontiers of Siberia and the steppe. It is within the context of these early ethnographic missions that detailed descriptions providing information about the migration patterns, land-use strategies, sociopolitical organization, and commercial activities of societies living in Semirech'ye were compiled (Levshin 1840; Valikhanov et al. 1865; Aristov 1894; Aristov 1896).

SOURCES USED IN THIS CHAPTER

Among the first individuals to have studied various aspects of geography and ethnography of the steppe region (Lunin 1973), there are relatively few whose work contains specific ethnographic and ethnohistoric details of the populations living in Semirech'ye, the Dzhungar Mountains, or the Koksu River valley (but see Bartol'd 1962–1963). Three of the most detailed nineteenth century ethnographic studies of this region are those by Alexis S. Levshin (1840), Chokan Ch. Valikhanov (1865), and Nikolai A. Aristov (1894). Levshin (1799–1879) was a Russian historian who traveled throughout Semirech'ye during the first quarter of the nineteenth century, compiling some of the earliest systematic studies of the economic and social organization of the "Kazakh-Kyrgyz."[3] Chokan Valikhanov (1835–1865) was himself a Kazakh, conscripted in Semipalatinsk by the Russians, and was a talented linguist and expeditionary. His father, Chengis, was a noted Kazakh ethno-historian and, as a result of his father's tutelage, Chokan was well instructed in the ethnohistory of steppe cultures at an early age. In 1856, the Russian Geographic Society commissioned him to lead a geographic and ethnographic expedition through Semirech'ye and the Tian Shan Mountains (Lunin 1973, 36). Valikhanov's work is considered amongst the most detailed ethnographic recordings of Semirech'ye, although his mission was cut short by his early death in the village of Tezeka at age thirty (Margulan 1984, 87). Nikolai Aristov (b. 1847), a lawyer and political station-agent, was concerned with demographic studies in Semirech'ye in the later half of the nineteenth century. He began his ethnographic writing after retiring from civil service, where he compiled data from his fieldwork among Kazakh populations from Turkestan and Semirech'ye (Aristov 1896). Aristov's demographic record of the Kazakh Great Zhus is recognized as one of the most accurate of its time (Lunin 1973).

In addition to these early field-based sources, this chapter draws from compiled ethnohistorical and ethnological studies by authors such as V.V. Bartol'd, who studied the history and ethnography of Semirech'ye in the late nineteenth century (1893–1894) (Bartol'd 1963–1977; Bartol'd and Gibb 1928; Bartol'd 1943), and A.D. Carruthers, who traveled in the Koksu River valley and Dzhungaria in the early twentieth century (Carruthers and Miller 1914). This chapter also gains from the synthetic work of contemporary ethno-historians (Abramzon 1973; Argynbaev 1973; Kurylev 1977; Masanov 1995), whose research and interpretations are derived in a large part from these earlier sources. As this chapter is meant to provide an overall ethnographic picture of the variable strategies of societies living in the Semirech'ye region rather than a comprehensive ethnohistory, I have limited myself to a close reading of these particular authors rather than undertaking a broad consideration of all the available early ethnohistorical and ethnographic sources concerning the Eurasian steppes.

ETHNOGRAPHY OF SEMIRECH'YE AND THE DZHUNGAR MOUNTAINS

According to the corpus of ethnographic work outlined above, the way of life in the territories of eastern Kazakhstan was predominantly based in mobile pastoralism until the first decade of the twentieth century (Argynbaev 1973; Fedorovich 1973; Masanov 1995). Ethnographers have suggested that agricultural production was relatively rare in the region until the turn of the twentieth century (Brill Olcott 1981; Kurylev 1977). Argynbaev (1973, 155) notes, that "at the start of this century dry farming in the Semirech'ye province was introduced only under conditions of small plots, scattered throughout mountain fields." Many early ethnographers suggest that the decision not to practice agriculture was a social conviction of Kazakh pastoralists, who looked down upon settled life and valorized a mobile pastoral existence (Valikhanov 1961–1972, III:22; Levshin 1840, 314, 316, 413). Nevertheless, the fact remains that irrigated agriculture was practiced along the southern boundaries of the Ili and Chu Rivers long before, from at least the seventh century CE (cf. Bartol'd 1962–1963, 82) and throughout the early history of the region as evidenced by the existence of large towns with clearly documented agricultural production (Baipakov 1984; Bartol'd and Gibb 1928). Furthemore, recent paleobotanical studies of Saka and Wusun settlements in the Talgar-fan region have shown conclusive evidence of millet agriculture as part of a mixed agro-pastoral economy in the loessic plains to the south of the Ili River during the Iron Age (c. seventh–second century BCE) (Miller-Rosen et al. 2000; Benecke 2003). Agricultural products such as millet and wheat were readily traded for domesticated animals and commodities such as textiles, metals, and manufactured goods, as part of the active caravan trade throughout southern Semirech'ye during the eighteenth and nineteenth centuries (Valikhanov 1961, vol. II, 148; Levshin 1840, 413)—another testimony to the existence of agriculture in the area between the Ili and Chu Rivers before recent centuries.

Bartol'd (Bartol'd 1962–1963, 122) suggests, however, that during medieval times, political conflict between nomadic tribes over the rich pastures of the nearby upland areas led to the abandonment or destruction of agricultural settlements from the thirteenth century, so that the "cultivation of the land [Semirech'ye] was resumed only in the nineteenth century by Sarts and Russians." Therefore, we may characterize the primary socioeconomic strategy of populations living throughout the mountain regions of Dzhungaria and Semirech'ye in terms of mobile pastoralism, around which a variety of more locally specialized systems were practiced to greater or lesser success given fruitful political, social, and environmental conditions. Mobile pastoral strategies therefore ranged from vertically transhumant and seasonal pastoralism, small-plot seasonal farming in conjunction with pastoral mobility, and more substantial irrigated agriculture in the Ili valley and southern part of Semirech'ye (Hudson 1938; Fedorovich 1973; Abramzon 1973). Variation within pastoral strategies in the mountain zones—the focus of this study—can be traced through ethnographic data concerning the geography of mobility and land use, the degree of trade and regional economic interaction, and the nature of sociopolitical communication, all of which define the extents of the sociopolitical landscape of populations living in the region.

MOBILITY PATTERNS AND SEASONAL ASPECTS OF MOBILE PASTORALISTS

The territorial organization and patterns of mobility of pastoralists in Semirech'ye and the Dzhungar Mountains reflect the pervasive interdependency between environmental and societal pressures that condition socio-economic systems. Galaty and Johnson echo this opinion concerning pastoral societies generally, noting that "[mobile] strategies to fulfill animal requirements interact with the constraints of domestic and political interaction, which in turn define rights to the land, through which pasture, water, and mineral resources are secured" (Galaty and Johnson 1990).

From at least the seventeenth century, Kazakhs of the "Great Zhus"[4] occupied the Semirech'ye region and extended from Lake Balkhash and Lake Ala-kul in the north to the Syr-Darya in the south (Levshin 1840; Brill-Olcott 1981; Masanov 1995). Levshin documents the territorial distribution of the Great Zhus stating "The tribes we have spoken with camp along the 'Su' rivers, the Talasu, the Ili, Koksu, Karatal, Chirchik, Syr, Sarysu, around lakes such as the Karakul, Ala-kul, Alsu, Anamas, in villages such as Kulcha, Kachkar, Kokan, Tashkent, Turkestan, in the Karatau, Tarbagatai, Zhengis-tsazan mountains, and in the region of the Seven Rivers"[5] (Levshin 1840, 308).

Population estimates for the Great Zhus at the end of the nineteenth century range from 450,000 to 700,000 (Demko 1969; Masanov 1995, 56). Masanov provides a reliable reconstruction based on various corroborative ethnographic surveys of the late 1800s and indicates that the population of the Dzhungar Mountains and Semirech'ye region was approximately 180,000, derived from three of the eleven clans of the Great Zhus: the Suany, Ysty, and Zhalairy. The Suany were localized in the southeastern ranges of the Dhzungar Mountains and on the Ili River plain. The population of the Suany was approximately 30,000 at the beginning of the twentieth century (Masanov 1995, 57). The Ysty generally inhabited regions closer to Lake Balkhash, and migrated south to summer pasture in the Zailisky Alatau. Their population at the turn of the twentieth century was approximately 40–50,000. Finally, the Zhalairy were localized in the mountain valleys and foothill zones of the Dzhungar Mountains, with winter pastures between the Ili and Karatal Rivers and in the pre-Balkhash Desert. Their larger population, between 100–110,000 people at the end of the nineteenth century, accounted for a wider distribution across the territories of Semirech'ye (Masanov 1995, 58). Contact between these clans and the clans of the Middle Zhus (of central Kazakhstan) was known for the time, as members of neighboring clans from other regions are known to have married into the clans of the Great Zhus (Valikhanov et al. 1865), likely skewing the demographic assessment of tribal affiliations.

PATTERNS OF PASTORAL MIGRATION

Movement patterns of Kazakh pastoralists living in the Tian Shan and Dzhungar Mountains are well documented in the early ethnographies. The distance of seasonal migration, the pattern of movement, and the strategic scheduling of relocation varied according to local environmental and political factors (Masanov 1995, 86–87). The mobility patterns of pastoral groups in the Semirech'ye region from the late nineteenth century to the turn of the twentieth century were notably different from the typical migration pattern of central and southern Kazakhstan at the same time (fig. 28; Abramzon 1971; also Levshin 1840). Specifically, migratory "orbits" of Kazakh pastoralists of Semirech'ye did not reflect north–south migration. Instead, these groups traditionally migrated east and west, exploiting changes in pasture composition and climatic conditions according

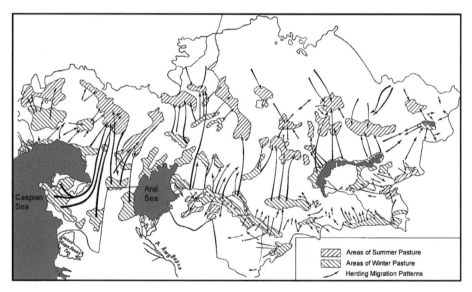

FIGURE 28
Traditional Kazakh migration patterns. After Abramzon 1971.

to vertical (altitudinal) zones between lowland arid plains and upland subalpine meadows (Carruthers and Miller 1914, 377; Valikhanov 1961–1972, I:531). Pastoralists sought richer pastures and cooler weather by traveling "up" in the Dzhungar mountain region instead of "north" as in the open steppe of central Kazakhstan. Changes in altitude reduce the actual migration distance necessary to supply fodder for herds in winter and summer pastures. However, migratory distances varied considerably from year to year, and from group to group. Hudson remarks that for Kazakh pastoralists of the nearby Tian Shan Mountains

> It is difficult to get precise information in the distances covered by different groups in the seasonal migrations. There appears to be a great deal of variation. My own information indicates that such journeys were much shorter than is usually assumed to be the case, but this may be because both principal informants belong to groups which lived near the mountains, so that it was only necessary to go a short distance to find good pasturage in the valleys and foothills. Karabaiev's group, for example, went only about nine kilometers, while Tlenshiev's group used to go twenty or thirty kilometers or perhaps farther if the conditions in any particular place proved unfavorable. In any case, they were not familiar with migrations covering hundreds of miles.
>
> (Hudson 1938, 26)

Paradoxically, variation in migratory distances should be considered the "norm" for Kazakhs living in the mountains of Semirech'ye. Valikhanov remarks on the different migration patterns of the Great Zhus tribes living in the Tian Shan Mountains, noting that the Alaban tribe migrates short distances from the Ili valley to the upland pastures of the Turgen River (approximately 50 miles), whereas pastoral groups of the Dulat tribe may migrate as much as five times farther (Valikhanov 1961–1972, III:18). This, he explains, is due to "their large population, warlike character, and wealth"[6] (Valikhanov 1961, III:18).

As a response to the array of environmental and social variables throughout the river valleys and foothills of Semirech'ye, a range of settlement patterns and mobility strategies were regularly employed between summer and winter (Masanov 1995, 87). Some populations of the region were known to stay in the foothill valleys during the winter, while others made longer migrations to the piedmont plains. For the longest migrations, the deserts and semi-deserts of the "pre-Balkhash" region were used for winter pasture.[7] The location of the winter camp had an impact not only on the nature of winter pastoral activity but also on the scheduling of spring and summer movements. For those groups who wintered in the lowland hills and mountain river valleys, the distance to summer pastures rarely exceeded 100 km. Thus, the seasonal "orbit" between alpine summer pastures and winter camps in the lowlands actually demanded only a semi-annual migratory schedule. Migration essentially only took place for two to three months of spring and autumn and was punctuated by three- to four-month periods of stability during the winter and summer (Bartol'd 1962–1963, 164). Pastoralists would also travel around their winter camps in a radial fashion but lived in well-established locales. For those who established winter camps in the less productive desert steppe of the pre-Balkhash zone, periodic moves during the winter were sometimes necessary due to lack of productive pastures. Nonetheless, the pattern of movement was generally restricted to short relocations around a defined encampment or settlement similar to a semi-permanent village (*aul*).

SEASONAL CAMPS

Traditionally, Kazakh pastoralists of Semirech'ye established their winter camp (*aul*) in an area where their herds would most productively survive the cold conditions of eastern Kazakhstan's continental winter climate (Valikhanov 1961–1972, I:531). This motivation is noted generally for other regional pastoralists as well. Levshin reports, "In order to protect themselves from the misfortunes and unpleasantness which winter causes them, the Kazakhs choose for their winter camps the middle of some grove, reeds, hills, or sands in the southern part of the steppe" (Levshin 1840, 311). He further remarks, however, that "their camps, winter as well as summer, cannot be exactly determined and are not always occupied by the same inhabitants. Nevertheless, they are quite constant in the choice of the former, because not all localities present the necessary conditions for a winter camp to the same degree and because the depth of snow does not allow them to move" (Levshin 1840, 311–312). In the late 1800s, the ethnographer Medvedskii recorded a checklist of "characteristics" of attractive winter camping grounds. "The [location of the] winter house (zimovka) should: a) be well protected from wind; b) not be covered in deep snow; c) have grassy areas under the snow; d) have a convenient water source; e) have the possibility to gather fuel in large quantities and without excessive work; f) be nearby dry forage, grasses, or fuel" (Masanov 1995, 88). These accounts illustrate that winter camps were not haphazardly occupied; to the contrary they were valued locations in the landscape and important in the construction of meaningful landscapes of interaction—concepts to which we will return in our archaeological reconstruction of the settlement geography of prehistoric winter camps in the study zone.

Hilly areas of medium elevation and river valleys in the foothills represent typical places for the establishment of winter lodging in the Dzhungar Mountains. The winter camp typically represented a collection of as many as forty to fifty households, which, except in the case of those that wintered in extremely dry deserts, was stationary from the month of November until mid-April. These groups did not necessarily settle all in the same location but rather set up smaller settlement groups in the many ravines and canyons throughout the lowland areas of river valleys. Winter in the region can be extremely cold, with average January temperatures below minus 20 °C. In order to protect herds from freezing overnight, stables are commonly constructed around the camp. These enclosed corrals are constructed of stone, wood, shrubs, sod, or brushwood interleaved across vertical posts (personal observation; Masanov 1995).

The primary selection criteria for the situation of the winter camp area, however, were still the accessibility of grass and water (Valikhanov 1961–1972, I:533). Pasturing of herds in the winter entailed exploiting ranges where the snow cover was less than 10–15 cm. Cattle and sheep cannot access grass beneath snow deeper than 15 cm unless horses break the snow cover before them. Yet horses were often let to roam in winter herds (*kos*), at substantial distance from the winter camp, therefore offering little help in breaking the snow near the settlement (Masanov 1995, 95). Thus, in order to ensure that sufficient pasture was found, herding usually took the form of daily radial excursions from the camp-center at a distance of 5–10 km. If local pastures were heavily covered by snow, a system of "cooperatively staged"[8] pasturing was used, where horses, then cattle, then sheep would be sequentially herded over the range, thus taking advantage of the horses' "snowplow" effect to provide access to grass for the cattle and sheep (Masanov 1995, 100). In years of extremely cold weather, famine (*jute*) could strike more than 50 percent of domestic herds. Famines[9] of this scale were recounted to occur on average every 10 years or so (Masanov 1995, 100).

Summer pastures of the Great Zhus were typically located in alpine and subalpine meadows of the Dzhungar and Tian Shan mountains (Valikhanov et al. 1865; Carruthers and Miller 1914; Chekeres 1973). These alpine pastures (*dzhailyau*) are highly productive and are often located near the sources of naturally occurring springs (Fedorovich 1973). Availablity of fresh water and the natural composition of pastures each played a major role in the selection of summer pastures (Masanov 1995, 107–108). The pattern of yurt relocation during the summer was largely associated with the capacity and productivity of upland meadows and annual climatic conditions. Typically, pastoralists spent the early summer months in upland pastures between 1200–1600 m, because the higher subalpine meadows were still under deep snow. After three weeks or so at these pastures, the group would move further up to take advantage of fresh grass and cool temperatures available at higher altitudes (Valikhanov 1961–1972, I:533). Groups might rest at these pastures for three to four weeks, and then begin to descend again. By this time the subalpine pastures would have regrown (Larin 1962), and be grazed again en route to lowland winter camps.

SOCIOPOLITICAL LANDSCAPE IN SEMIRECH'YE AND THE DZHUNGAR MOUNTAINS

Most of the ethnohistorical details concerning the social and political interactions of mobile pastoralists in Semirech'ye refer to Turkic tribes and post-Mongol clans whose hierarchical social organization can be traced no earlier than the first few centuries of the current era in association with the Wusun and Xiong-Nu nomads of Semirech'ye or alternatively take their most representative form after the thirteenth century CE (Bartol'd and Gibb 1928; Krader 1980; Golden 1992). However, archaeological studies of graves in Semirech'ye and northeastern Kazakhstan, such as the princely kurgans of Issyk

(Akishev 1978), Pazyryk (Gryaznov 1929), and Berel (Baipakov and Francfort 1999), suggest that from the seventh to the fifth century BCE a well structured political hierarchy was in place across Semirech'ye, Dzhungaria, and the southern Altai Mountains. In the Koksu valley, large kurgan burials illustrate that the populations living there during the first millennium BCE also played a part in the regional political economy of the Saka throughout Semirech'ye (Chang et al. 2003).

Athough Turkic and Mongol social and political organization was different from that in prehistory, we may benefit from understanding how individual and group status were codified and how the negotiation of social positions vis-à-vis neighboring populations was accomplished through the control of regional territory and local resources. Social and economic alliances had the effect of extending the perceived scale of pastoralist landscapes by linking individual groups through social and political interactions. The nature of interaction depended largely on the relationships between regionally defined groups and their leaders, which is indexed by the acquisition of exotic materials as tribute as well as the control of large herds of domesticated animals (Krader 1963).

For the Kazakhs, social alliances between pastoral clans were the defining order in the appropriation of summer pasturelands (Masanov 1995, 110). "Normally there existed rules regulating the use of summer pastures . . . every summer pasture is allocated for use only for certain groups of Kirghiz [Kazakhs], nearly always of the same clan, according to which pasturing is limited to specific clans or their sub-segments . . ." (Kuftin 1926). Thus, in order to have access to the best pastures or to ameliorate the effects of a dry season, alliances were developed between groups in both political and economic senses. Social and political interaction resulted in the joining of clans to create large migratory groups distributed throughout the upland ranges of the Dzhungar and Tian Shan Mountains (Valikhanov 1961–1972, III:18). Allied pastoral groups frequently shared routes and pastures, although they were rarely crowded atop one another (Levshin 1840, 312). Nonetheless, migratory camps commonly consisted of twenty yurts or more clustered across particularly rich summer highland meadows. Ethnographic accounts speak of coalitions of groups coming from distant winter camps sharing summer highland pastures, sometimes even joining different clans with numbers ranging to several thousand yurts (Levshin 1840, 164; Masanov 1995, 108). Bartol'd refers to great numbers of mobile pastoralists who had their camps in the lower Koksu valley (along the Karatal River), gathered under the powerful Khan Qasim in the early sixteenth century (Bartol'd 1962–1963, 153). Thus, the political potency of certain clans and their leaders affected the allocation and conditions of use of seasonal territory.

Winter as well as summer camp organization was established according to landscape divisions that reflected genealogical and political relationships between regional populations. "Although the descent lines and tribes of the Kazaks, who are constantly moving from one place to another, cannot have fixed habitations just for this reason, nor can they possess lands, strictly speaking, still, in order to avoid disputes, each group stays as much as possible in the same camping places, especially during winter. Only reasons of greatest importance can make them go against this custom" (Levshin 1840, 313–314). Within the boundaries of tribal pastures and migration orbits, internal conflict and interactions of various kinds also affected the selection of the kinds of contexts for settlement. Valikhanov provides a story of a local clan leader who wished to move up in the ranks of local power vis-à-vis the other leaders. "Bursuk . . . was aiming at securing the footing of hereditary chief, and carried on a constant depredatory warfare, or 'baranta,' [tribal raiding] with all the Kirghiz [Kazakh] aristocrats, in order to enrich himself. He was obliged, consequently, to chose the most secure and inaccessible positions for his auls [camps], at a distance from the general camping grounds" (Valikhanov 1865–1972, 87).

In addition to active disputes and political interactions, other factors such as the location of burial grounds and ritualized locations in the landscape influenced the selection of camps and the determination of migration routes. According to Valikhanov "Many ancient and more recent burials (kurgans) are scattered across the steppe. These monuments of the Kazakhs were much more important [to them] geographically, than in a historical sense, namely because these graves stand in the mouths of generations of people and the Kazakhs decide their migration routes according to the landscape[10] of these burials" (Valikhanov 1961–1972, III:29). This example shows that the ethnography of the seasonal behavior of mobile pastoralists is important to examine not only in terms of economic and political spheres of life, but also in reference to ideological practices.

The seasonality of various social and ritual events is also a contributing factor in the formation of contexts of interaction. For mobile pastoralists of mountain regions, the seasonal landscape is constructed in part by the environment and its effect on herding activities, and by the temporal and spatial geography of social behavior. In winter, groups may disperse and batten down against the cold, whereas in the summer the open pastures provide contexts for gaming and social interaction. "Summer was also the time when many rituals and festivals were conducted, including annual burial and memorial rites, initiation rites, weddings, and other ceremonies" (Masanov 1995, 110). Levshin notes that autumn is also an important season for festivals, and was also a popular season for political raids (*barantas*). He remarks, "this season is favorable [for raids] because of the darkness of the nights and the vigor of the horses, which have been restored in good pastures for a whole season and are all the better disposed for long-distance travel and galloping" (Levshin 1840, 311–12). This example illustrates the complex relationship between the concurrent and oscillating impact of seasonal environmental conditions on the health of herds and their role in more than simple subsistence needs: namely sociopolitical and ritual interactions.

LOCAL AND REGIONAL INTERACTION, TRADE AND COMMUNICATION

We have already discussed how both environmental conditions and social and political factors affect mobility and land use. We now turn to the processes by which information and materials are passed from mobile group to mobile group and between villages and agricultural settlements to landscapes more intensely generated by mobile pastoralists. Ethnography shows how social and economic strategies such as trade, gifting, tribute, and brokerage complement established mobility patterns and how conflict between groups competing for political power can drastically alter their accessibility to territory and their ability to balance the needs of their herds within regional political arenas. We have shown how in certain regions there are mobility patterns that become more common, such as seasonal transhumance in mountainous or high altitude valleys, and that these "norms" are surprisingly internally malleable given social dynamics. In order to understand how these strategies are affected by social conditions such as identity and group status, it is important to focus on the contexts that frame interaction between and among pastoral groups, merchants, and mobile traders and how these encounters contribute to the mixing of material culture of different populations in territories that seem peripheral to major centers of production.

TRADE, GIFTING, AND TRIBUTE

At the turn of the twentieth century, the river valley corridors oriented east to west through Semirech'ye and the Dzhungar Mountains were well-trodden pathways of trade and communication between China, Siberia, and Central Asia (Valikhanov 1961–1972, II:148; Levshin 1840). Levshin (1840, 106) comments that the Russian traveler Monsieur Zibbershtein "assures that all the caravans that pass along the frontier of Siberia, from the towns of little Boukharie [sic] to Kokant, are necessarily dispatched towards the Kara-tal River, on a route along the Kouk-Sou River to the town of Kouldji past the Iakchy-Altyne-Emel Mountains, which run toward the Ili River."

For the Kazakh pastoralists of Semirech'ye, trade was highly entangled with political relationships, personal status, and economic prosperity. On this point, Valikhanov (1865, 72) provides an illustrative example of interactions in the mountains of Dzhungaria:

> After traversing a distance of seventy miles daily, the caravan usually came to a halt in the cool of the evening and pitched its tents under the shade of a high poplar or silver-leaved wild olive, on the brink of some brawling rivulet . . . The Kirghizes [sic], encamped in the vicinity, would likewise make their appearance with sheep, which they offered for sale, while their more distinguished chiefs approached with the view of receiving a "bazarlyk," or present. They would approach the caravan with great ceremony, accompanied by numerous suite, making the inquiry, "Who is the richest?" On this, each owner of a tent, in

his turn, usually treated the dignitaries of the horde to tea, biscuits, and dried fruit, which the Kirghizes stowed away about their person, and, after soliciting a present, would speedily withdraw.

Valikhanov's ethnography abounds with accounts of combination trading, gifting, and tribute—all part of negotiating social interactions within the tribal pastoralist territories of the Dzhungar Mountains. For example, he lists the materials among the tribute paid to the agents of the ruler of the Sairam Lake region (50 km to the west of the Koksu River valley on the caravan route to Xinjiang) to pass his territory:

> As a gift we gave 1 manlik (Chinese silken textile), 1 skein of silk, 4 shan-maty, 100 tszinei [about 125 lbs] of wheat, 10 tszinei [12.5 lbs] of cotton paper, 1 brick of tea, 1 sheep (for the agent) [sic], a jug of wine in its wrapper and Chinese tea-cups, different medicines against eye infections, and 16 kilograms of plaster to destroy eye infections.

> Valikhanov 1961–1972, II:149

This seemingly random array of items exchanged as tribute is significant for the current study because it highlights how the control of landscapes by mobile pastoralists through local political structure influenced the influx of highly variable material culture into the possession of members of some parts of a tribal group. Of course, these items were exceptionally exotic because they were part of a larger commercial caravan system. Nonetheless, the process is one that may be useful for understanding the way political and economic interactions played a role in the diversification of materials according to the ordered variability of interactions across prehistoric pastoral landscapes proposed here. For example, organized trade of particular commodities, especially made from animal and agricultural products, was related to the natural cycles of the harvest (of agricultural groups of the region) and successes of summer pasturage on the part of mobile pastoralists. Animals such as camels and horses were sought-after commodities in the fall market trade, especially after begin fattened during the summer. Therefore domestic artisans (largely women) also worked diligently in the summer period on textiles and manufactured goods, so that by autumn they would have a variety of items, like carpets, felts, leather bags, and textiles, to exchange for stock in regional market centers (Valikhanov 1961–1972, II:151). Thus, even traders, who were not themselves pastoralists, participated in reinforcing the seasonal tempo for trade; often initially set by mobile herders. "The center of a nomad empire was always a great attraction for merchants of various countries. Here they found a good market for their wares . . ." (Bartol'd 1962–1963, 82). In effect, trade, gifting, and even coincident interaction were all tied to the nature of seasonal habitation throughout the mountain passes of Dzhungaria as it related to the schedule of pastoral activity, which, in practice, served to promote and bolster the status of individuals and groups in a regional political system.

The examples above illustrate types of coincidental, opportunistic, or even passively organized interactions that were part of the social landscape of pastoralists living in the Dzhungar Mountains and Semirech'ye. Many of these mobile groups also took an active role in changing their status and power vis-à-vis regional political systems through strategies that generated wealth and promoted regional alliances. Partly because they were knowledgeable of the mountainous terrain, and partly because they controlled pack animals like camels, pastoral herders who camped in the Koksu valley and other major mountain passes often were hired as escorts, or brokers, for caravans that were moving through their territory (Valkihanov 1961–1972, II:148). For these local escorts, brokering transport for a foreign caravan between different tribal territories not only could improve their personal wealth but also could accrue for them legitimate power to negotiate internal relationships and alliances between Kazakh tribes, especially if different groups coordinated to have tribute paid to their respective leaders. These intricate dealings often produced imbalance in local power structures, which were also regulated by less mercantile means such as raiding or tribal warfare (Levshin 1840, 433).

The efficacy of pastoral political organization rests in a group's ability to negotiate its movements through a network of social relations and across territorial and genealogical boundaries (Beck 1991; Irons 1974; Khazanov 1994). Institutionalized forms of political reciprocity, such as raiding (for livestock), trade, tribute, brokerage and caravan escorts, marriage arrangements (Bacon 1958), and a host of other social interactions could reorient certain individuals in terms of local and regional power structures (Bartol'd 1963–1977). For pastoral groups of eastern Eurasia, the dynamics of social, economic, and political interactions rested in both historically forged relationships, as well as in opportunities for the promotion of oneself, or one's group, to a higher order in the segmentary system (Krader 1963). Often these opportunities were conditioned by the various spatial and temporal patterns of an overarching pastoral landscape, defined though the related experiences and dynamics of pastoral herding strategies, settlement geography, and socioeconomic negotiations.

Through a review of the ethnohistory and ethnography of Semirech'ye and the Dzhungar Mountains, we have developed a view of a particular type of social landscape that is defined by mobility patterns and flexible networks of interaction. Adaptation to a restrictive environment and negotiation of economic settings, social experiences, and political motivations of other populations conditioned the spatio-temporal experience of pastoralist in regionally localized contexts. These elements are in fact inherently variable, differentially contributing to a practical form by which mobile pastoral societies generally carry out their way of life. Yet, this way of life was also regularly reshaped according to ever-evolving needs and conditions. This chapter has illustrated that the variation in pastoral strategies and their rich cross-stitch of various strategic threads led to the development of social interactions within a rather localized territory of Semirech'ye and Dzhungaria from the sixteenth through nineteenth centuries, where materials, languages, people, and animals were exchanged and brought together in common times and spaces across the territory.

Such interactions had far-reaching effects in the region beyond these local systems and in terms of larger geo-historical processes. These ethnographic examples may serve to illustrate, if only in part, some of the globalizing processes that brought Central Asia into the center of world history by the late nineteenth century (Golden 1992; Hopkirk 1994). For the purpose of this study, the ethnographic information provided in this chapter provides useful analogies for conceptualizing some of the relationships between the ecology of pastoral strategies in the Dzhungar Mountains and Semirech'ye and the construction of political and social networks that played an equally important role in structuring social interaction during the Bronze Age and throughout prehistory.

5

A PASTORALIST LANDSCAPE IN SEMIRECH'YE

Archaeology of the Koksu River Valley

The previous chapters presented detailed investigations of the environment and ethnography of the Koksu River valley and Semirech'ye region that characterize it as a rich ecological context for mobile pastoral ways of life, prehistorically and more recently. Environmentally, the seasonal variability and resources of different altitude zones help to shape the strategies of transhumant mobility between lowland winter settlement areas and highland summer pastures, typically ranging less than 50 kilometers per season. From a long-term paleo-environmental perspective, the productive capacity of the various ecotones described for the Kosku valley was shown to be relatively stable, drawing into question an environmental pressure for extensive migration or relocation on the part of the local pastoral populations at various times in prehistory. The regional ethnographic and ethno-historic record illustrates that pastoralists of Semirech'ye employed a pattern of annual migration consistent with the vertical distribution of range resources and seasonal ecology described above but also significantly extended and reshaped the range of their territorial boundaries and networks of interaction according to social, economic, and political factors. From these two sources of information, we have an image of a generally structured but significantly variable pastoral landscape with considerable chronological continuity (Frachetti and Mar'yashev 2007).

This chapter presents a synthetic view of the archaeological record of the study region, in order to focus on pastoralist landscape formation from its earliest prehistoric expressions to more recent historical iterations. Specifically, recent archaeological survey of the Koksu valley documents the geography of settlements, burials, rock-art, and other

anthropogenic features from as early as 2500 BCE (Frachetti 2006c). This survey serves
as the basis for conceptualizing the structure and variability of pastoralist strategies from
a long-term perspective and in comparison to the region's dynamic ecology. The archaeology is characterized by both continuity and change in the distribution, function, and
significance of pastoralist sites through time, while it also highlights the contribution of
local populations in the formation and re-formation of a local landscape with ties to a
wider regional network of interactions. This chapter sets the stage for an alternative view
of Bronze Age pastoral life in which social, economic, and political systems evolved in
step with pastoralists' strategic manipulation of their ever-shifting landscapes.

GEOGRAPHY AND DISTRIBUTION OF ARCHAEOLOGICAL EVIDENCE

The data discussed in this chapter is documented primarily within the Koksu River valley and the surrounding piedmont of the Dzhungar Mountains (fig. 29). The boundaries
of the study zone correspond largely with the environmental limits of the Koksu river

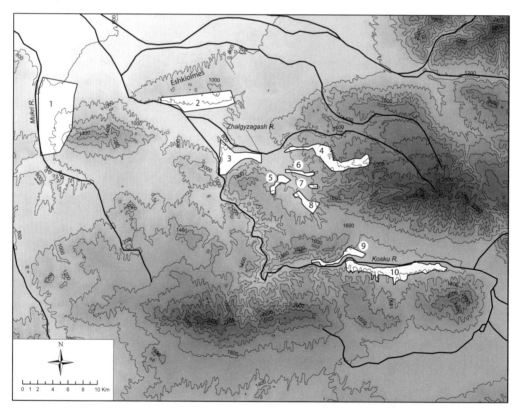

FIGURE 29
Survey polygons (2002) in the Koksu River valley.

system and nearby natural pastures.[1] In the west, the study zone boundary lies at the border between natural grassland ranges and the modern irrigated plain, which the Soviets modified heavily in the 1950s and 1960s. At its westernmost extreme the study zone corresponds with the transition from an arid-steppe environment of the Koksu lowlands to the sandy, barren Sary-Esik desert. Two high mountain ranges border the Koksu valley on the north and south with peaks as high as 3500 m above sea level. To the east, the study zone is limited by the national border of China, which also corresponds with extreme peaks of the Dzhungar Range (more than 4100 m above sea level). Within this general study zone, smaller study polygons were delimited for archaeological survey based on their geographic location, with the plan to span the area's ecological transition from the lowlands to the highlands.

We recorded 382 archaeological features within the study area. For the purpose of general statistical comparison, I categorized sites as low, middle or high altitude features. Lowland areas reflect elevations less than 800 m, middle altitude areas range from 800 m to 1200 m, and high elevation zones are above 1200 m. These categories correspond with vertical boundaries reflecting compositional variation in rangeland vegetation (Goloskokov 1984).[2]

The broad chronology of archaeological features recorded in the study zone ranges from the Neolithic to the contemporary era. Upon initial recording, it was often difficult to assign an accurate chronology to every feature, thus all archaeological features recorded within the study areas were documented using a standardized system and were assigned to gross chronological periods only after analysis (Frachetti 2006c). Archaeological features were attributed chronological periods according to three lines of evidence: datable ceramics or other diagnostic finds in shovel tests; datable construction or feature type according to structural typologies (e.g., kurgan burials); and datable motifs or stylistics of rock-art. By cross-referencing these factors for each feature as much as possible, a general chronological phase was attributed to each site and, when possible, a more precise period. This general chronology has been justified by radiocarbon dates at excavated sites within the dataset such as Begash and Mukri (Frachetti and Mar'yashev 2007). From the general chronology of sites, we may illustrate the geography of the primary site types (settlements, rock-art, and burials) of the Bronze Age, Iron Age, and historical periods (figs. 30–32). In each period, the distribution of archaeological sites across the study zone corresponds with trends of elevation and geographical setting.

In the lowland polygons, the primary feature categories were burials (kurgans and stone arrangements) and settlement structures. The majority of burials are classified as "kurgans" (large earthen tumuli) generally dating from the "Saka" period and later (i.e., later than the seventh century BCE) (Yablonsky 1995). Two notable Bronze Age cemeteries, Talapty and Kuigan, had been previously excavated revealing stone cists and Late Bronze Age material culture typical of the late Andronovo phases of Semirech'ye (Mar'yashev and Karabaspakova 1988; Mar'yashev and Goryachev 1993). These lowland cemeteries were revisited, but not re-documented in detail (see Goryachev 2004 for

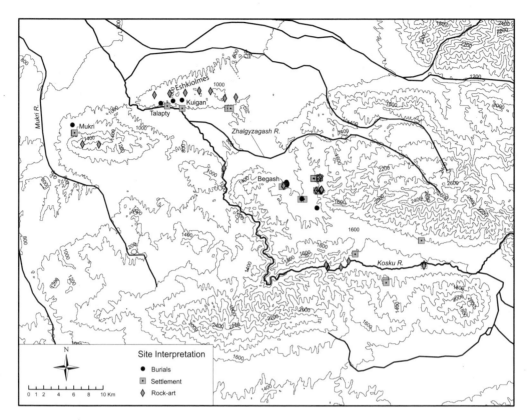

FIGURE 30
Bronze Age sites of the Koksu Valley.

detailed accounts of these sites in English). In addition to burials, settlement structures were found to be more abundant in lowland areas than previously recorded. Nearly 35 percent of the total sites in lowland areas were settlements. Finally, a considerable number of rock-art panels are found adjacent to burials and settlements, often in the immediate hillsides and crags of lowland settlement contexts. This is especially notable in the Eshkiolmes range and near the site of Mukri on Mount Alabasy—a newly documented locale of rock-art. Although many of these rock-art groups are chronologically and socially associated with lowland settlements, the absolute elevation of the rock-art areas is often higher than 800 m, so many statistically fall into the middle elevation class.

In the midland polygons, the percent composition of features is generally comparable to those in the lowlands, but the total number of sites is much larger. Noticeable increases in the number of burials (both kurgans and stone arrangements), rock-art and settlements at midland altitudes, suggest increased activity in this zone. Ecological models of seasonal transhumance explain how midland altitudes are productive in both spring and fall, whereas high and low altitudes are only used in the summer and winter, respectively. This seasonal routine may partly account for the increased percentages of

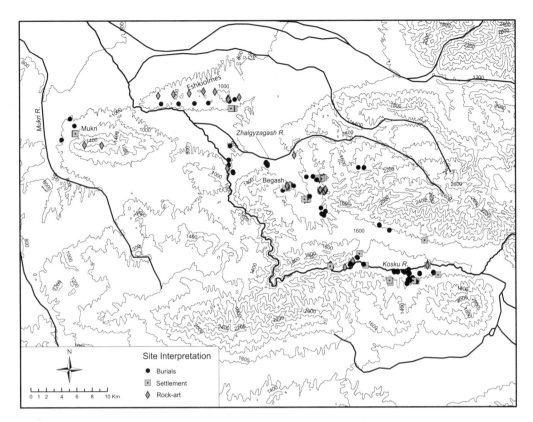

FIGURE 31
Iron Age sites of the Koksu Valley.

feature types, such as settlements, in areas occupied for more than one season (Frachetti 2006a).

Considerably fewer sites are documented in the highland polygons. The most notable change, however, is an increase in percentage of Saka (Iron Age) kurgans. The relative increase in upland kurgans may reflect a conscientious utilization of highlands as burial grounds in the Iron Age, but more likely the change in statistical trend merely reflects the difficulty in locating settlements in upland meadows versus the easily distinguishable mound burials. During the months when high altitude zones are free from snow, they are also overgrown with high meadow grass, which mitigates site recovery. Additionally, the relative lack of stone in the upland pastures means that constructions would likely have been built of less durable wood, sod, or felt, further adding to the ephemeral nature of highland settlements. Although site recovery in the highland territories was poor, we must assume that the ecological pressure to migrate to the upland meadows meant that those pastoralist groups living in lowland winter settlements inhabited the highlands during the summer. Given these general trends in the geography and chronology of archaeological sites survey in the Kosku valley and surrounding mountains, we

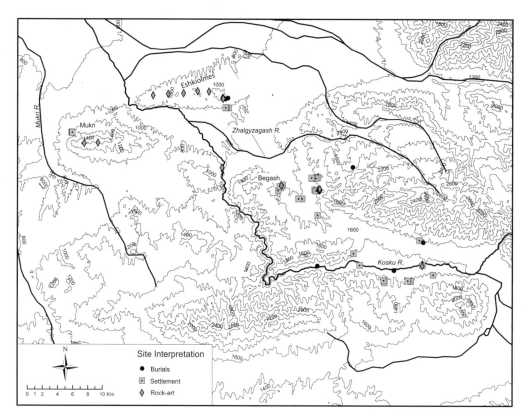

FIGURE 32

Turkic and later sites of the Koksu Valley.

now turn our attention to the formation and reiteration of the pastoralist landscape from the Bronze Age through historical times.

THE PASTORALIST LANDSCAPE THROUGH TIME
THE FORMATIVE PERIOD (2500–1000 BCE)

The earliest concrete evidence for pastoralist communities in the Koksu valley comes from the settlement of Begash, dating as early as 2460 BCE[3] (Frachetti and Mar'yashev 2007). Begash also provides the earliest evidence to date of mobile pastoralism anywhere in Semirech'ye. The site is located in the midland altitudes of the study zone and reflects a center of pastoralist activity from the Early to Middle Bronze Age. Begash is only one of a number of settlements nestled into small ravines at the edge of the piedmont and riparian terrace of the Zhalgyzagash tributary (fig. 33). Beyond the domestic structures at Begash, the broader site context consists of a large nearby burial ground (Begash 2 and 3) and rock-art in the surrounding cliffs. Although exceptional in its level of documentation, the site at Begash reflects a multi-featured Bronze Age context commonly found in the Koksu valley and throughout Semirech'ye. These archaeological

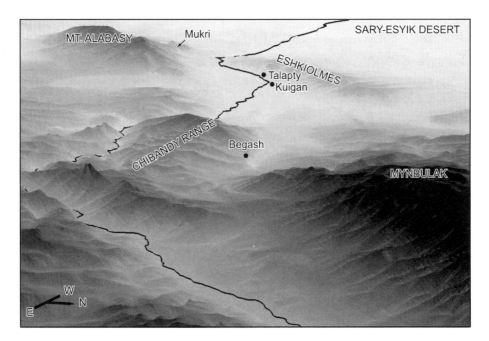

FIGURE 33

Location of Begash, Talapty, and Kuigan, and topography of the Koksu River valley. View facing southwest.

complexes have been recorded in midland zones, as at Begash, and in the lowland territories near Eshkiolmes at Talapty and Kuigan (Goryachev 2004) and Mukri . Eshkiolmes is best known as an extensive rock-art sanctuary, with over 10,000 engravings distributed across two kilometers of steep crags and cliffs. On the shrubby, arid terraces below these steep basalt cliffs are a number of Bronze Age burial grounds and settlements.[4] Although many Bronze Age burials on this terrace have been archaeologically documented (Goryachev 2004), only two settlements near Eshkiolmes are excavated: Talapty and Kuigan. Nonetheless, a number of newly discovered settlements indicate that pastoralists regularly occupied this lowland territory throughout the Bronze Age and later periods. In fact, amongst the forty settlements recorded within the study zone, over two-thirds are located in the lowland and midland territories, and can be associated with Bronze Age (and later) burials and rock-art.

Economic evidence from settlements in the Koksu valley illustrates an unambiguous pastoral character. Faunal remains excavated from Talapty illustrate that domestic cattle were the dominant herd animal throughout the Bronze Age, followed by sheep and goat. Although detailed statistics are not yet available from more detailed faunal analysis of Begash, preliminary figures show a faunal assemblage richer in sheep and goat remains. Correlating this economic evidence with the detailed chronology of occupation at Begash, the animal remains also show a considerable percentage of wild animals in the diet of the site's earliest inhabitants (5–10%, Benecke, pers. comm.). Throughout the second millennium BCE, the pastoral economy in the valley became increasingly centered on domestic sheep and cattle. In fact, faunal evidence recovered in shovel tests of recovered sites illustrates a clear pastoral signature at all of the settlements in the valley. All the shovel-tested sites revealed remains consistent with those recovered at Begash, which provisionally indicates that all settlements were part of a similar mobile pastoral adaptation in the valley during the Bronze Age.

The geographic distribution of settlements like Begash offers important insights into the way the region was used by various pastoralist groups. The earliest dated settlement zones are located in the lowlands and midlands and illustrate part of the seasonality of pastoral life in the Koksu valley. The lowland and midland settlements in the Koksu valley are, first and foremost, ecologically well situated for winter settlement. Most have year-round spring sources for water and are located in climatic micro-niches created by the warming effects of solar radiation off the black cliffs that surround the settlements. Settlement contexts within ravines and along south-facing cliffs in this territory can have a relative temperature as much as two to three degrees warmer than those in the open plain. These domestic contexts formed focal points in the landscape, as populations would settle and return to these locations seasonally. Material recovered from shovel tests of settlement contexts illustrates that at least 70 percent of the settlements are multi-period, many with remarkable continuity from the Bronze Age to historical periods. Excavation and radiocarbon dating at Begash documents this continuity in detail. From the perspective of settlement ecology, we must conclude that pastoralists selected their settlement locations in part because of specific, favorable environmental conditions and returned to them both for practical reasons and for the social and historical significance accrued through repeated use.

Detailed variation in the nature of Bronze Age settlement types is difficult to assess, since only four settlements in the Koksu valley have been excavated to date. From these excavations, however, we can discuss minimally two settlement classes: semi-subterranean houses and small camps. Semi-subterranean houses are defined as rectilinear habitations with substantial stone foundations, such as Begash and Talapty (figs. 34 and 35). These settlements archaeologically demonstrate long-term reuse and local continuity as well as considerable ideological and social investment in the form of large associated burial grounds and rock-art. The elaboration of these settlement contexts with burials and rock-art likely contributed to their formation as nodes in the broader landscape. Small camps, although sometimes similar to semi-subterranean houses in construction technique, illustrate shorter-lived occupations with less elaboration and social investment in the location. This fact is documented archaeologically by a lack of elaborative features such as on-site burials as well as longer periods of site abandonment in the camp's stratigraphy. For example, the archaeological stratigraphy of the small camp at Mukri[5] illustrates an extended period of site disuse with a rubble fill layer over 40 cm thick separating phases of occupation. Elsewhere I have suggested that small camps represent settlement options within the dynamic landscape of opportunities available to regional pastoralists during periods of environmental or social risk (Frachetti 2008).

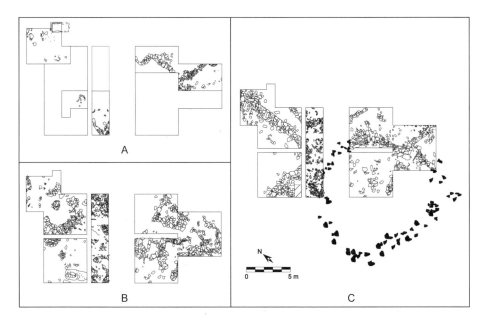

FIGURE 34

Three phases of architectural development at the settlement of Begash, Koksu valley: (a) Bronze Age;
(b) Iron Age; (c) medieval/early historic. After Frachetti and Mar'yashev 2007.

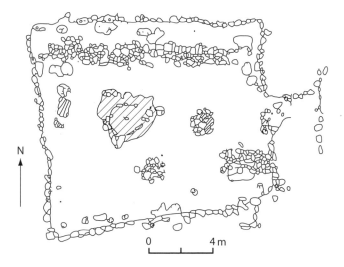

FIGURE 35

Plan of Bronze Age settlement at Talapty. After Mar'yashev and Goryachev 1996.

The oldest burial contexts in the Koksu valley are associated with Early and Middle
Bronze Age houses and are arranged in nucleated burial grounds. Bronze Age burials in
the Koksu valley consist of stone slab cists, with stone alignments surrounding them
(sometimes called "fences"). Cist burials are well documented at Begash, Kuigan, and
Talapty (near Eshkiolmes), and elsewhere in the valley (fig. 36). Bronze Age cemeteries

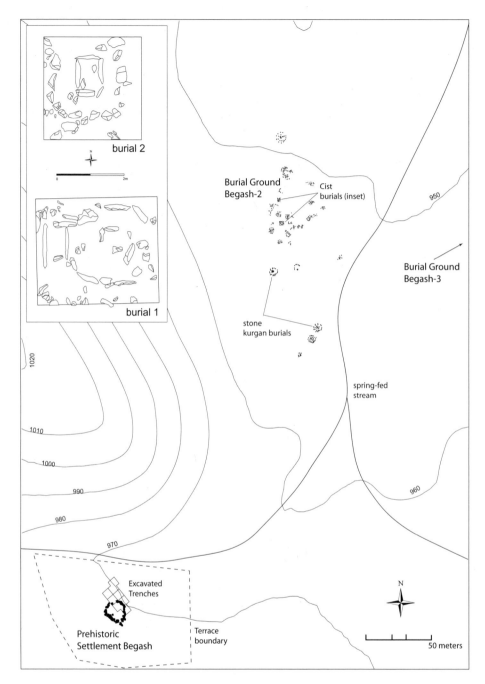

burial 2

burial 1

Burial Ground
Begash-2

Cist
burials (inset)

Burial Ground
Begash-3

stone
kurgan burials

spring-fed
stream

1020

1010

1000

990

980

970

960

950

Excavated
Trenches

Prehistoric
Settlement Begash

Terrace
boundary

N

50 meters

FIGURE 36

Location and plan of Bronze Age burial ground Begash-2. Inset: Excavation plans of burials 1 and 2. (after Mar'yashev and Frachetti 2008).

are typically nucleated on flat terraces with burial groups ranging in size from three to five stone arrangements to more than fifty. Each stone arrangement can contain numerous burials; typical ranges are from one to seven individual cists within a stone fence.

The absolute chronology of Bronze Age burials in the Kosku valley is a subject of debate. The undecorated coarseware ceramic forms documented in Late Bronze Age levels (1950–1700 BCE) at Begash are commonly found in burial contexts at Talapty and Kuigan. In his summary of excavated Bronze Age burials from the Koksu valley, Goryachev (2004, 132) dates these burials to the final Bronze Age (c. 1200–1000 BCE) based on typological correlates using the traditional (uncalibrated) Andronovo chronology. Goryachev's analysis is robust as it correctly illustrates ties between the ceramic and metallurgical traditions of Semirech'ye and neighboring regions. However, given the strength of the new radiocarbon evidence from Begash, we must assume that the Bronze Age sites near Eshkiolmes are at least 500–600 years older than has been previously considered. In spite of the chronological inconsistencies, the burial grounds of Talapty and Kuigan reveal a substantial use of the Eshkiolmes range for social and ritual purposes.

The variation in the size and nucleation of Bronze Age burial groups may reflect the social flexibility of groups among the pastoralist communities of the region throughout the second millennium BCE (Frachetti 2008). Recent burial excavations at three new Bronze Age cemeteries, Begash 2 and 3 and Karatal, have further expanded the database of early burial contexts in the study zone (Mar'yashev and Frachetti 2008). Discovered in 2002, Begash 2 and Begash 3 reflect sizable burial grounds in the Begash area, numbering thirty-seven and fifteen burial arrangements, respectively. These cemeteries stand in contrast to smaller contemporaneous Bronze Age burial sites, such as Begash 1. Begash 1 was discovered and excavated by Karabaspakova in the late 1970s, though few details are published (Karabaspakova 1987). The site consists of fewer than seven burials, although the materials of the site, as well as the construction of the burials are similar in form to the burials at Talapty 1 and Begash 2 (Mar'yashev, pers. comm.). Smaller burial groups such as this may have been constructed during periods of community fragmentation or division among lineages, or may simply reflect periodic choices to construct new, ritually important locales across the landscape. In both larger and smaller Bronze Age cemeteries, burials marked the landscape through the use of large visible stones, which may have served to ideologically "inter" the communities who built them as part of the visible landscape—an idea concerning the ritual landscape discussed in chapter 6. In addition to burials, rock-art provides another perspective on the social investments of mobile populations in their local landscapes associated with the first emergence of pastoralism in the region.

Rock-art is widely distributed in the Koksu River valley and the surrounding mountains and canyons. It is found in all elevation ranges, either in proximity to other feature classes such as burials or settlements or without associated contexts. The occurrence of rock-art is dependent on the existence of suitable rock surfaces, which means that rock-art is found also on the cliffs and crags of steep ravines, which are difficult to access.

Although over thirty new rock-art groups were recorded within the survey, a detailed study of the imagery of these new panels has not yet been completed. However, most of the rock-art[6] in the Koksu River valley has been extensively studied in terms of chronological associations and stylistic taxonomy so that we can make some conclusions about the role of rock-art in social life during the Bronze Age and later periods (Mar'yashev 1994; Mar'yashev and Goryachev 2002).

Like settlements, rock-art in the Koksu River valley represents a historically continuous form of social engagement with the landscape from the Bronze Age to contemporary times. Nearly all rock-art panels in the valley contain motifs contributed over the last 4000 years. Images commonly superimpose one another, illustrating the reuse and revisitation of rock-art locales as part of the historical nature of the landscape. In addition to highlighting those places that represent arenas for communication or ritual expression, certain types of rock-art can be interpreted as markers, used to designate boundaries or relationships translated from the social landscape to the geographic one. Examples include motifs placed in association with settlements or burials, or individual boulders carved with cup-stones placed in, or selected for, their unique location in the landscape (fig. 37).

Rock-art is notoriously difficult to date accurately using absolute methods. Although this methodological limitation applies to Central Asian rock-art, decades of stylistic analysis, material correlation with motifs, and serendipitous discoveries of rock engravings in archaeological contexts, has produced a good general chronology for rock-art

FIGURE 37
Boulder with cupstone carvings in the Koksu valley. Inset: Detail of carvings. Photo by the author.

in the region. Considering the known rock-art and additional panels recorded within the scope of the current study, Bronze Age rock-art motifs in the Koksu valley typically depict wild animals such as deer, mountain goats, and saiga (Eurasian mountain caprids) as well as domestic animals such as horses, bulls, and dogs (fig. 38). Within the Bronze

A

B

FIGURE 38

Bronze Age animal motifs of the Koksu Valley (Eshkiolmes): (a) bulls, dogs, and humans; (b) deer and wild goats. After Mar'yashev and Goryachev 2002.

Age typology, these animals are stylistically depicted with large block bodies, and smaller extremities (Mar'yashev 1994; Rogozhinski 2001; Mar'yashev and Goryachev 1998; Mar'yashev and Goryachev 2002). Occasionally, Bronze Age animal depictions are also carved using a graffiti style where only the outline of the image is incised into the rock. Bronze Age motifs of human figures and block style animals have been recovered on rocks extracted from radiocarbon-dated archaeological contexts at the site of Tamgaly in southeastern Kazakhstan. These images are common to the rock-art found in the Koksu valley, and date to between 1220–900 BCE, which partially helps to justify the stylistic chronology within the Late Bronze Age (Rogozhinski 1999).

In addition to animals, human figures are documented within the array of Bronze Age rock-art motifs. Ubiquitous human motifs are simple stick figures engaged in group interactions or activities such as warring or group hunting with bow and arrow (fig. 39). In addition to quotidian human forms, there is also a well-developed typology of deistic figures, known as "sun-head" deities (fig. 40). These figures are found throughout Semirech'ye, most notably at Tamgaly, and from rock-art sites throughout the wider region such as Saimaly-tash in Kyrgyzstan. Sun-head motifs are also well known in the shamanistic imagery of the Altai mountains and southern Siberia (Devlet 1980; Devlet 1998). The identifiable chords and hanging elements of the costumes in some Bronze Age sun-head images in the Dzhungar mountains, such as at Eshkiolmes

FIGURE 39

Bronze Age human motifs of the Koksu Valley (Eshkiolmes): (a) human motifs in conflict; (b) horse tamers; (c) (ritual?) battle scene. After Maryashev and Goryachev 2002.

A

B

FIGURE 40
Sun-head figures from the Dzhungar Mountain Region: (a) sun-head "deity" (Eshkiolmes); (b) sun-head
deity (shaman?) (Byan Zherek). After Mar'yashev and Goryachev 2002.

and Byan-Zherek, have been convincingly associated with Eurasian shaman costumes of
the Altai, which suggests that shamanism also played a role in the ritual and ideological
practices of Bronze Age peoples in the Koksu valley (Samashev 1998). This interpretation is supported by the frequent association between shaman-like figures and wild
animals, indicating that animal veneration or totemism was also a part of the social and
political organization of societies in the Koksu valley.

Another notable motif that is prevalent in the Koksu valley rock-art is the chariot
(fig. 41). Chariots are common throughout the panels at Eshkiolmes as well as in the
Terekty gorge. Chariots are interpreted here as a sign of status, or political position, perhaps associated with distant alliances or political ties. No material evidence of actual
chariots has been found in the Koksu valley, although they are well known from
Sintashta-type burial contexts in the trans-Urals region (Anthony 2007). Similar images
of chariots have, in rare cases, been used to decorate Late Bronze Age ceramic vessels,

FIGURE 41

Bronze Age chariot motif from Eshkiolmes. Scale not published in original. After Mar'yashev and Goryachev 2002.

such as that found at Sykhaya Saratovka, in the Volga region (Kuz'mina 1994, 433). Thus, imagery of chariots may have been used for an associative effect, to illustrate the wider geographic links that local populations had developed during the Late Bronze Age.

Taken together, the distribution and variation of Bronze Age settlements, burials, and rock-art illustrate a considerable investment in specific locales across a number of environmental settings. At the earliest stages, it seems that settlement locales were chosen according to their ecological character, though quickly this factor became only one consideration among many, including the degree of social importance and history imbued in particular locations. Considering the scale of pastoralist communities, the archaeology illustrates that populations were dispersed across the lowlands and midlands, especially during the winter months, in small to medium-sized groups. The area of most of the settlements could accommodate a group no larger than twenty-five to thirty people per settlement. Thus, interaction would demand the development of social networks across these settlement nodes. The active landscape was also reinforced by the construction of nucleated burials, where groups would return for interment rites while also reiterating their genealogical tie to particular settlement areas. For those cases of burials unassociated with settlements, we may suggest that the same social pressures that draw communities together can also cause them to fragment periodically, depending on the particular strategies and motivations of the groups involved.

The earliest archaeology illustrates that although the lowlands and midlands of the Koksu valley provided rich social venues in the early and Middle Bronze Age, from an economic perspective these territories could not effectively support pastoral groups year round. Since the range potential of the upland territories was many times more productive, seasonal migration to the upland pastures set the populations in the Koksu valley on dynamic trajectories of interaction. These patterns are further explored in chapter 6. We now turn to the way in which the archaeology of later periods illustrates continuity and change in the pastoral landscape of the Koksu valley.

THE LANDSCAPE EXPANDS (750–50 BCE)

The Iron Age landscape of the Koksu valley reflects both a continuous transition from the Bronze Age and a scalar expansion in the constructed social and ritual venues employed by pastoralists. Continuity is evident in the consistent reoccupation of a large percentage of earlier settlement contexts during the Saka period (750–50 BCE) and in the continued use of nearly all of the Bronze Age rock-art locations presented above. Throughout the first millennium BCE, however, expansion in the demography of the Koksu valley is reflected in a formal and scalar shift in burial practices from nucleated cemeteries to monumental kurgans widely distributed across the landscape. Furthermore, a proportional increase in the number and size of settlements and the proliferation of Iron Age motifs at rock-art sites all index demographic and economic growth during the Saka period.

The continuity of Bronze Age settlements into the Iron Age in the Koksu valley is documented through ceramic material recovered by shovel testing at a vast majority of the known settlements. To date, however, Begash is still the only excavated Iron Age settlement in the Koksu valley (Frachetti and Mar'yashev 2007). At Begash, a period of social fragmentation marks the transition from the Bronze Age to the Iron Age (950–600 BCE) as the site seems to be occupied less regularly. Subsequent to this phase in the early Iron Age, Begash experienced substantial growth and renewal. The site's architecture and material illustrate that the settlement was used more regularly after 550 BCE, which corresponds with the construction of three stone foundation domestic structures. The domestic consolidation documented in this period also correlates with the foundation of a number of new contemporaneous settlements of similar scale across the valley. Although the slightly wider distribution of Iron Age settlement sites provides a broad indication of demographic growth and expansion, the emergence of widely distributed and numerous kurgan burial contexts more clearly illustrates how the scale of organization and interactions of Saka groups transformed the pastoralist landscape of the Koksu valley in the middle of the first millennium BCE.

The demographic expansion suggested by the settlement archaeology of the Koksu valley may be explained in part by a corollary transition in the domestic economy in the eastern steppe around 750 cal BCE. Specifically, recent excavations of contemporaneous settlements in the Talgar plain of southern Semirech'ye have provided the first evidence of the integration of agriculture into the productive economy of regional pastoralists (Chang et al. 2003). The extent to which agriculture was a widespread endeavor at the start of the Saka period is yet unclear. Currently few Iron Age settlements have been systematically analyzed for either micro- or macro-botanical remains (but see Miller–Rosen et al. 2000). Yet even if agricultural production was still only a local practice, the availability of this new food source may have contributed to the expansion of trade networks and possible social divisions between mobile pastoral specialists and those increasingly tied to their agricultural fields. The amplification of social hierarchy, indexed by the rapid expansion in the size and ubiquity of kurgan burial mounds in the Koksu valley and throughout other regions of Semirech'ye, may well be linked to this critical transition in domestic production and demographic growth.

"Kurgan" is a general term for earth and stone tumulus burials. Across the steppe region, kurgans have a widely variable chronology and typology. However, in the Koksu valley, a few notable subtypes are evident. The first subtype includes low, stone kurgans (diameter of 3–5 meters across and less than one meter high), which often are situated in the landscape within the same context as Bronze Age stone cist burials. Not infrequently, these oval stone mounds superimpose Bronze Age burials, such as at Begash-2, which may reflect a transition from stone cist construction to stone mound building some time in the Late Bronze Age or Early Iron Age. More detail concerning these smaller stone-mound kurgans is precluded by the fact that priority has traditionally been placed on excavation of larger kurgans in lieu of these smaller monuments.

The more comprehensively studied and numerous type of kurgan is the earthen kurgan. Earthen kurgans are the most common burial type of the Iron Age, and these mounds range in size from smaller burials, approximately five to seven meters in diameter and one meter in height, to extremely large monumental mounds, 30 meters or more in diameter and five to eight meters in height (fig. 42). Kurgans of this subcategory are typically dated to the Saka period (seventh to third century BCE) based on countless excavated analogies from the Semirech'ye region and beyond (Akishev 1989).

In the Koksu valley, kurgans are typically found in midland hills, clustered in alignments from three to more than twenty, in a generally north-south orientation. The distribution of kurgans into linear groups distributed on the crests of low, grassy hills reflects a major change from typical Bronze Age use of the landscape for burial. As noted, Bronze Age stone cist burials were localized in nucleated cemeteries and their borders were deliberately defined on flat terraces. By distinction, kurgans are widely distributed throughout the landscape, with an apparent emphasis on orientation and regularity of burial form.

When viewed on a larger scale, Iron Age kurgan burials reflect what may be considered a shift in social planning of the larger landscape. The orientation and alignment of kurgans delineates groupings often as large as twenty mounds, often situated along the contours of low bluffs or prominent points in the landscape. The overt placement of kurgan groups may indicate a new attention to territorial arrangement engendered by social and political changes around the mid first millennium BCE (fig. 43). Without detailed excavations, it is difficult to know if the linear burial groups correspond to differences in

FIGURE 42
"Kurgan" burial in the Koksu valley. Photo by the author.

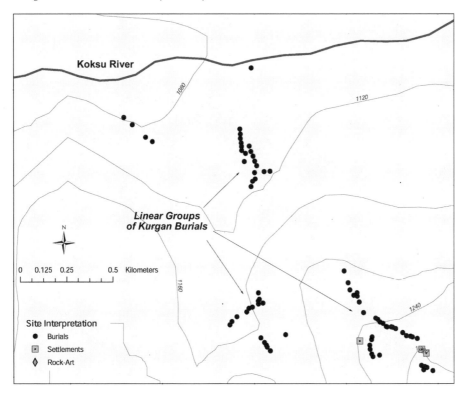

FIGURE 43
Linear alignments of kurgan burials in the Koksu valley.

social affinities, periods of time, or some other defining criterion. However, the material objects and construction scale of kurgan burials, which have been researched in Semirech'ye for over thirty years, are indicative of a new degree of social and political cohesion among a population with more extensive geographic contacts.

Iron Age kurgans from eastern Kazakhstan and Semirech'ye have produced some of the clearest evidence for the expanding political and economic scale of Sake agro-pastoralists. The kurgan mounds at Issyk, where the infamous "Golden Man" was recovered, illustrate the vast wealth and status of some sectors of society and the labor organization that those individuals were able to mobilize for construction of monumental graves.[7] Akishev (1978, 55) suggests that "the large number of so-called 'tsar's kurgans' speak to the sharp social differentiation that developed with Semirech'yean Saka herding in the VII–IV c. BCE."

Iron Age rock-art is dated by association with a well studied stylistic phenomenon that pervades steppe art and material culture during the second half of the first millennium BCE: the "animal style" (Jettmar 1965). Formal similarities between metal artifacts excavated from Iron Age contexts of Semirech'ye (Akishev 1975; Akishev and Akishev 1984) and rock-art imagery have provided archaeologists with a basis for the chronology of specific motifs of Iron Age rock-art (Mar'yashev and Goryachev 2002) (fig. 44). The prevalence of animal style rock-art confirms the occupation of the Koksu valley by pastoralists during the Saka period (750–250 BCE) and its stylistic evolution suggests continuity with the Wusun phase (250 BCE–200 CE) and eventually the early Turkic period of the Common Era. Stylistic similarities between rock-art motifs and material culture have also

FIGURE 44

Deer and goat motifs in Saka "animal style." After Mar'yashev and Goryachev 2002.

been used to link the stylistic grammar of various Iron populations from the Altai to the Pamir Mountains, and as far as Siberia. These wide semiotic ties may also be an effect of the demographic and geographic expansion proposed above for the early Iron Age.

REITERATION OF THE PASTORALIST LANDSCAPES IN THE TURKIC, MEDIEVAL AND HISTORICAL PERIODS

Archaeological research on pastoralists from historic periods (Turkic, medieval and later) is considerably less detailed than that of prehistoric phases. The prevalent research in Semirech'ye for this period has focused on larger towns of the silk route, which have produced a rich record of expanding trade networks and inter-regionalism in the material culture of "silk route" sites such as Otrar and medieval Talgar (Baipakov 1998).

In decidedly pastoralist territories, such as the Koksu valley, the majority of historic period settlement sites recovered through archaeological survey were visible on the surface in their most recent construction, even though most settlement locales are used throughout history to various extents. Given that prehistoric occupation levels are typically found more than a meter below the current ground level, the longevity of use and geographic continuity in the pastoralist settlement landscape enabled the recovery of prehistoric camps from more recent surface evidence. Although the reuse of specific habitation locales show that pastoralist settlement geography in the Koksu valley was largely continuous, the scale and construction of medieval and historical settlements show considerable change from prehistoric periods. First, the construction technology of lowland and midland settlements is different from those documented in the Bronze Age and Iron Age. For example, medieval and later pastoralist settlements at Mukri were constructed with mud brick and flagstone foundations. The use of mud brick has not been documented elsewhere in mountain contexts of Semirech'ye, although it is a typical medieval (and later) construction method for urban centers in more arid zones of southeastern Kazakhstan and the Ili valley.[8] Other medieval pastoralist settlements in the valley were predominantly made of stone, likely with wooden superstructures. The recovery of iron nails at Begash also suggests that carpentry was part of the construction of houses in historical periods.

The supplemental use of grains in the diet of local pastoralist is also documented at domestic contexts of the medieval and historical periods. Preliminary botanical analysis of soils from medieval hearths at Begash has identified charred remains of pearl millet (*Panicum miliaceum*) and rice. Agricultural productivity of these domesticates is also documented in the southern regions of Semirech'ye as early as 750 BCE (Miller–Rosen et al. 2000)—so it is not surprising that pastoralists included these products in their diet in the historical period. The soils and environmental conditions of the Koksu valley are not particularly well suited for raising millet or rice, which suggests that perhaps mobile pastoralists in the mountain zones were trading with agriculturalists in the south for these components of their subsistence.

Included in the broad category of "early historic burials" are essentially all burial forms that are neither typical Bronze Age stone-cist burials, nor typical Iron Age kurgans. This loose classification is limited by the lack of archaeological excavation and knowledge concerning medieval and later burial forms in the region of southeastern Kazakhstan. Also included in this category are "Kazakh" burials of the past three hundred years, many of which are marked with Islamic gravestones or stele commemorating the dead. Older Kazakh burials tend to have a central earthen mound covering the interred, with an earth or stone enclosure built around the mound. Rich or literate Kazakhs of the past few centuries were buried in mud brick mausoleums (Bartol'd 1963–1977), whereas more recent Kazakh burials (of the past fifty years) tend to have stone or iron fences around the central grave. In addition to these more classically Islamic burial styles, some historical Kazakh burials illustrate a local burial tradition in tribal pasturelands or ancestral locales, with graves demarcated by a standing spear or staff stuck into the burial with a white flag tied to it (fig. 45). Contemporary Kazakh burial grounds are located frequently in the same location as medieval or Turkic-period mound burials as well as prehistoric kurgans and earlier stone-cist burials. This tradition of historical land use may suggest a conceptual continuity in the geography of ritual landscapes over the past few centuries, as in the Late Bronze Age transition to stone kurgans.

Historical rock-art motifs are dated by association with depictions of artifacts such as standards, which were widely used from at least the third century CE and later periods

FIGURE 45
Contemporary Kazakh burial in the Koksu valley. Photo by the author.

to designate political affiliations among Turkic and Mongolian steppe nomads (Khudyakov 1986). The motifs also include riding archers with compound bows and armor (Mar'yashev and Goryachev 2002). The style of rock-art from Turkic and historical periods in the Koksu valley conforms to a tradition of rock-art that stretches from Mongolia to the oases of southern Central Asia. Though unsurprising as an index of known nomadic empires such as the Mongols, these images raise a compelling question about whether the artists who produced this engraved archive were local pastoralists reacting to changing social and political arenas, or foreigners who were marking their own likeness on the landscape of those who received them. I propose that, similar to prehistoric rock-art, the archive of historical motifs should be viewed as part of the complex array of investments in the landscape on the part of local pastoralists, who used this artistic form to non-discursively communicate their occupation of meaningful locations across dynamic social, political, and economic currents of history.

In addition to settlements, burials, and rock-art, other anthropogenic features are attributable to the historical landscape. For example, stone monuments represent constructions likely designed to demarcate or define locales or boundaries within the landscape. The first type of stone monument is ethnographically similar to the Mongolian *oba*[9] and usually appears as a mound of stones piled at the tops of the highest peak within a group of hills (fig. 46). These stone configurations function practically as well

FIGURE 46
Stone "oba" on peak in the Chibandy Range, at approximately 1400 m, Dzhungar Mountains. Photo by the author.

FIGURE 47
Standing stones, Mukri river drainage. Inset: nearby small plantings. Photo by the author.

as ritually. They have been described as markers designating common migration pathways and also are known to hold meaning in terms of ancestor veneration, geomancy,
and other traditional ritual practices employed by pastoral societies of the steppe region
over the past centuries (Humphrey 1996). In addition, stone constructions are used to
accent functionally unique locations within the landscape. For example, a site along the
Mukri river consists of an anthropomorphic stack of stones (fig. 47) near a group of discrete agricultural plantings (fig. 47, inset). The stack apparently serves the dual purpose
of garden locator and scarecrow. Although this example is contemporary, the location of
stone or other landscape markers (such as the aforementioned cup stone) are indicators
that the extents of the pastoral landscape were socially designated at locations in addition
to settlements and burials.

The archaeology collected within the survey of the Koksu valley illustrates two main
points. First, the study zone has been occupied continuously from prehistoric times to
the present day, and was densely inhabited by Bronze Age, Iron Age and historical populations. The pastoralist landscape enfolds the geographic distribution of settlements
from as early as the middle third millennium BCE into the experienced geography of
historical pastoralists. Bronze Age cist burials from as early as the second millennium
BCE occupy the same terraces as Iron Age kurgans and Kazakh cemeteries, which
demonstrates the impacted relationships among pastoralists over the past 4000 years.

The palimpsest of rock-art illustrates a similar local trajectory among regional pastoralists. From the distribution and density of these sites in the Koksu valley, we may conclude that pastoralist populations structured their social, ritual, and domestic activities through a tacitly formed history of pastoralism conferred through the common patterns of adaptation among groups of different chronological epochs.

This historically cumulative landscape also records the geographic distribution of various types of settlements and burials of the Bronze Age and later periods and illustrates that all segments of the population did not use the environment or the social contexts of the Koksu valley in a uniform way. The variations in the selected placement of Bronze Age burial grounds such as Talapty, Kuigan, Begash, and other smaller Bronze Age burial areas suggest that there were internal political and social affiliations that contributed to the heterogeneous shaping of the landscape among the Bronze Age and later populations. Broadly contemporaneous settlement contexts can be differentiated according to their construction style, scale, environmental location and the degree to which they formed complex site groups. In all periods, larger sites tend to be associated with rock-art and burials, and thereby define social, economic, and ritual focal points in the landscape. The geographic location of these elaborated complexes attest to the diverse array of social and environmental factors that determined how domestic spaces were selected, such as their suitability for summer or winter pasturage or the availability of water or stone resources. These locations also reflect the changing considerations for settlement on the part of mobile populations, such as the environmental suitability, access to trade, and the possibility that some settlement locations were preferable to others for social or political reasons. The archaeology of the Koksu valley presents a complex and variable array of prehistoric and historic feature types, which document the diverse adaptations to dynamic environmental conditions as well as the impact of changing historical and economic currents on the patterns of pastoralist life in the region. The following chapter explores in depth what these formative constellations of environment, politics, and social identity may have been in the Bronze Age and how the shape of the earliest pastoralist landscape in the Koksu valley was tied to social and economic change at a more global scale.

6

BRONZE AGE PASTORALISM, LANDSCAPE, AND SOCIAL INTERACTION

MODELING PASTORAL LANDSCAPES AND CONTEXTS OF INTERACTION

The pastoralist landscape in the Koksu River valley is shaped through a combination of economic strategies related to the management of herds and through the construction of, investment in, and iterated use of social, ritual, and political locales. These practices together organized the spaces and times of human interactions throughout the landscape (Ingold 1993). The following sections explore the ways in which Bronze Age pastoralists of the Koksu valley experienced their pastoral landscape by reconstructing the spatial and temporal intersections of ecological and social forces. Specifically, this chapter explores the constellation of pastoral mobility and pasture use, selection of settlement locations, and the elaboration of domestic and ritual complexes as formative components of the economic, ritual, and social landscapes of Bronze Age populations. Ultimately, the Bronze Age archaeology of the Koksu River valley illustrates how a state of "ordered variation" in the practices of these groups produced diverse scenarios for social interaction which, although spatially and temporally flexible, systemically facilitated opportunities for the influx of exotic materials over a variety of geographic scales.

THE ECONOMIC LANDSCAPE

The most likely subsistence economy for societies living in the Koksu River valley during the second millennium BCE was a vertically transhumant form of mobile pastoralism, predominantly based in herding sheep, goats, and cattle between upland pastures in the summer and lowland regions in the winter. This conclusion is based on four lines of evidence, presented in previous chapters. These include the diagnostic assemblage of domestic fauna recovered from excavated Bronze Age settlements in the study zone; the vertical zonality and restrictive nature of the mountain steppe environment in the Koksu valley; ethno-historical documentation that the region has been inhabited by vertically transhumant mobile pastoralists since the third century BCE; and the provisional "lack of evidence" from Bronze Age archaeological contexts for alternative subsistence strategies, such as the cultivation of domesticated plants (especially grains). Such a general observation, however, is only the first step toward understanding the landscape that was formed by Bronze Age mobile pastoralists. The critical step is to reveal the variability in the patterns and extents of this transhumant lifestyle and to focus on the kinds of interaction this herding strategy would have produced, using relevant archaeological and environmental data.

To understand how economic aspects of mobile pastoralism in the Koksu valley were organized in space and time during the Bronze Age, we must model patterns of movement between various environmental niches (which offer pasture resources for herds) and archaeologically documented domestic contexts. The primary data used to model pastoral migration patterns include the location and variable productivity of pastures in the Koksu River valley[1] and the seasonal location and variable geography of settlements, burials, and rock-art.

LOCATION AND VARIABLE PRODUCTIVITY OF PASTURES

Chapter 4 provided ethnographic information demonstrating that one of the most important economic considerations for the movement strategies of pastoralists in the Koksu River valley is the availability and productivity of green pasture and water sources. Whereas water sources are highly abundant throughout the Koksu valley, the size and productivity of pastures in the study zone are restricted by variations in seasonal climatic conditions and altitude. As a general rule high altitude pastures (higher than 1400 m) are three to six times as productive as pastures below 800 m during the months of June, July, and August (table 4). Therefore, the geography of pasture resources in the study zone can be rectified according to known botanical horizons at different altitudes, and pasture areas can be assigned "quality" based on their ability to support herd animals during different parts of the year (Sobolev 1960). Seasonally, upland pastures are prospective locations for summer herding,[2] whereas lowland areas are more suitable for winter habitation.

By modeling the seasonal qualities of the landscape as they pertain to pastoral strategies, we can qualify the above parameters (resources and elevation, grazing propensity) into a map of seasonal pasture fitness from an economic point of view (fig. 48). This map summarizes the relative fitness of particular locations for the success of seasonally mobile herding. Given this general seasonal classification, more detailed assessments of

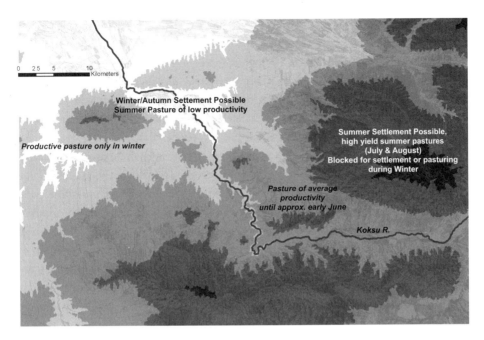

FIGURE 48
Seasonal ecology of settlement and pasture zones in the Koksu valley.

mobility and interaction can be generated from the actual geography of discrete pastures and constructed locations.

As discussed in chapter 5, prehistoric settlements are distributed throughout the Koksu River valley in lowland areas and in midland elevations. The settlements in these areas are either "semi-subterranean houses" or "small camps." Excavated Bronze Age settlements such as Begash, Talapty, and Mukri present good evidence that lowland settlements were used seasonally in the winter by mobile pastoralists (as opposed to year-round by settled herders).[3] Of the other twenty-five lowland and midland settlements recorded from the archaeological survey, roughly 70 percent of those shovel tested revealed ceramic forms typical of the Late Bronze Age or early Iron Age, which suggests that the geography of archaeological settlement locations in the Koksu River valley is relevant for use in reconstructing settlement and mobility patterns for prehistoric periods. Significantly, these settlements are not identical; they exhibit variation in size and construction as well as variation in their degree of elaboration through corollary archaeological contexts such as nearby burials or rock-art. To understand the range of mobility patterns in terms of the archaeological distribution of sites, settlement locations are used to define concrete nodes in the study zone for migration routes to and from pasture locations.[4]

The variability of pastoral land use is first assessed in terms of herding migrations delimited by the availability of optimal grass resources. Here we assume that herders would be more likely to move their animals over pathways where the animals can feed along the way, whether en route to summer highland pasture locations or returning to known social arenas (e.g., winter settlements). Admittedly, this economic optimization only partly reflects reality, in that the ethnographic record shows instances of nomadic migrations over areas without adequate pasture resources (Bradburd 1990; Tapper 1979). However, from an economic standpoint, it is less likely that pastoralists explicitly avoid rich pastures while moving their herds, other factors being equal (Dakhshleiger 1978). Archaeologically, Bronze Age settlements in the Koksu valley are often located in water-fed ravines, which typically have greater availability of grass resources than open exposed plains, especially during the winter. Thus, to link herding routes to corridors of rich grass should be taken as one structuring factor in the spatial and temporal distribution of pastoral groups.

Simulating these geographic parameters using Geographic Information Systems, I calculated a network of pathways that reflects a dynamic "flow" of people and animals across a landscape of qualitatively "preferred" ranges. Figure 49 illustrates a map of herding pathways throughout the Koksu River valley derived by accumulating the grazing productivity of "rich pastures" by traveling between Bronze Age settlement camps and highland meadows, classified according to the capacity of the pasture to support relevant herd animals. This simulation produces a geographic approximation of pathways for feeding herds and illustrates the formation of arenas where neighboring populations would come together during the summer.[5]

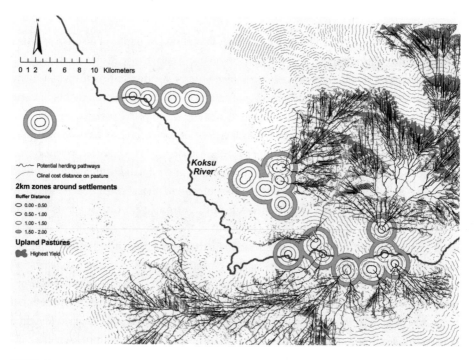

FIGURE 49

Projected herding routes from settlements to best pastures in the Koksu valley and Dzhungar Mountains (shortest distance).

Although the qualitative "value" of grazing capacity ranges may theoretically be iterated along a continuum from the maximum (upper limit of pasture carrying capacity) to the minimum (zero cumulative pasture productivity), an upper-bound grazing capacity to support forty thousand sheep was used to delimit the most attractive ranges as "destinations," and to separate them from less productive pasture areas. In part this tempers the availability of pasture; in reality more areas would be available to pastoralists. Using only the richest pastures polarizes the mobility of pastoralists and serves as a form of standardization to account for inherent inaccuracies in the calculation of range capacity. Forty thousand sheep is roughly equivalent to the herd holdings of forty Kazakh "tents," and is based on ethnographic accounts of maximum herd sizes of Kazakh populations in such upland pastures throughout the summer grazing period (Masanov 1995). A Kazakh "tent" typically housed one or two families (Hudson 1938), which is an analogous demographic size for the Bronze Age settlements given that the average size of semi-subterranean houses, like Begash, in the Koksu valley could easily support similarly sized populations. In addition, the settlement locations are "buffered" by a radius of two kilometers, representing a catchment area around each location that includes burial grounds, rock-art areas, and other foci of activities indexed by archaeological features. These data parameters also force us to examine alternative motivations for mobility, and as is further reconstructed below, the layering of economic and social factors motivates populations to behave in ways that may not be economically logical.

In addition to the productivity of pastures, the location of pastures used here is also an approximate variable. Although in general the Bronze Age environment was shown to be comparable to the one used in this model, we cannot assume that the location of specific patches of pasture is constant throughout time. Today these pasture zones vary slightly from year to year. Therefore, the pathway map reflects theoretically optimal routes for traveling across the study zone according to the aggregate grass resources that collectively can support the designated herd size. The goal in modeling pathways is to understand the general nature and extent of movement patterns as they relate to animal needs and pasture quality, and to understand the extent of mobility that would feasibly support sheep and cattle herds in numbers relevant to the Bronze Age record.

The mapping of potential pathways based on the availability of grass may best reflect the movement of pastoralists if their only consideration was providing good pastures and fresh water for their herds in the summer. However, the availability and productivity of grass in upland pastures does not speak to the motivations for the selection of wintertime settlement locations or other socially determined pressures. In the case of winter settlement, ecumenical lowland settlement areas appear to have been selected partly in light of favorable environmental conditions, but, as the archaeology and ethnography of the study region shows, sociopolitical and historical factors were also a major concern. Non-environmental considerations for settlement location, based on proximity to social and ritual contexts, include locales where groups might regularly meet with kinsmen, avoid hostile or inhospitable neighbors, be close to ancestral burial

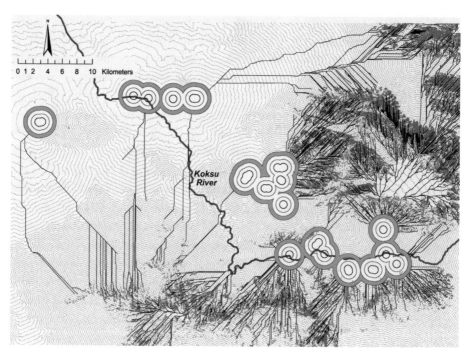

FIGURE 50

Projected herding routes from settlements to best pastures in the Koksu valley and Dzhungar Mountains (maximum distance).

grounds, or take advantage of other resources for social purposes, like rock outcrops for rock-art. Thus, the second simulation presented emphasizes the distribution of settlements because they most reliably reflect human occupation and contexts for social interaction.

By placing emphasis on settlement options, a second land use simulation illustrates that more extensive mobility is need to travel between proposed summer and winter zones, while maintaining a suitable accumulation of pasture resources (fig. 50). The extended routes reflect the "best" way to provide grass resources and still reach all of the settlement locations. This model is calculated by changing the "quality" assessment of the various environmental niches in an iterated fashion: incrementally making areas in the lowlands more "attractive," and lessening the cost of travel to those niches, until pathways extend to all settlements. However, this model conceptually illustrates that in rich environments like the Koksu valley, settlement choices were made not only according to ecological fitness. Instead, migratory distances were likely variable according to social and economic impulses.

In this second case, all settlement locations were routed to pastures, even those that were located at greater distances from rich ranges (e.g., in arid lowlands). These pathways and settlement locations should be considered among the different options available to pastoralists, for example, when naturally occurring variations in the environment may have caused them to alter their selection criteria for winter settlements and mobility schedules, or when social pressures restricted the use of larger settlement centers or encouraged departures from them. Based on this method of analysis, we can only speculate as to why different choices were made; these variations may have been responses to documented environmental inconsistency in the Dzhungar Mountains, or perhaps sociopolitical motivations played a role in decision making. Ethnographic cases discussed in chapter 4 suggest that in many cases pastoralists decided to occupy different areas to negotiate trade, access rare goods, acquire tribute, or to inhabit traditional territories on principle. The calculated routes presented here, which are tied to the real geographic extent and layout of prehistoric settlements and pastures in the study zone, provide a reliable, albeit not exhaustive, reconstruction of the varied migratory distances and interactive geography of Bronze Age pastoral communities.

The above illustrations characterize the Bronze Age mobile pastoral economy as a variable strategy of transhumance throughout the Koksu valley and surrounding mountains. Both simulations illustrate that mobility patterns would have been variable, in the sense that some groups would have migrated as much fifty kilometers to access rich upland pastures whereas others needed only to migrate ten to twenty kilometers to provide adequate pasturage for their herds during the summer. This routine may have also extended and shifted over time according to both environmental and sociopolitical factors. In addition, we should envision these routes as periodically active, and periodically unused, thereby situating the population within an ordered but variable schedule of movement. The network of pastoralist pathways depicted here illustrates how the geography of seasonal pastures and socially important locations together shape the economic landscape. The socioeconomic concerns of mobile groups activate regularly shifting zones of population overlap in summer pastures as well as through the use of winter settlements in various locations. Both of these settings provide different qualities for the maintenance of herd animals and for potential social responsibilities, while they also demonstrate how individual decisions by pastoralist groups may have affected the timing and geography of social interactions throughout the landscape. We now turn our attention to the archaeological evidence for some of these social variables.

THE RITUAL AND SOCIAL LANDSCAPES

Bronze Age groups constructed a socialized and ritual landscape demarcated by such features as rock-art sanctuaries, cemeteries, and other socialized spaces, which played a role in the organization of experiences in space and time in the Koksu River valley. The primary data sources used to reconstruct the social and ritual aspects of the landscape include the geography and semiotics of rock-art, and the geography and construction of burials.

GEOGRAPHY AND SEMIOTICS OF ROCK-ART

In the Koksu River valley, rock-art, burials, and settlements are found in clusters, generally within a radius of less than 800 meters and often closer. Together these site classes form social "complexes" through the combination of ritual and domestic contexts. For example, in the territory of Begash nearly every settlement is associated with centers of rock-art and a nearby cemetery. For the settlement at Begash, cemeteries Begash-2 and Begash-3 are less than 500 meters away, and there are rock-art panels as close as 200 meters. In addition, the major rock-art center of the Terekty gorge is approximately one kilometer across the plain from Begash, in full view from the settlement and cemetery. Along the Eshkiolmes range, the settlement of Talapty is located less than 300 meters from large rock-art panels, while Bronze Age burials are located within a radius of less than 500 meters around the settlement (Mar'yashev and Karabaspakova 1988). Along the same terrace, a similar feature organization is recorded at Kuigan (Mar'yashev and Goryachev 2002). The spatial relationship among rock-art, burials, and settlements, coupled with the seasonal economic patterns proposed above, allow for some initial interpretations concerning the land use schedule and sociopolitical interactions that resulted from group investment in specific locations in the landscape.

The location of settlements provides information concerning the seasonal use of the landscape, which can be tied to social and political strategies. The Bronze Age settlements at Talapty and Kuigan are located in dry lowland areas and likely represent winter or autumn settlements. Begash is located at a slightly higher elevation (approximately 950 m), although, given its situation in a protected canyon it also likely represents a winter settlement. According to the seasonal economic reconstruction above, these settlement areas were variably inhabited for three to seven months during the late autumn, winter, and early spring, and would likely have been unoccupied for about three to six months during the late spring and summer while groups migrated to, and inhabited, upland pastures.

The existence of the complex of features (rock-art and burials) near these winter settlements may indicate that investments in the landscape partly served to communicate ownership or control over domestic locations while the population was away at highland pastures in the summer. Significantly, there is little rock-art in the upland areas, even though ample rock outcrops exist. Since the upland pastures are treacherously cold and uninhabited during the winter, it is unlikely that there would be significant human traffic there except during the summer. Logically, there would be no need to protect or mark settlement areas in the highlands. Furthermore, since the nature of the summer pasture resources is much more variable from year to year than winter conditions, marking areas of settlement might actually serve to limit the possibilities of claiming prime locations from year to year. Most likely, the boundaries of summer pastures and settlement zones were negotiated at the time of migration, when pastoralists came together while providing for their herds in the limited territories of highland pastures.

Although it may have been unnecessary to mark summer settlement areas, lowland winter settlement areas were accessible to any group that would be passing through the area year-round, so more overt displays of control, power, and status, such as symbolic invocations of shamanism, folklore, and ancestry, were encoded into the landscape near choice settlements using rock-art in specific places and constructing megalithic-like burials. By socializing these areas with ritual and ideological signs, specific groups could signify their definition of territorial boundaries and could communicate their engagement in specific locations, even though their overall patterns of movement led to periods when these sites were physically unoccupied.

Interpretation of the meaning of rock-art is not without problems; at best we can hope to offer plausible explanations based on a number of correlated lines of argument to provide insights into the way rock-art helped to define landscapes (Frachetti and Chippindale 2002). Prevalent motifs in the Late Bronze Age rock-art in the Koksu valley suggest some meaningful themes used to communicate social or political status between groups. These themes include military strength, hunting prowess, and control of prestigious domesticated animals.

Among the thousands of engravings in the Koksu valley, a dominant theme nearby the settlements of Talapty and Kuigan along the Eshkiolmes range is warring and conflict, which is depicted through different motifs. The most obvious panels illustrate large battles with archers, horsemen, and hand-to-hand combatants (shown in fig. 39). In addition to battle scenes, scenes illustrating the conquest of extraordinary beings are also suggestive of political commentary embedded in the Bronze Age rock-art near settlements. These scenes depict what Russian archaeologists refer to as "giants" being attacked by smaller individuals with bows and arrows. In the Eshkiolmes range there are three such panels, while in the Terekty gorge (near Begash) there are also large scenes of mounted archers. Warring scenes of this nature may be interpreted as illustrating the potency of the area's population and recalling mythological or epic battles through artwork.

A. N. Mar'yashev, who has studied the rock-art of the Koksu River valley for decades, suggests that these images may refer to canonized regional folklore, which was cultivated by local groups to strengthen their social and political position by evoking associations with supernatural beings (Mar'yashev, personal communication). He bases this interpretation on the fact that similar scenes are known throughout the Dzhungar and Tian Shan mountain regions with surprising consistency (Mar'yashev and Goryachev 2002). Yet even if these images are not representative of the broader folklore of Bronze Age populations in Semirech'ye, the motifs unequivocally depict opposing individuals as grossly disproportionate in size to one another, perhaps reflecting a theme of resistance and power imbalance, which may be interpreted as a sign of political engagement on the part of the groups occupying the Koksu River valley.

In addition to fighting and battle scenes, the imagery of the rock-art depicts many scenes of hunting. According to faunal evidence recovered from settlement contexts, wild animals made up a relatively small percentage of the diet of Late Bronze Age groups. Hunting nonetheless figures prominently in the themes of rock-art panels and may have been used to illustrate a spiritual connection with the natural world, or to lionize the groups that occupied the territory of the Koksu valley. These spiritual worlds may have been channeled through shamanistic practices, referenced by the sun-head images discussed in chapter 5 (Samashev 1998). Hunting scenes typically depict small groups of archers and riders pursuing long-horned mountain goats, deer, bears and wolves. Ethnographic studies suggest that hunting for predatory beasts by Eurasian pastoralists was often associated with concepts such as hunting magic, animism, and geomancy (Humphrey 1996; Sarkozi 1976; more generally Ingold 1993). Therefore, by registering hunting scenes alongside settlements, individuals or groups may have sought to promote themselves or their ancestors, in order to improve their status or power by depicting their role in ideologically significant activities while marking their settlements in the process.

Prestige and status were likely attributed to control over domestic animals as well. Like wild animals, horses make up only a small percentage of the faunal assemblages recovered from Bronze Age settlements. Nonetheless, the rock-art depicts a clear association of horse riding, hunting, and war (Maryashev 1994). Horse riders are typically set within the above mentioned scenes that depict individuals conquering giants, vanquishing opponents, or hunting beasts of prey. As horses were a limited component of the domesticated fauna in the Koksu valley during the Bronze Age, control or ownership of a horse would likely have distinguished individuals or groups in the relative pecking order of local politics. Historically, pastoralists of this region held horses in high regard and from the seventh century BCE[6] through medieval periods incorporated them into living rituals and in burial rites. Horses were not killed and interred in Bronze Age burials in the Koksu valley during the Bronze Age, yet I propose that the semiotic inclusion of horse motifs in ritual contexts, rather than actual horses, may have been used to convey status, strength, or control associated with the ownership of these animals.

In addition to images of horse riding, there are more than one hundred images of horse-drawn chariots in the Koksu River valley. These motifs likely date to the Bronze Age, based on their stylistic association with actual chariots excavated in Bronze Age contexts in the western steppe zone (Kuz'mina 1988) and their positional association with other motifs associated with the Bronze Age (Mar'yashev 1994). There is no archaeological evidence that chariots were in use in the Koksu region itself, so that chariot motifs may be associative references to powerful groups outside the immediate region. Throughout the history of rock-art in this region, there is frequent use of marked political associations, signified by motifs such as horsemen with identifiable banners and standards, which historically were associated with potentates based at regional centers in Dzhungaria (northwestern China) and southwestern Semirech'ye (Bartol'd 1943). Thus, if medieval and later rock-art can be used as an analogy, the Bronze Age carvings of chariot riders and horsemen may have also demarcated political relationships beyond the local pastoral landscape.

The motifs discussed here are among the most prevalent Bronze Age images. Given their association with settlements and burials I suggest that they were used, in part, to mark the territory of pastoral groups and to designate the status and nature of the populations who controlled social and ritual spaces throughout the Koksu River valley. The semiotic significance of the rock-art is highly complex and must be used cautiously to make meaningful interpretations about the social themes that resonated with Bronze Age societies. Nonetheless, from a landscape perspective, the prevalence of specific rock-art motifs, and their particular distribution alongside settlements and burial contexts, reflects how ritual and social concepts were embedded in the landscape, and how they may have affected the dynamics of Bronze Age communication between populations living in, or moving through, the Koksu River valley.

BURIALS

In addition to rock-art, burials represent fixtures in the social and ritual landscape whose construction and geography figured prominently in relations of Bronze Age populations. Bronze Age cist burials in the Koksu valley are characterized by stone arrangements, usually constructed from large boulders set into oval or rectangular formations, with a slab-lined central cist (Karabaspakova 1987; Goryachev and Mar'yashev 1998). An important quality of these constructions is their visibility on the surface. Bronze Age burials were likely completely exposed on the surface upon their construction and the central cists would have been easily accessible to passers-by. The pseudo-"megalithic" monumentality of these burials would have been significant in the designation of territory as ritual space (Barrett et al. 1991), given that typically burials of this nature are found in large configurations of thirty or more stone circles, each containing numerous burial cists. With their close proximity to settlements and rock-art, these burials would have likely elicited recognition that the territory was tied ancestrally to an incumbent group.

In addition to the monumentality of the burials, it is significant that some Bronze Age burial cists were not categorically robbed or disturbed, in spite of the ease of access to the cists and the Bronze Age burial tradition of interment with rich grave goods. Furthermore, the reuse of specific geographic locations as burial grounds over many centuries, as well as the placement of multiple burials within one stone configuration during the height of the cist burial tradition (1900–1300 BCE) suggests their representation of ancestral territory. The maintenance of cist burials suggests a social respect afforded to the dead, coupled with the long-term investment in ritual locations through both burials and rock-art. During the Bronze Age, an ideological importance was placed on ancestral relationships, which was translated into deference to the importance of burials and ritual spaces.

The coherence of these sociological associations was clearly challenged by documented intrusions into Bronze Age cists during later periods of antiquity: for example, Bronze Age cists were robbed in the Iron Age at Kuigan (Mar'yashev and Goryachev 1996) as well as at Begash 2. Nevertheless, the placement of kurgans of later epochs in the same locations as Bronze Age cist burials suggests that the ritual nature of burial ground locations was somewhat preserved, even if the status of the previously interred individuals had already lost significant resonance with the later populations.

Given the seasonal attributes of both the social and environmental contexts within the Koksu River valley, the migration patterns that most effectively provided forage for even relatively large herds of cattle and sheep averaged about twenty-five kilometers and in many cases winter settlements were constructed as close to summer pastures as was feasible given snow cover. The settlements in the mid-land elevations, such as Begash, exhibit limited evidence of horses, which means that to a small degree snows deeper than fifteen centimeters could be opened for other animal types (Argynbaev 1973). However, variation in the location of lowland settlements indicates that sometimes the population was either willing or forced to employ migrations of as much as fifty kilometers, thereby representing a wider extension of their sphere of interactions. In fact, it may be that these groups played an inadvertent role in extending the local boundaries of the social and political landscape as well.

The network of potential migration routes reflects the variation in the way the environment can be exploited for herding, and also provides a proposed framework for understanding when and where groups would have interacted in the landscape. From our discussion, the pathways illustrate that different locations of winter settlements might have encouraged the use of certain summer pastures over others and this division of pasture resources would bring groups settled in disparate winter camps into common spaces, at least during the summer migration period. By combining our archaeologically derived model with probable behavior assimilated from ethnographic studies, we may suggest that these interaction spheres in the upland pastures were places where social alliances may have been forged through institutions such as marriage, trade, gaming, festivals, and even everyday activities such as tending herds (Masanov 1995, 110).

Summer activities around the domestic sphere would have likely been more focused on work related to herding and on processing secondary products such as milk, leather, and other material culture. Ethnographic sources note that while Kazakh men and boys may spend time away from their summer yurts looking after herds, women devote considerable attention in the summer to the production of butter, cheese, curd, and other products for use during the winter months (Masanov 1995, 110–111). The archaeological remains of such activities may be few, but by establishing the likelihood of movement to upland pastures for herding, it is reasonable to suggest an intermingling of social group and domestic group activities.

The winter settlement geography in the lowlands illustrates a dispersal of the population into discrete and separate locations. These niches may have been ranked according to their environmental attractiveness as well as their proximity to socially significant locations such as burials and rock-art. It would seem that during the winter smaller groups came together to solidify their social connections in the domestic context. The domestic locations of the Bronze Age are documented contexts for weaving and ceramic production (Frachetti and Mar'yashev 2007), activities known from ethnographic accounts to be highly socially significant practices that entail generational folklore, story telling, and meta-cultural discourse (Barber 1994; Beresneva 1998).

The Bronze Age landscape in the Koksu valley did not only reflect a conceptual understanding of the relationship of territory, temporal patterns of occupation, and the social status of those who controlled ritual locales. Cemeteries such as Kuigan and Begash 2 and Begash 3 represented areas in the landscape that acted as nodes in a ritually designated and socially defined territory. Therefore, burial grounds in the Bronze Age offered contexts for social and political interaction as well as the performance of religious rites.

An artist's reconstruction of steppe burial ceremonies provides a compelling visual representation of how burial rituals may have been experienced in antiquity (fig. 51). The image illustrates the construction of a large kurgan burial in a general steppe context, but these large kurgan burials are typical of planned burial grounds of the Iron Age in the Koksu River valley as well. In a similar vein, the planned arrangement of Bronze Age stone configurations and the visibility of stone cist burials also suggest that considerable work hours and cooperative engagement at discrete locations in the landscape were necessary to construct burial contexts such as Begash 2. Some of the stone arrangements at Begash 2 contain an empty cist with no stratigraphic evidence of being robbed, which may indicate that planning in the layout and construction of Bronze Age cemeteries was conducted before the time of death (i.e., not on a person-by-person basis).

FIGURE 51

Artist's reconstruction of steppe burial ceremony: diorama at Kiev Archaeological Museum, Ukraine. Photo by the author.

I suggest that the planning and construction of Bronze Age cemeteries were organized as social events, while layout of the burials was set up according to social and political status (Potemkina 2002). Group efforts are indexed by the size of many Bronze Age burial grounds: for example, the complex at Kuigan contains more than sixty stone configurations, and Begash 2 has more than thirty. At Begash 2, the shape and orientation of the stone configurations suggest that there were either two phases of construction, or a social distinction in burial construction. To the southern side of the cemetery, burials have oval or circular stone fences, while on the northern edge they tend to be rectilinear.[7]

From the patterns of Bronze Age burial layout, it appears that cemeteries in the Koksu valley were planned before the death of an individual. Since access to the superficial cists would have been relatively uninvolved, bodies could easily be placed in preordained graves by relatively few individuals. From this perspective, burial construction may have elicited large scale social gatherings, perhaps on a seasonal basis. At the time of a death, locals who participated in the construction of the burial grounds might readjourn to participate in the interment of the dead, but this ritual may not compare to the social significance of actually planning the cemetery. Corollary to the construction of cemeteries, such gatherings likely fostered other interactions, such as localized trade, family introductions, or other social contacts (Barth 1964, appendix 1).

Taken together, Bronze Age burials and rock-art reflect a conceptual landscape that associates elements of everyday social interaction with experiences of ritual and ideological communication. The mechanisms of this communication are both active and passive and take place during prescribed interactions such as at burial ceremonies, as well as through non-discursive yet highly indexical semiotic forms such as rock-art. Rock-art acts as an index to the occupation and definition of the landscape by a local population, as well as a referent to the character and political potential of the particular groups that occupy niches within the landscape. Although we do not have access to the exact meanings of the motifs carved into rock faces, these fixtures contribute to the production of meaningful social locales. We may interpret these locales on a number of scales, ranging from their local socioeconomic suitability to their role in the formation of a conceptual landscape that defined social and political interactions of Bronze Age pastoralists. Thus, the creation of ritual spaces serves as a proxy for the negotiation of social and political relationships, pressed together into a seasonally variable and spatially diverse landscape.

WIDER EXTENSIONS OF THE PASTORAL LANDSCAPE

The sections above have presented reconstructions and interpretations of the spatial and temporal patterning of Bronze Age economic, ritual, and political landscapes in the Koksu valley. From these patterns, a seasonally based geographic pattern emerges in relation to the movement, settlement, and interactions in social contexts of the Bronze Age pastoralists who occupied the valley and surrounding upland meadows at different times of the year. These reconstructions also illustrated that there was likely a consider-able degree of variation inherent in the strategies that Bronze Age societies used to exploit their environment through mobile pastoralism, as well as in the way they con-structed social spaces. Variations in the geographic and seasonal pattern of migratory routines and interaction at social, ritual and domestic contexts illustrate how Bronze Age populations differentially employed the landscape in the Koksu valley during the later part of the second millennium BCE. If the extents of the local landscape are defined by the ordered variation in pastoral routines and the construction of contexts for interaction that are activated and deactivated at different times, then the extent of the macro-land-scape or the "global" scale for Bronze Age pastoralists was reflected in the acquisition and reproduction of exotic objects, imagery, and domestic products.

The geographic scale of the pastoral landscape during the Bronze Age was constantly changing and was being defined by the cross currents of individual and group strategies and interactive opportunities. Periodic changes in movement patterns, settlement geog-raphy, or social and ritual contexts produced considerable opportunities for local agents to expand their "mental map" of experienced landscapes. A variety of "reasons" may account for agents acting outside of their local system. Trade relationships, politics, con-flict, and geographic deviations in mobility patterns might all contribute to new config-urations of the pastoral landscape and to the propensity for exogenous materials to become available within the material assemblage of local populations.

MATERIAL DIVERSITY

The geographic and archaeological distribution of exotic materials among the Bronze Age sites of the Koksu River valley and generally across Semirech'ye illustrates how or-dered, yet variable, landscapes of interaction served to instantiate the nodes of local net-works within a wider-scale structure of transmission throughout the region. Specifically, Bronze Age settlements, burials, and rock-art document a variable distribution of exotic material culture in Semirech'ye.

Bronze Age settlements in the Kosku valley are admittedly humble in their construc-tion and outward appearance. One can envision a typical pastoralist settlement: relatively small with semi-subterranean stone walls, and a roof of branches, felt, or sod. Yet, for such prosaic living contexts, sites such as Begash reveal a highly exotic assortment of ce-ramic forms and metals. Of all the diagnostic sherds recovered at the site, over 25 per-cent are decorated vessels, and of these more than half can be associated stylistically with forms typical provenienced beyond Semirech'ye. This array of exotic ceramics includes forms typologically comparable with Fedorovo ceramics known from central and eastern Kazakhstan, as well as forms typically found in the Altai and southern Siberia.

To examine the inventories of Bronze Age settlements in similar environmental con-texts across Semirech'ye, we see that the occurrence of exotic styles within ceramic as-semblages from Bronze Age settlements and burials is common throughout the region,

Begash	Talapty/ Kuigan	Kyzlbulak/ Kulsai	Tamgaly	Acy/ Turgen
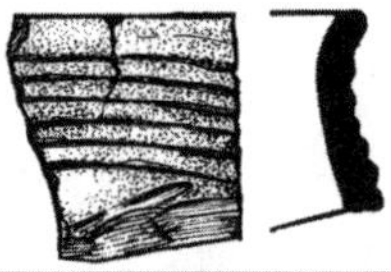	X			X
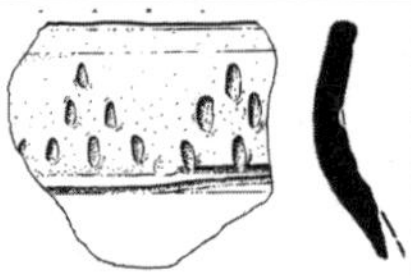				
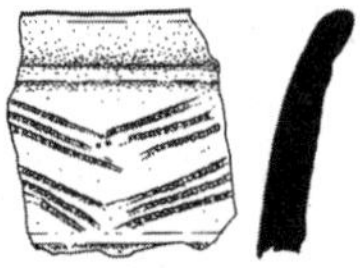			X	
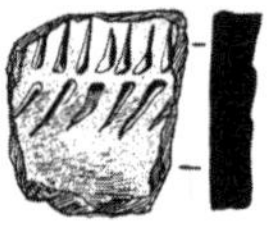	X			X
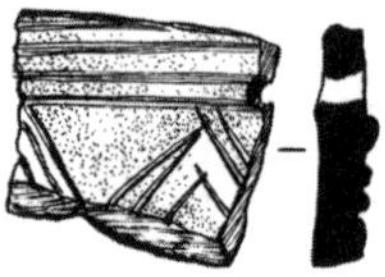			X	
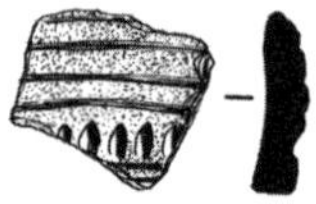	X			
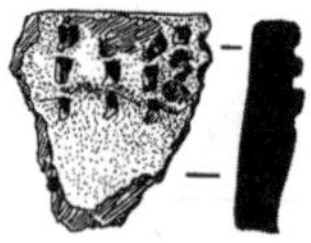				
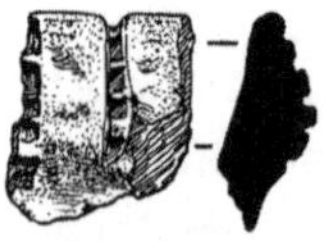				

FIGURE 52

Occurrence of specific ceramic motifs from Begash at main Bronze Age settlement sites of the Semirech'ye region.

but the decorative details of these assemblages are different for each site. Bronze Age settlements across the Dzhungar Mountains and Semirech'ye, such as Talapty, Kuigan, Acy, Kyzylbulak, and Tasbas all share a common set of coarseware jar forms with Begash; these likely represent domestically produced quotidian ceramics. However, each of these sites also has a unique and rich set of decorated ceramics, which are associated with stylistic analogies from beyond the region, for example from the Tian Shan mountains, central Kazakhstan, southern Siberia, and the Altai Mountains (Goryachev 2004; Rogozhinski 1999). By comparing decorated ceramic forms from seven prominently documented settlements of Semirech'ye (Begash, Kuigan, Talapty, Tamgaly, Acy, Kyzylbulak and Tasbas) we can see that there is only limited overlap in the occurrence of particular decorative motifs. Figure 52 illustrates the decorated forms at Begash, and the occurrence of these particular designs at the other sites mentioned. This regional variation may reflect the different opportunities of the population for acquiring exotic goods; perhaps an effect of their variable interactions within a mobile pastoral lifestyle. The local distinction between decorated forms is important, not necessarily to illustrate where these forms originate but rather to elucidate the variability of dynamic social connections through which exotic forms circulated into local assemblages.

The metal objects excavated at Begash 2 and Begash 3 further document the variable distribution of exotic material forms that are associated with pastoral societies of the Koksu valley (fig. 53, Frachetti 2006b). For example, burial-1 at Begash-2 produced a bronze bell-form earring that finds its closest analogy in the forest steppe zone of southern Russia, within the Elovskaya material package (Bader et al. 1987, 390). At nearby Begash-3, burial 1 contained a gold-leafed spiral pendant, which is a form typically associated with Bronze Age burials in central Kazakhstan and the Tian Shan foothills (Margulan et al. 1966). This adornment is also typically associated with female dress (Baipakov et al. 1998, 34), which entices the idea that women were prominent agents in the transmission of exotic materials and styles.

Rock-art motifs in the Koksu valley also illustrate the products of regional communication, as many motifs are commonly found throughout the mountains from the Altai

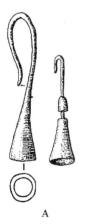
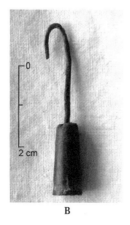

A B

FIGURE 53

(a) Bell-shaped earring from the Elovskaya Culture of Southwestern Siberia. After Bader et al. 1986, 390. (b) Detail of bronze earring from Begash-2, burial 1.

to the Pamirs (Samashev 1993; Mar'yashev 1994). Specifically, "sun-deities" have been regularly recorded throughout Semirech'ye, most notably at Tamgaly (Rogozhinski 2001), Byan-Zherek, Eshkiolmes in the Koksu valley, and Anrakhai (Mar'yashev and Goryachev 2002). These images show direct stylistic associations with sun-deities known from the Tian Shan Mountains at the sites of Saimaly-Tash and Chopan-Ata (Kyrgyzstan). Sun-deities are among the most prevalent rock-art motifs that are found throughout the region, though many other motifs attributed to the Bronze Age also reflect highly transferable semiotic currencies across the region.

In a comparison with the Kosku valley, Rogozhinski (1999) argues that Tamgaly, located in the southwestern part of Semirech'ye, functioned primarily as a ritual center, while practical and economic life was carried out on the site's "periphery." The first period of ritual centralization is represented by the burial ground Tamgaly 1, which chronologically correlates with the late Alakul/Atasu period (1600–1400 BCE). The second period of intense construction (at Tamgaly 2 and 4) reflects a later "mixed" cultural phase in Semirech'ye corresponding to the Final Bronze Age (1400–1000 BCE).

The two major cemeteries at Tamgaly provide some indication of the varied scale of sociopolitical interactions across Semirech'ye. The stone-cist burials at Tamgaly-1 are arranged in a burial group with a central cist and associated cists dated as early as 1600 BCE (uncalibrated C^{14}: Rogozhinski 1999). Based on Rogozhinski's comprehensive comparative analysis, the ceramics and metallurgy from Tamgaly 1 illustrate close stylistic similarities with late Alakul and Atasu materials from as far as the southern Urals and central Kazakhstan (Rogozhinski 1999, 17). In fact, the ceramic assemblage collected from the fourteen burials at Tamgaly 1 is consistent in its decoration, which may indicate that the dominant population was engaged in more highly institutionalized relations of exchange across an extensive, but formally organized, socioeconomic arena. Given the ecological constraints of the arid region around Tamgaly, the population was more likely engaged in longer migratory orbits, perhaps as far as the steppes of central Kazakhstan or beyond. Ethnographic studies of seasonal movements of nineteenth century Kazakhs lend additional support to this hypothesis, at least from an ecological point of view (Abramzon 1971). What is clear, however, is that Tamgaly provides us with a discrete set of semiotic and material forms, which may be an indication of formalization in the social and political engagements of those who controlled this important location.

Although the Koksu valley also boasts impressive rock-art, the sanctuary at Tamgaly presents a highly centralized and formalized ritual context. The control of this site, as well as the environmental demand to migrate longer distances throughout the year, may have promoted the population's ability to develop more highly institutionalized interactions than those that characterized the political economy of other parts of Semirech'ye. The diverse material artifacts recovered in the Koksu valley speak to the prevalence of interactions among pastoralists living across Semirech'ye. However, there is little evidence to suggest that pastoralists in territories like the Koksu valley were highly mobile or controlled expansive political or social geographies during the Bronze Age. Instead, it appears that the boundaries of their pastoralist landscape were sufficiently porous to absorb an array of crossing technologies, products, materials, and people through time, while maintaining a fundamentally stable pattern of local exploitation. Crossing currents of ceramic forms, metals, semiotic forms, language, and population sometimes flowed rapidly along periodically interlocked social coduits. Sometimes these currents trickled through articulated channels of communication and interaction. Both were dependent upon the successful negotiation of varied social and ecological pressures on the part of locally situated populations.

This chapter has presented a synthetic reconstruction of the economic, social, ritual, and political aspects of the pastoralist landscape of the study zone. The landscapes described above are interpreted vis-à-vis data presented in earlier chapters to present a dynamic representation of pastoralist life as it may have been experienced in the Bronze Age. Economically, Bronze Age pastoralists strategically exploited their mountain ecology to raise cattle and sheep using seasonal, vertical migrations, but their patterned movements were not only a means to economic success. Their mobility must be understood along with their settlements, burials, and rock-art, which collectively framed the geography and timing of social interactions and conditioned the metamorphasis of their material culture, ideology, political economy and social interactions through time. Through their participation in a dynamic local network of social and economic exchanges, mobile pastoral populations of the Koksu valley energized the diffusion of a wider array of exotic materials beyond the local range of their practices. When the social geographies of neighboring populations were aligned, materials and technology could rapidly transfer, as if "flashing" through a temporarily connected conduit. As regional groups readjusted their strategies, such networks of communication and diffusion fragmented and reformed to produce new structures articulated across wider territories.

This chapter presented this generative model of pastoralist landscapes through the archaeological details of the Koksu River valley and suggested that the pastoral landscape that defines this specific region was analogous in adjacent contexts throughout Semirech'ye. Since the model presented depends on a detailed view of a highly complex process in a specific location, it cannot simply be cut and pasted in the form that fits one context, into other regions of the steppe to explain how analogous archaeological contexts and transmissions of material culture are produced. Each region has its own pressures and ecology, and reflects a unique context that is defined by its own internal variation. Nevertheless, the model presented enables us to view the wider "global" extent of the steppe zone as a highly variegated region with potentially hundreds of "local" systems that could be linked through their respective systems of interaction and communication.

CONCLUSION

SYNCOPATED RHYTHMS OF PASTORALIST LANDSCAPES

This book set out to provide a clearer understanding of the formation of pastoralist landscapes across Eurasia through time. Starting from the earliest documented evidence of mobile strategies of herd management, the structure and durability of Eurasian pastoralist landscapes were presented as the result of human experiences and practices spatially and temporally reiterated in relation to a number of dynamic pressures. These included regionally discrete environmental variation and ecological fluctuation, locally conceived social and political relationships, and the historical resonance of meaningful places constructed through the knowledge of intersecting mobile pastoral groups. The foregoing chapters also contributed the idea that the shapes of pastoralist landscapes mutate in concert with syncopated rhythms of social, political, and economic conditions outside the locally experienced context. This thesis reorients our historical perspective on Eurasian societies from one of cohesive groups that emerge or decline as regional entities toward one of a process of socio-geographic metamorphosis brought about at the interstices of coincident worldviews and interactive experiences.

The underlying focus of this book has been the development of these pastoralist landscapes during the Bronze Age in the steppe zone of central Eurasia. I have argued that previous conceptualizations of the chronological and geographical spread of key innovations in this period have been couched in an academic paradigm that positioned the archaeological record at odds with the practical realities of pastoralist ways of life. Specifically, the mechanisms cited to explain the remarkable distributions of material culture and the diffusion of domestic strategies, technology, and language associated with the Andronovo culture seem inconsistent with the way pastoralists occupied and invested in their territories in a quotidian fashion, both in the Bronze Age and in later epochs. Improvements in our scientific understanding of the chronology and character of the earliest herding societies in the steppes enable us to recast the archaeological elements of a complex matrix of pastoralist societies across the steppe from the middle of the third millennium BCE. This study has reinvestigated the archaeological particulars of the steppe from a vantage point of regional continuity to show how, through time, flexibility in the scalar complexity of early nomadic landscapes shaped the contextual frames of Eurasia's long-term history.

Toward this goal, we have explored a particular pastoralist landscape—the Koksu River valley of Semirech'ye—and characterized it vis-à-vis the environmental, ethno-historical, and archaeological particulars of the study zone. Taken together, these data suggest that societies living in the Koksu valley have been variously engaged as mobile pastoralists for more than four thousand years, and their lifestyle has been generally characterized by short range migrations across a dynamic social landscape. Their general migratory pattern, however, has changed through time while it also reproduced an embedded sense of social history in the region. The practical timing and scalar extent of pastoralist mobility, variations in economic strategy, negotiated trade relationships, and political engagements were differently experienced by societies of different periods on the local scale as a result of their confluence with overlapping time-space geographies of their neighbors: broadly, their interactions. At the same time, the experience of every pastoralist group in the Koksu valley was filtered through the spatial and temporal legacy of those before them: the geography of their burials, settlements, pastures, rock-art, and environmental impact.

This legacy is imprinted on the landscape by archaeological data that document the formation of complex social locations, which superimpose domestic, ritual, and sociopolitical realms of Bronze Age and later societies. Material assemblages from excavated sites, coupled with the geographic distribution of other settlements, burials, and rock-art documented throughout the study zone, illustrate that Bronze Age and later societies had developed a variable landscape that presented a variety of options for mobility, settlement, and social interaction. The vertical zonality of the environment was assessed in terms of pasture resources relevant to the proposed Bronze Age economic strategy and contributed to an archaeologically and environmentally derived reconstruction of the Bronze Age mobile strategy of land use. Mobility patterns were viewed in light of the simultaneous need to provide for a subsistence economy based in herding and to negotiate a diverse social landscape. It was demonstrated that the mountain-steppe ecology of the Dzhungar region played a role in the spatial and temporal experience of the landscape, as the geographic variability of seasonal pasture resources contributed to the places where populations settled, how far they moved, and where they interacted. Yet, the environment was not the only input; social locations were also important areas, evidenced by the archaeological co-occurance of domestic, ritual, and sociopolitical features in revisited locales.

Ethnographic data bolstered the archaeology to understand other factors that may have contributed to the interactive geography of pastoralists throughout the past. It was suggested that the motivations for social interaction were both economically practical and highly sociological including, for example, the need to feed herd animals in a restrictive environment and the desire to promote social and political status within a constantly changing social landscape. In negotiating their social landscape—which reflects the socially produced spaces and times of practical interactions—mobile pastoral societies played an integral part in a process of extending their social geography by incorporating a host of exotic materials. By expanding the scope of their material world they also reduced the physical and conceptual geography that separated societies of the Eurasian steppe before the Bronze Age.

The thesis presented in this book also contributes to the broader study of the so-called "Andronovo Cultural Community" by reorienting the way material culture is seen as a proxy for social groups. Material diversity is presented in this study as a form of currency that affected the discourse of interaction of individuals, groups, and societies of the Bronze Age. Yet social organizations, akin to "communities," were formed through the reiteration of pastoral landscapes whose boundaries were constantly reconfigured by practical strategies. Tracing the way Bronze Age pastoralist landscapes iteratively affected wider-scale material distributions and social diffusions throughout the second millennium BCE illustrates the dialectical relationship between local and global contexts and contributes to our understanding of processual change from a tangible perspective.

The conceptual paradigm of this study allows the widest "global" extents of the steppe zone to be viewed as permeable and interconnected, potentially with hundreds of "local" landscapes linked through their respective syncopated rhythms of interaction and communication. Therefore, in order to assess the potential utility of this landscape model, we should see how it may reorient our perspective of the interactive geography of the "Andronovo Cultural Community," or other material distributions that illustrate macro-scale homologies and local-scale diversity.

THE SEIMA-TURBINO RECONSIDERED

A concise problem within studies of the Andronovo period that may be reconsidered through the lens of the thesis presented here is the widespread distribution of metal objects within the Seima-Turbino phenomenon (described in chapter 2). The complexity of the developmental processes of the Seima-Turbino phenomenon crystallizes some of the questions that plague other material and cultural studies of the Late and Final Bronze Age archaeology of the steppe, such as ceramic or language transfer. Namely, how can materials, in this case metals provenienced to the Altai Mountains, find their way into archaeological assemblages in the Ural Mountains and beyond? What were the processes that displaced these materials? Did societies of the Altai region undertake mass migrations as "warrior-horsemen," as suggested by Chernykh (1992)? The evidence for the travel of Seima-Turbino metal objects is substantial, but can this be equated with demic diffusion as well? In fact, the argument for mass migration of a warrior horseman class from southwest Siberia to the west rests on a platform of corollary archaeological evidence, which may be reconceptualized in light of the model presented in this study.

First, Chernykh (1992, 228) suggests that differences in material goods among burials at Seima reflect ethno-cultural differences in the population, with one in five burials reflecting materials of the Abashevo culture to the west, whereas others reflect typical Seima-Turbino materials (i.e., populations from the east). He suggests that this difference is reflective of a mixing of populations, potentially reflecting an emerging class structure, with Seima-Turbino groups at the top of the pecking order because they controlled metallurgical production.

The current study, however, has illustrated that material variations may in fact highlight differential access to a diversity of interactions that occur within the ordered variation of local pastoral systems, which would not mandate that those individuals buried with Seima-Turbino materials be attributed genetically or ethnically to the same population that collected and transported tin-bronze from the Altai Mountains. The current study suggests that various patterns of localized interactions could facilitate the transfer of materials through a network of routinized but often periodically varied contexts, which may account for their uneven distribution and mixture with other forms (e.g., Abashevo materials) within large burial contexts such as at Reshnoe (Chernykh 1992, 228). Thus, the differentiation of burials at Seima does not necessarily reflect population movement but may instead reflect differential access to commodities through strategic and coincidental interaction across a flexible network.

Second, Chernykh suggests that the thin chronological horizon within which Seima-Turbino materials were distributed across a wide territory is an indicator of a rapid influx of populations from the east, followed by intergroup assimilation. Yet perhaps this rapid influx reflects a pulse of material distribution fostered by interactions between seasonally mobile populations who were motivated to procure a finite source of exotic materials by slightly extending or changing their pastoral orbits. This interpretation may also explain why the Seima-Turbino materials are not ubiquitous in the Ural and Tobol regions. Like exotic ceramic forms in Semirech'ye, there appears to be differential access to Seima-Turbino metals within archaeologically consistent areas, such as around Sintashta (Chernykh 1992, 231). The suggestion that a burst of fine metals was actively transferred along a discrete network of local populations, perhaps over only a short period of time, is also supported by what Chernykh recognizes as copying of Seima-Turbino metals within local metallurgical traditions (1992, 231). If there was not a constant or organized supply of the original objects, there was likely a lucrative developing "market" for good copies during the later part of the second millennium BCE.

The model presented in this study offers a different and fruitful way of explaining complex systems of interaction by rooting them in the multivalent motivations of local populations whose varied practical experiences of trade, ritual communication, political negotiation, herding migrations, and exploitation of resources played a role in the distribution of materials across the steppe. To attempt to account for all the potential situations and contexts for interaction across the steppe would be beyond the reliability of the archaeology presented in this study. The model presented here, however, can lead archaeologists to reconsider the way we create generalized categories from archaeological data, by illustrating that concepts such as mobile pastoralism, the Andronovo culture, or the Seima-Turbino phenomenon, for example, are not objects to be recovered whole.

From the data presented in this study, it appears that Bronze Age mountain pastoralists of the Koksu valley did not have a highly institutionalized strategy for long-distance trade nor did their migrations take them deep into exotic territories. Their environment provided them with a comfortable, economically productive niche that did not demand extensive mobility for successful exploitation. Nonetheless, their ability to strategically negotiate the ecological and social pressures of their local context actually produced a scenario whereby they could transcend the boundaries of their landscape to participate in a wider "globalizing" network of interaction that brought together material culture from dissociated contexts. I argue that this process is at the root of the spread of material culture throughout the steppe during the second millennium BCE and may also be a useful framework to approach the spread of other "transferables" such as metallurgy, language, and technology.

The model proposed to explain the material diversity of Bronze Age archaeological contexts is supported by two main conditions. First, the scale of pastoralist landscapes across the steppe should be considered local and continuous on the basis of recoverable patterns of economic, sociopolitical, and ritual practices of mobile pastoralists. Remarkable continuity in settlement geography, ideological investment, and a geographically durable definition of the local landscape was documented in the study zone. At the same time, variation and change in these patterns fostered periodic extensions in the boundaries of the landscape. In the simplest terms, the ability of mobile pastoral populations of Eurasia to foster a diffuse array of exotic materials and exogenous relationships is an effect of the variable and nonlinear spatial and temporal patterns inherent in their pastoralist strategies. These strategies are multivalent and cumulatively contribute to a historical geography of syncopated interactions with other groups filtering in and out of the social landscape.

This approach steps away from the organic modeling of Bronze Age steppe societies and away from the concept of "blocks" of material culture presented as indexes of social groups. This study rests its interpretations on the flexibility of pastoral landscapes and the identies of those who give them meaning. It refocuses how we describe the relocation of materials over space and time from a linear process to a nonlinear one. Objects such as ceramics, metals, textiles, animals, and many other commodities contribute to the reformation of social relationships, while access to and re-valuation of exotic materials may have provided opportunities for societies to extend the boundaries of their perceived social world and their personal and group identities.

This study has presented an approach that emphasizes local adaptations to social and environmental conditions, which produced a variety of contexts for interaction. The material diversity documented in the archaeology speaks to broader extensions of the landscape, but should not be confused as an equation with a cohesive population that occupied real space and time. Instead, the steppe societies of the Late Bronze Age, like those living in the Koksu River valley, can be better understood by trying to trace incrementally the variable factors that affected their everyday practices and way of life and by recognizing that the boundaries of their society were changeable according to their own ontological diversity.

What do these notions say about the existence of regional cultural groups and broader processes during the second millennium BCE? How has the archaeology conducted in this study moved us past an ethnographic understanding of mobile pastoral systems in prehistory?

The model presented in this study suggests that culture groups of the steppe are creations of archaeologists, and although these are useful as heuristic guides for classifying data, they can obscure the flexible continuities of pastoralist landscapes through time (Hodder 1990). This would suggest that for mobile pastoralists of the second millennium BCE, for example, regional identities were always being altered in response to different impulses that conditioned their porous landscapes. New forms of material culture, new people, new social opportunities, and new economic opportunities may have been a few of these. The material culture they traded or the languages they spoke did not simply affix to them an identity (Kopytoff 1986). These characteristics were malleable and multifaceted—much as they in are contemporary contexts (Appadurai 1984; Ong 1999). Cultural identity was not necessarily imported through the acculturated pockets of long-distance immigrants but was transfused through the networks of interaction shaped by strategic variations. Historically recognizable populations are associated with archaeologically meaningful geographies, whereas their identities change along with the spatial and temporal currents of their social landscape. The structures of pastoralist landscapes were constantly regenerated by the variation that characterized the economic and social strategies of different groups, which helped them get along in the world (Giddens 1984). These structures were also affected by exotic materials that were opportunistically infused within, and thereby changed, the landscape itself.

The macro-scale currents of material transfer, technological diffusion, and semiotic assimilation documented in the Bronze Age and beyond were constantly being filtered through the practical scales of local landscapes. Considering the institutional frames created by this dialectic, the global scale never actually exists as an ontological reality. In fact, the global scale of cultural and economic homologies across the steppe in the Bronze Age is a meta-narrative that may seldom have been realized by pastoralist in the negotiation of their local practices. Bronze Age mobile pastoralists may have strategically expanded the geography of their interconnections and may have been aware of the political and social currents of their neighbors near or far. Yet the iterated network through which their mutual innovations and sociopolitical, economic, and personal concerns were communicated was not the result of extensive boundaries of conformity or geographically protracted negotiations. Instead, knowledge and participation in the "global" world was iteratively sprinkled into the lives of Eurasian pastoralists and only sometimes poured full force. What is certain is that their landscapes stand as a durable testimony to the ways in which their dynamic and strategic lives bridged these scalar extremes to phenomenal ends.

Archaeology is a science of time, and the future holds bright prospects for answering many questions concerning the Bronze Age of the Eurasian steppe zone. This book has potentially generated more questions than it has answered; yet it is offered as an incremental step toward more concrete knowledge concerning pastoralist societies of Eurasia and the dynamic landscape that is reflected in their archaeological and ethnographic records.

NOTES

PROLOGUE

1. "Kazakh" is used here as a national and multi-ethnic category, not to be confused with Kazakh ethnicity.
2. The scale of developmental change in Almaty was dramatic from 1999 to 2007 and in urban contexts the population of Kazakhstan is rapidly defining an important node in global networks of international finance and commerce.
3. The phrase *"ransho ne bilo"* was commonly expressed after comments concerning rising crime or political corruption, lower wages, lack of work, or other conditions that were endemic and apparently newly recognized in the immediate years after the collapse of the Soviet Union.

INTRODUCTION

1. Agro-pastoralism has also been suggested for Bronze Age steppe communities (Zdanovich 2002a), although this economy has been proposed mostly for regions of the western steppe and the trans-Urals. In the eastern steppe and central Kazakhstan, few studies have produced concrete evidence for the presence of agricultural production, leaving a vague concept of "pastoralism" as the dominant model of subsistence during the Bronze Age (but see Margulan 1979 for discussion of potential proto-irrigation systems).
2. Baipakov (1998) also notes that the medieval city of Talgar in Semirech'ye was sacked by Mongolian armies in the 13th century.
3. Semirech'ye is also known as "Zhetisu" in Kazakh.

CHAPTER 1

1. Bourdieu (1977, 73; 85) defines "practice" as the behavior and action of human agents within experienced social and physical locales.

2. Environmental, political, and ideological considerations of the Makran Baluch of western Pakistan result in various patterns of interactions related to territorial and social affiliations at local and regional scales (Pastner 1971, 175–180). Pastner emphasizes how localized patterns of mobility, or the "micro-pastoral orbit" used by the Makrani nomads to accommodate the demands of herd animals and social groups in a marginal environment, are also extended for purposes of resource exploitation and socioeconomic strategies not specific to herd needs. Alternative aims, such as trade, raiding, itinerant agriculture or the sale of labor introduce unique mobility patterns and bring nomads into close interactions with sedentary villagers while nomads are settled in peripheral residence camps near agricultural villages. For the Makran Baluch, the year-to-year variability of mobility strategies in their nomadic search for pasture also brings about interaction and overlap between various contiguous micro-pastoral orbits, forming what Pastner calls a "macro-pastoral orbit" or territory. This macro-pastoral orbit generates for the pastoralists a wider range of regional alliances and political affiliations between groups (Pastner 1971, 182).

3. Claudia Chang's recent economic studies of the Saka-Wusun Iron Age reveal a mixed agro-pastoral economy in the greater Semirechye region by the eighth century BCE (Miller-Rosen et al. 2000), but the productive economy of the Late and Final Bronze Age (roughly 1500–1000 BCE) is still poorly documented by archaeology. Honeychurch and Amartuvshin (2007) illustrates that agricultural communities were related to pastoralists early in prehistory in Mongolia, however this is likely a diffusion of agricultural innovations from regions to the south, in present day China.

4. The environment reflects climatic and biospheric conditions far beyond the range of most pastoralist groups. Thus, although anthropogenic change is significant to the experience of pastoralist landscapes, environmental conditions are to a large part affected by trends beyond the impact of local pastoralists. This idea challenges the idea of the "tragedy of the commons" popularly associated with pastoralists and their impact on climate change.

5. Scale in this case is used as a qualitative and quantitative reference to the geographic extent, social organization, political influence, military strength, and connectivity of various societies which occupy a region.

CHAPTER 2

1. "*Assyk*" is a children's game common in Kazakhstan (personal observation), known by other names throughout Central Asia. The object is to toss sheep knucklebones close to a pile of other bones, and the closest toss wins the pile.

2. The ceramic ornament description continues for another page. See Sorokin and Gryaznov (1966, 6–7) for a full description.

3. Of course, Marxist models of social processes are not uniquely Soviet. The Soviet model of ethnic division actually finds antecedents in the social movements of late 19th century

Russia although ethnos as a formal paradigm was not highly developed until the mid 20th century in the Soviet Union (Shlapentokh 1996; Gellner 1988).

4. Recent studies of the paleoclimate of the steppe are constrained by a lack of localized detail within the second millennium BCE, so that regional climatic conditions are only beginning to emerge. Where regional climatic studies are being developed, as in Semirech'ye and the greater Tian Shan region (see paleoclimate section in chapter 3), they present scenarios contradicting the consensus that there was a widespread change in the steppe vegetation during the second millennium BCE.

5. The impact of calibrated radiocarbon dating may seem "old hat" to archaeologists working in the western tradition, but this method has only been systematically applied in the steppe region for about the past 10–15 years.

6. It is important here to remind ourselves that the Bronze Age is a heuristic category, not a historical event. Thus, there is no earliest Bronze Age society of the steppe (Rassamakin 1999). For the purpose of this study, we will focus on those societies which illustrate significant and multivalent innovations in their technology, economy, and sociopolitical organization specifically associated with pastoralism as the start of our discussion of distinctly pastoralist landscapes.

7. Given the complication of chronology between western and eastern domestic herding economies, the introduction of sheep/goat and cattle to southwestern Siberia, Semirech'ye, and other regions of the Inner Asia in the late fourth and early third millennium BCE is of eminent concern. To date, the argument has been that domesticates in southern Central Asia were introduced along with agriculture in the Neolithic, though, currently, evidence to demonstrate a link between these mixed economies and those that emerge in the steppe zone and inner Asian mountains in the early Bronze Age is sparse (Hiebert 2002). Interactions between settled agricultural communities and mountain communities of the fourth millennium BCE at the site of Sarazm (Lyonnet 1996), however, may be related to the introduction of domestic animals through the Pamir Mountains, diffusing northward by 3000 BCE. Substantial qualitative and quantitative research remains to sufficiently demonstrate this hypothesis.

8. Pashkevich (2003) provides a coherent summary of botanical remains from Bronze Age sites of the Ukrainian steppes and western steppe, which do show continuity in agricultural production from Neolithic times. Here I am referring to the steppe zone beyond the north Caspian, where botanical correlates for plant domestication are scarce.

9. Although this may reflect a determinism of the archaeological survey strategy.

10. The depth of Soviet and post-Soviet research concerning this material is not represented in the bulk of the literature accessible in most western libraries. During the Soviet era, hundreds of regional volumes or "sborniki" were printed, which systematically presented decades of excavation and research conducted by Soviet archaeologists. However, for many of these volumes, the production run was limited to less than 100–200 copies, making them difficult to find outside of Russia or the Newly Independent States. Even within the national academic libraries of these countries, limited funds after the breakup of the Soviet Union restricted the purchasing of these publications. The most

common circulation of the material was by direct exchange between the archaeologists themselves. Thus, for western scholars working from their institutional libraries, much of the detailed literature concerning the Steppe Bronze Age is largely inaccessible.

11. Many "culture" groups were established a priori from the first excavations at namesake sites like Fedorovka or Alekseevka.

CHAPTER 3

1. The most recent dated sample (which the authors note was likely disturbed due to its proximity to the surface salts of the lacustrian deposit) dates to approximately 330 years BP. Therefore, the last reliable sample (dated to 1140 yrs. BP) is used here to represent the most contemporary climatic maximum.

2. 4220±220 BP (uncalibrated), 3100–2450 BCE (calibrated 1 sigma range) (Frachetti and Mar'yashev 2007).

3. More detailed studies of the paleo-climate are under way, and we hope to hone our picture of the Bronze Age environment through continued sampling of archaeological contexts and coring in regional salt flats. At present, and for the purpose of environmental modeling in this study, we will assume that the vegetation and climate of the study region during the middle and late second millennium was broadly similar to contemporary conditions.

4. Range management is the science and art of planning and directing range use so as to obtain maximum livestock production consistent with conservation of range resources (Stoddart and Smith 1943, 1). Range science is the organized body of knowledge upon which such development and utilization of ranges is based (Vallentine and Sims 1980, 3). This study is not concerned with range management in the disciplinary or applied sense (Provenza 1991); rather this discussion applies knowledge generated from range science to derive potential and round figures concerning the comparative grazing capacity of rangelands of different zones in the Koksu valley, expressed in their potential to support herds of domesticated cattle, sheep, and horses.

5. Rangelands are defined as "uncultivated grasslands, shrublands, or forested lands with an herbaceous and/or shrubby understory, particularly those producing forage for grazing and or browsing by domestic and wild animals..." (Vallentine and Sims 1980, 1). This section is concerned with the characterization and utilization of rangeland pastures, which for this case study are limited to native grasslands and shrubby ranges harvested directly by grazing animals (i.e., arid and grassy steppes and meadows). Although not relevant to the current discussion, pastures also include "cultivated perennial, temporary, and crop aftermath" contexts (Vallentine and Sims 1980, 1). Forage is defined as "that proportion of the vegetation actually grazed by the animal or fed to the animal" (Van Dyne 1969, cited in Cook and Stubbendieck 1986, 51).

6. To render the pasture resources in the study zone accurately, a Normalized Difference Vegetation Index (NDVI) image was calculated in Arc-View Image Analyst using Landsat TM 7 base data. An NDVI image assigns values ranging from −1 to 1 to land-cover, according to the intensity of reflected chlorophyll in the vegetation (i.e., "greenness"). Using ArcGIS 8.2, the NDVI image was reclassified, assigning the ranked "productivity

values" discussed above to the visible vegetation indices greater than zero. This revalued NDVI image was then resolved into four classes of grassland types according to known botanical composition of pastures at various altitude horizons (Goloskokov 1984; Sobolev 1960).

7. "Vernal aspect" is defined as "lack of a short-lived plant cohort in the spring."

8. The discrepancy between the suggested capacity of the Dzhungar region and those suggested by Zhu's and Gomboev's calculations may also be a product of their methodological choice to calculate productivity using "dry matter" weights rather than "edible green mass." Russian plant scientists tend to use "edible green mass" when calculating the productivity of natural pastures, since the animals would in fact be eating green grass as opposed to harvested hay. Thus, if one were to multiply the capacity yield suggested in these studies by 2.5–3 (the suggested correlation between dry and green yield), the results of their pasture carrying capacity are closer to those presented for steppe pastures of the Dzhungar Mountains.

CHAPTER 4

1. The Kara-Khitai ruled over the territory of Semirech'ye during the twelfth though thirteenth centuries CE (Golden 2003).

2. The Kalmykh original maps and Renat's copy are held at the Uppsala University Library. The two original maps plus the copies by Renat were presented as gifts to the library in 1743 (*Alla Tiders Kartor: A Treasury of Maps* 1988).

3. Ethnohistorical texts concerned with the eastern regions of Eurasia (present day Kazakhstan) often refer to the populations living throughout Semirech'ye as Kazakh-Kirghiz, or Kirghiz. This older moniker most likely reflects the tribal affiliations that exhisted between groups living throughout the territories that today are divided into Kazakhstan and Kyrgyzstan. From an ethnographic perspective, this general naming conevention simply represents the common macro-identity attributed to these segmentary tribal societies by European travelers and ethnographers in the eighteenth and nineteenth centuries.

4. Also referred to as the "Great Horde."

5. "Seven rivers" is the translation of the Russian "Semirech'ye", known in Kazakh as "Zhetisu".

6. Likely a reference to large herd sizes (Bartol'd 1943).

7. An archaeological survey by the author in 2007 recorded the use of desert-steppe regions such as the Ushkara plateau by pastoral communities, though the earliest evidence recorded is attributable to the Saka period. No Bronze Age archaeology was documented by the survey.

8. Author's translation of "*sovmestno-posledovatel'noe.*"

9. On famine as a general problem, see Valikhanov (1961, I:530).

10. The literal translation is "according to the layout (*polozheniem*) of these burials". I have liberally translated this term as "landscape" to comply with the thesis forwarded in this study that there is social significance in the historical layout and geography of monuments and burials.

CHAPTER 5

1. Current research is underway exploring the archaeology of the Sary-Esik desert, located west of the piedmont environmental zones of the Dzhungar Mountains. Preliminary excursions into this region suggest a significant break in the archaeological character of Bronze Age sites in the desert, thus the current boundaries of the study zone should be considered as non-determinant for the patterns and distributions of archaeological sites in the Koksu valley.

2. In mountainous environments, categorizing the features according to elevation reveals preliminary associations between ecological conditions and human strategies.

3. 3870±35 BP (uncalibrated), 2460–2290 BCE (calibrated 1-sigma range) (Frachetti and Mar'yashev 2007).

4. To date, absolute chronologies for the sites Talapty and Kuigan have not been published. From a material perspective, these sites are comparable with Begash: minimally during the Late Bronze Age, or from 2050–1700 BCE and 1650–1000 BCE, respectively (ibid.). In the literature, these sites are tradionally attributed to the Late and Final Bronze Age (1400–900 BCE) on the basis of relative dating (Goryachev 2004).

5. The publication of the settlement excavations at Mukri are in preparation by the author.

6. Prior to the current survey, only the largest rock-art areas in the Koksu valley were known and well studied, with the exception of those atop Mount Alabasy, first recorded by the author in 2006.

7. The "golden man" is an Iron Age individual excavated by Akishev from the Issyk kurgan group in southeastern Kazakhstan (Akishev 1978). The interred individual was adorned with goldern plaques, headdress, and weaponry dating to the fifth century BCE.

8. Mud brick construction is common to medieval cities such as Otrar, located in arid territories of southern Kazakhstan (Baipakov 1998).

9. Humphrey 1996.

CHAPTER 6

1. Recent paleo-climatic studies conducted in the Dzhungar region suggest that the climate of the second millennium BCE was broadly comparable with that documented today (chapter 3). This is a topic of debate, as paleo-climatologists working in other parts of the Eurasian steppe, namely the western steppes and northern Kazakhstan, have argued that the climate (vs. vegetation) of the second millennium was different from that of today (e.g., Kremenetsky 2003). However, paleo-botanical reconstructions in the Koksu Valley suggest that the steppe vegetation during the second millennium BCE at Begash was comparable to the contemporary vegetation (Aubekerov et al. 2003). Therefore, for the purpose of modeling pastoral migration patterns, the modern environment serves as an approximation of the conditions that might have been experienced during the Bronze Age. Future research will enable a more accurate reconstruction of the vegetation and climate during the second millennium BCE.

2. The qualified land-cover data along with the grazing capacity figures calculated in chapter 3, as well as the seasonal changes in these figures are used as the base data

sources to delimit the spatial and temporal cycles of available pastures during the summer (i.e., the most productive growing season).

3. At Begash, this interpretation is supported by the iterated infilling shown in the stratigraphy and formation of the site, as well as the seasonality of recovered botanical remains.

4. Commonly, all of the settlements used for modeling are interpreted as winter settlements based on their locations in areas of low summer pasture productivity and their construction details. Furthermore, faunal remains of cattle, sheep, and horses are documented at approximately 90 percent of the settlements that were shovel tested, and also from formally excavated settlements in the Kosku valley such as Talapty, Kuigan and Begash, which ties them all to populations engaged in herding. At all these sites, sheep and cattle represent the greatest proportions of bones, followed by smaller numbers of horses (Mar'yashev and Goryachev 1996).

5. The methodology for these simulated patterns of pastoral mobility is described in Frachetti 2006a.

6. Iron Age kurgan burials such as Pazyryk and Berel in northeastern Kazakhstan offer clear evidence for horse veneration through the interment of numerous horses in ritual fashion.

7. Begash 2 has not been comprehensively excavated to determine whether this represents a social or chronological difference.

BIBLIOGRAPHY

Abramzon, S. M. 1971. *Kirgizy i ikh etnogeneticheskie i istoriko kul'turnye sviazi*. Leningrad: Nauka.

———. 1973. Vliyanie perekhoda k osedlomu obrazu zhizni na preobrazovanie sotsial'nogo stroya, Semeinobytovogo uklada i kul'tury prezhnikh kochevnikov i polukochevnikov (na primere Kazakhov i Kirgizov). In *Ocherki po Istorii Khozyaistva Narodov Srednei Azii i Kazakhstana*, ed. S. M. Abramzon and A. Orazob, 235–248. Leningrad: Akademiya Nauk.

———. 1978. Family-group, family, and individual property categories among nomads. In *The Nomadic Alternative: Modes and Models of Interaction in the African-Asian Deserts and Steppes*, ed. W. Weissleder, 179–188. Paris: Mouton, The Hague.

Abuseitova, M. K. and IU. G. Baranova. 2001. *Pismennye istochniki po istorii i kul'ture Kazakhstana i TSentral'noi Azii v XIII-XVIII vv (biobibliograficheskie obzory)*. Almaty: Kazakhstanskie vostokovednye issledovaniia "Daik-Press".

Adams, R. M. C. 1974. The Mespotamian social landscape: a view from the frontier. In *Reconstructing Complex Societies*, ed. B. Moore, 1–11. Chicago: American Schools of Oriental Research.

Akhinzhanov, S. M., L. A. Makarova, and T. N. Nurumov. 1992. *K Istorii Skotovodstva i Okhoty v Kazakhstane*. Almaty: Gylym.

Akishev, A. and K. A. Akishev. 1984. *Iskusstvo i mifologiia sakov*. Alma-Ata: Izd-vo "Nauka" Kazakhskoi SSR.

Akishev, Kemal A. 1975. *Drevnosti Kazakhstana*. Almaty: Qazaq SSR ghylym akademiiasy.

———. 1978. *Kurgan Issyk*. Moscow: Nauka.

———. 1989. *Aktual'nye problemy istoriografii drevnego Kazakhstana arkheologiya*. Alma-Ata: "Nauka" Kazakhskoi SSR.

Alla Tiders Kartor: A Treasury of Maps. 1988. Uppsala: Uppsala University Library.

Andrews, P. A. 1999. *Felt Tents and Pavilions: The Nomadic Tradition and its Interaction with Princely Tentage.* London: Kölner ethnologische Mitteilungen Melisende.

Anikin, A. V. 1988. *Russian Thinkers: Essays on Socio-Economic Thought in the 18th and 19th Centuries.* Moscow: Progress Publishers.

Anshuetz, K. F., R. H. Williams and C. L. Scheick. 2001. An archaeology of landscapes: Perspectives and directions. *Journal of Archaeological Research* 9(2):157–211.

Anthony, David W., 1990. Migration in archaeology: the baby and the bathwater. American Anthropologist, 92:895–914.

——. 1998. The opening of the Eurasian steppe at 2000 BCE. In *The Bronze Age and Early Iron Age Peoples of Eastern Central Asia,* ed. V. Mair, 94–113. Philadelphia: University of Pennsylvania Museum Publications.

——. 2007. *The Horse, the Wheel, and Language: How Bronze-Age Riders from the Eurasian Steppes Shaped the Modern World.* Princeton (NJ): Princeton University Press.

Anthony, David W. and Dorcas R. Brown. 2000. Eneolithic horse exploitation in the Eurasian steppes: Diet, ritual and riding. *Antiquity* 74(283):75–86.

Anthony, David W., D. Brown, E. Brown, A. Goodman, A. Kokhlov, P. Kosintsev, P. Kuznetsov, O. Mochalov, E. Murphy, D. Peterson, A. Pike-Tay, L. Popova, A. Rosen, N. Russel, and A. Weisskopf. 2005. The Samara Valley project. Late Bronze Age economy and ritual in the Russian steppes. *Eurasia Antiqua* 2005:395–417.

Antipina E. E. 1997. Metody rekonstruktsii osobennostei skotovodstva na yuge vostochnoi Evropy v epokhy bronzy. *Rossiskaya Arkheologiya* 3:20–32.

——. 1999. Kostye ostatki zhivotnykh s poseleniya Gornyi. *Rossiskaya Arkheologiya* 1: 103–116.

Appadurai, A. 1986. *The Social Life of Things: Commodities in Cultural Perspective.* New York: Cambridge University Press.

——. 1996. *Modernity at Large.* Minneapolis: University of Minnesota Press.

Argynbaev, Kh. 1973. Nekotorye osobennosti khozyaistva Kazakhov Kopal'skogo uezda Semirechenskoi oblasti (v kontse XIX– nachale XX v.) In *Ocherki po Istorii Khozyaistva Narodov Srednei Azii i Kazakhstana,* ed. S. M. Abramzon and A. Orazob, 154–160. Leningrad: Akademiya Nauk.

Aristov, N. A. 1894. Opyt vyyasneniya etnicheskogo sostava kirgiz-kazakov Bolshoi ordy i karakirgizov na osnovanii rodoslovnykh skazannii i svedenii o syshchestvuyushchikh rodovykh deleniyakh i o rodovykh tamgakh, a taakzhe istiricheskikh danniykh nachi-nayashchikhsya antropologicheskikh issledovanii. *Zhivaya Starina* III–IV:391–486.

——. 1896. Zametki ob etnicheskom sostave tyurkskikh plemen i narodnostei i svedeniya ob ikh chislennosti. *Zhivaya Starina* III–IV:277–456.

Arkheologicheskaya Karta Kazakhstana. 1960. Almaty: Akademiya NAUK Kazakhskoi CCP.

Arutiunov, S. 1994. Ethnogenesis: Its forms and rules. *Anthropology and Archaeology of Eurasia* 33(1):79–93.

Arutiunov, S. A. and I. V. Bromlei. 1989. *Narody i kul'tury—razvitie i vzaimodeistvie.* Moskva: Nauka.

Asad, T. 1979. Equality in nomadic social systems? Notes towards the dissolution of an anthropological category. In *Pastoral Production and Society,* 419–428. Cambridge: Cambridge University Press.

Ashmore, W. and A. B. Knapp. 1999. *Archaeologies of Landscape*. Malden (MA): Blackwell.

Aubekerov, B. Zh., S. A. Nigmatova, and M. D. Frachetti. 2003. Geomorfologicheskie Osobennosti Raiona Archeologicheskogo Pamyatnika Begash Severnoi Zhongarii. In *Aktual'nye Problemy Geosistem Aridnykh Territorii*, 287–289. Almaty: Kazakh National University.

Aubekerov, B. Zh., R. Sala, S. A. Nigmatova, and Sh. Zhakupova. 2001. Paleoklimaticheskie usloviya zony Semirech'ya v epokhu bronzovogo i rannego zheleznogo vekov. In *Prirodnye i sotsial'nye problemy geografii aridnykh territorii*. Almaty: Kazakh National University.

Averkieva, Iu. 1932. Sovremennaya Amerikanskaya Etnografiya. *Sovietskaya Etnografiia* 2:97–102.

Bacon, E. 1958. *Obok: A Study of Social Structure in Eurasia*. Viking Fund Publications in Anthropology 25. New York: Wenner-Gren Foundation.

Bader, O. N., D. A. Krainov, and M. F. Kosarev. 1987. *Epokha bronzy lesnoi polosy SSSR*. Arkheologiia SSSR (Izdanie v 20 tomakh) Moskva: Nauka.

Baipakov, K. M. 1984. Arkheologicheskiye issledovaniya v yuzhnom Kazakhstane 1970–1980g. Alma-Ata: Nauka Kazakhstanskoi SSR.

_____. 1998. *Srednevekovye goroda Kazakhstana na Velikom Shelkovom puti*. Almaty: Nauka.

Baipakov, K. M. and H.-P. Francfort. 1999. *Recherches archéologiques au Kazakhstan*. Mémoires de la Mission archéologique française en Asie centrale. Paris: De Boccard.

Baipakov, K. M. and A. N. Mar'yashev. 2001. Novie dannye po izucheniyu poselenii epokhi rannego zheleznogo veka v Zhetisu. *Vestnik Instituta Arkheologii, Almaty (KZ)* 1:53–64.

Baipakov, K., G. Arbore Popescu, C. Silvi Antonini, 1998. *L'uomo d'oro la cultura delle steppe del Kazakhstan dall'età del bronzo alle grandi migrazioni*. Milano: Electa.

Bar-Yosef, O. and A. M. Khazanov. 1992. *Pastoralism in the Levant: Archaeological Materials in Anthropological Perspectives*. Madison (WI): Prehistory Press.

Barber, E. J. W. 1994. *Women's Work the First 20,000 Years : Women, Cloth, and Society in Early Times*. New York: Norton.

Barfield, Thomas J. 1981. *The Central Asian Arabs of Afghanistan: Pastoral Nomadism in Transition*. Austin: University of Texas Press.

_____. 1993. *The Nomadic Alternative*. Englewood Cliffs (NJ): Prentice Hall.

Barnard, Hans and Willeke Wendrich, eds. 2008. *The Archaeology of Mobility: Nomads in the Old and in the New World*. Cotsen Advanced Seminar Series. Los Angeles: Cotsen Insititute of Archaeology (UCLA).

Barrett, J., R. Bradley, and M. Green. 1991. *Landscape, Monuments and Society*. Cambridge: Cambridge University Press.

Barth, F. 1964. *Nomads of South Persia*. New York: Humanities Press.

_____. 1969. *Ethnic Groups and Boundaries*. Boston: Little and Brown.

Bartol'd, V. V. 1943. *Ocherk istorii Semirech'ia*. Frunze: Kirgizgosizdat.

_____. 1962–1963. *Four studies on the history of Central Asia*. Leiden: Brill.

_____. 1963–1977. *Sochineniia* (vols. 1–9). Moskva: Izd-vo Nauka.

Bartol'd, V. V. and H. A. R. Gibb. 1928. *Turkestan Down to the Mongol Invasion*. London: V. Luzac and Co.

Beck, L. 1991. *Nomad: A Year in the life of a Qashga'i Tribesman in Iran*. Berkeley: University of California Press.

Beck, U. 2000. *What is Globalization?* London: Polity Press.

Bender, Barbara. 2002. Time and landscape. *Current Anthropology* 43 (supplement):103–112.

Benecke, N. 2003. Iron Age economy of the Inner Asian steppe. A bioarchaeological perspective from the Talgar Region in the Ili River Valley, Southeastern Kazakhstan. *Euraisia Antiqua* 9:63–84.

Benecke, N., and A. von den Driesch. 2003. Horse exploitation in the Kazakh steppes during the Eneolithic and Bronze Age. In *Prehistoric Steppe Adaptation and the Horse,* ed. M. Levine, C. Renfrew, and K. Boyle, 69–82. Cambridge: Oxbow Books.

Beresneva, L. G. 1998. Rugs and felts of the Kazakhs, Kirgiz, and Karakalpak People. *Arts and the Islamic World* 33:80–84.

Bernshtam, A. N. 1952. *Istoriko-arkheologicheskie ocherki tsentralnogo Tian-shania i Pamiro-Alaia.* Moscow: Nauka.

Bichurin, N. Ya. (also Monk Iakinf). 1950. *Sobranie svedenii o narodakh, obitavshikh v Srednei Azii v drevnie vremena.* vol 1–4. Moskva: Izd-vo Akademii nauk SSSR.

Binford, L. R. 1962. Archaeology as anthropology. *American Antiquity* 28(2):217–225.

———. 1968. Methodological considerations in the use of ethnographic data. In *Man the Hunter,* ed. R. Lee and I. DeVore, 268–273. Chicago: Aldine Publishing Company.

———. 1981. Middle-range research and the role of actualistic studies. In *Bones, Ancient Men, and Modern Myths,* ed. L. R. Binford, 21–30. New York: Academic Press.

———. 1987. Data, relativism, and archaeological science. *Man* 22:391–404.

Biyashev, G. Z., B. A. Bykov, and V. P. Goloskokov. 1975. *Flora i rastitel'nye resursy Kazakhstana.* Alma-Ata: Nauka.

Boserup, E. 1965. *The Conditions of Agricultural Growth: The Economics of Agrarian Change under Population Pressure.* Chicago: Aldine Publishing.

Bourdieu, P. 1977. *Outline of a Theory of Practice.* Cambridge Studies in Social Anthropology 16. Cambridge: Cambridge University Press.

Bradburd, D. 1990. *Ambiguous Relations: Kin, Class, and Conflict Among Komachi Pastoralists.* Smithsonian Series in Ethnographic Inquiry. Washington: Smithsonian Institution Press.

Brill Olcott, M. 1981. The settlement of the Kazakh nomads. *Nomadic Peoples* 8:12–23.

Bromlei, Iu. V. 1974a. Ethnos and endogamy. *Soviet Anthropology and Archaeology* 13(1):55–69.

———. 1974b. *Soviet Ethnology and Anthropology.* Paris: Mouton, The Hague.

———. 1976. *Soviet Ethnography: Main Trends.* Problems of the Contemporary World. Social Sciences Today Editorial Board, USSR Academy of Sciences, Moscow.

———. 1981. *Sovremennyi problemu etnografii ocherki teorii i istorii.* Moskva: Nauka.

———. 1983. *Ocherki teorii etnosa.* Moskva: Nauka.

———. 1984. *Theoretical ethnography.* General Editorial Board for Foreign Publications, Moscow: Nauka.

Bromlei, Iu. V. and V. Kozlov. 1989. The theory of ethnos and ethnic process in Soviet social science. *Comparative Studies in Society and History* 31(3):425–438.

Brown, D. and D. Anthony. 1998. Bit wear, horseback riding and the Botai Site in Kazakstan. *Journal of Archaeological Science* 25(4):331–347.

Bykov, V. A. 1974. *Biologicheskaya Produktivnost' Rastitel'nosti Kazakhstana.* Alma-Ata: Nauka.

Carruthers, A. D. M. and J. H. Miller. 1913. *Unknown Mongoli: A Record of Travel and Exploration in North-West Mongolia and Dzungaria.* Philadelphia: Lippincott.

Clark, J. G. D. 1952. *Prehistoric Europe: The Economic Basis.* London: Metheuen and Co.

Clarke, John I. 1959. Studies of semi-nomadism in North Africa *Economic Geography*, 35(2):95–108.

Chang, Claudia, Norbert Benecke, Fedor P. Grigoriev, Arlene M. Rosen, and Perry A. Tourtellotte. 2003. Iron age society and chronology in south-east Kazakhstan. *Antiquity* 77(296):298–312.

Chavannes, E. 1900. *Documents sur les Tou-kiue (turcs) occidentaux recueillis et commentés, suivi de notes additionnelles. (Présenté à l'Académie impériale des sciences de St.-Pétersbourg le 23 ao ut 1900).* Paris, Taipei: Librairie d'Amérique et d'Orient; Adrien-Maisonneuve, Cheng Wen.

Chekeres, A. I. 1973. *Pogoda, Klimat i otgonno-pastbishchnoe zhivotnovodstvo.* Leningrad: Gidrometeoizdat.

Chen, K. T. and F. Hiebert. 1995. The late prehistory of Xinjiang in relation to its neighbors. *Journal of World Prehistory* 9(2):243–300.

Chernikov, S. S. 1960. The Eastern Kazakhstan Expedition, 1952. 126–134. Cambridge (MA): Harvard University Press.

Chernykh, E. N. 1992. *Ancient Metallurgy in the USSR: The Early Metal Age.* Cambridge (UK): Cambridge University Press.

———. 1997. *Kargaly: zabytyi mir.* Moskva: Institut arkheologii (Rossiiskaia akademiia nauk).

———. 2002. *Kargaly.* Moskva: Iazyki slavianskoi kul'tury.

———. 2004. Kargaly: The largest and most ancient metallurgical complex on the border of Europe and Asia. In *Metallurgy in Ancient Eastern Eurasia from the Urals to the Yellow River,* ed. Katheryn M. Linduff, 223–238. Lewiston: Edwin Mellen Press.

Chernykh, Evgenii, Evgenii V. Kuz'minykh and L. B. Orlovskaia. 2004. Ancient metallurgy of northeast Asia: From the Urals to the Saiano-Altai. In *Metallurgy in Ancient Eastern Eurasia from the Urals to the Yellow River,* ed. Katheryn M. Linduff, 15–36. Lewiston: Edwin Mellen Press.

Chernykh, E. N., L. I. Avilova and L. B. Orlovskaia. 2000. *Metallurgicheskie provintsii i radiouglerodnaia khronologiia (Metallurgical provinces and radiocarbon chronology).* Moskva: Institut Arkheologii RAN.

Chernykh, E. N., L. I. Avilova, L. B. Orlovskaya and S. V. Kuz'minykh. 2002. Metallurgiya v tsirkumpontiiskom areale: ot edinstva k raspadu. *Rossiiskaya Arkheologiya* 1:5–23.

Chernykh, E. N., S. V. Kuz'minykh, and N. I. Merpert. 1989. *Drevniaia metallurgiia Severnoi Evrazii seiminsko-turbinskii fenomen.* Moskva: Nauka.

Childe, V. Gordon. 1925. *The Dawn of European Civilization.* London: Kegan Paul.

———. 1951. *Man Makes Himself.* New York: Mentor Books

Chlenova, N. L. 1972. *Khronologiia pamiatnikov karasukskoi epokhi.* Materialy i issledovaniia po arkheologii SSSR; no. 182. Moskva:Materialy i issledovaniia po arkheologii SSSR.

———. 1994. *Pamiatniki kontsa epokhi bronzy v Zapadnoi Sibiri.* Moskva: Rossiiskaia Akademiia Nauk, Institut Arkheologii.

Christian, D. 1998. *A History of Russia, Central Asia, and Mongolia.* Malden (MA): Blackwell Publishers.

Cook, C. W. and J. Stubbendieck. 1986. *Range Research: Basic Problems and Techniques.* Denver: Society for Range Management.

Cribb, R. 1991. *Nomads in Archaeology.* Cambridge: Cambridge University Press.

Dansereau, Pierre 1975. *Inscape and Landscape: The Human Perception of the Environment.* New York: Columbia University Press.

Dakhshleiger, G. F. 1978. Settlement, and traditional social institutions of the formerly nomadic Kazakh people. In *The Nomadic Alternative,* ed. W. Weissleder, 361–369. Paris: Mouton.

Daly, P. T. 2003. *Social Practice and Material Culture : The Use, Discard and Deposition of Ceramic Material at Two Iron Age Hillforts in Oxfordshire.* PhD Dissertation, University of Oxford.

Danti, M. D. 2000. *Early Bronze Age Settlement and Land Use in the Tell Es-Sweyhat Region, Syria.* PhD Dissertation, University of Pennsylvania.

Demin, Yu. I. 1973. *Tablitsy rascheta kormovykh ploshchadey.* Moscow: Nauka.

Demko, G. J. 1969. *The Russian Colonization of Kazakhstan, 1896–1916.* Bloomington: Indiana University publications.

Devlet, M. A. 1980. *Sibirskie poiasnye azhurnye plastiny II v. do n.e.-I v. n.e..* Arkheologiia SSSR : svod arkheologicheskikh istochnikov. Moskva: Arkheologiia SSSR Izd-vo "Nauka".

———. 1998. *Petroglify na dne Saianskogo Moria gora Aldy-Mozaga.* Moskva: "Pamiatniki istoricheskoi mysli".

Di Cosmo, Nicola. 2002. *Ancient China and its Enemies: The Rise of Nomadic Power in East Asian History.* Cambridge (UK): Cambridge University Press.

Dincauze, D. F. 2000. *Environmental Archaeology: Principles and Practice.* Cambridge: Cambridge University Press.

Dragadze, T. 1980. The place of "ethnos" theory in Soviet anthropology. In *Soviet and Western Anthropology,* ed. E. Gellner, 161–170. New York: Columbia University Press.

Du Toit, P. C. V. 2000. Estimating grazing index values for plants from arid regions. *Journal of Range Management* 53(5):529–536.

Durkheim, E. 1933. *The Division of Labor in Society.* New York: Free Press.

Dudd, S. N., R. P. Evershed and M. A. Levine. 2003. Organic residue analysis of lipids in potsherds from the early Eneolithic settlement of Botai, Kazakhstan. In *Prehistoric Steppe Adaptation and the Horse,* ed. M. A. Levine, C. Renfrew and K. Boyle, 45–54. McDonald Institute Monograph. Cambridge: McDonald Institute for Archaeological Research.

Dyson-Hudson, R. and N. Dyson-Hudson. 1980. Nomadic Pastoralism. *Annual Review of Anthropology* 9:15–61.

Environmental Systems Research Institute. 1994. *Digital Chart of The World for Use with ESRI Desktop Software, Arcdata.* Redlands, CA, USA.

Epimakhov, A. V. 2003. Analiz Tendentsii Sotsial'no-ekonomicheskogo Razvitiya Naseleniya Urala Epokhi Bronzy. *Rossiskaya Arkheologiya* (1):83–90.

Erickson, C. 2000. The Lake Titicaca basin: A Precolumbian built landscape. In *Imperfect Balance: Landscape Transformations in the Precolumbian Andes,* ed. D. Lentz, 311–356. New York: Columbia University Press.

Fedorin, Yu. V. 1977. *Zemel'nye resursy predgornykh ravnin Kazakhstana.* Alma-Ata: Kainar.

Fedorova-Davydova, A. 1973. K probleme Andronovskoi Kul'tury. In *Problemy Arkheologii Urala i Sibiri,* ed. V. N. Chernetsova, 133–152. Moscow: Nauka.

Fedorovich, B. A. 1973. Prirodnye usloviya aridnykh zon SSSR i puti razvitiya vnikh zhivotnovodstva. In *Ocherki po Istorii Khozyaistva Narodov Srednei Azii i Kazakhstana,* ed. S. M. Abramzon and A. Orazob, 207–222. Leningrad: Akademiya Nauk SSSR.

Fleure, Herbert J. and Harold Peake. 1928. *The Steppe and The Sown*. New Haven: Yale University Press.

Formozov, A. A. 1951. K voprosu o proiskhozhdenii Andronovskoi kul'tury. *Kratkie Soobshcheniya Instituta Istorii* 39:3–18.

Frachetti, Michael D. 2002. Bronze Age exploitation and political dynamics of the eastern Eurasian steppe zone. In *Interaction: East and West in Eurasia*, ed. K. Boyle, C. Renfrew, and M. Levine, 87–96. McDonald Institute Monographs. Cambridge (UK).

———. 2004. *Bronze Age Pastoral Landscapes of Eurasia and the Nature of Social Interaction in the Mountain Steppe Zone of Eastern Kazakhstan*. Ph.D. dissertation, University of Pennsylvania. Ann Arbor: University Microfilms.

———. 2006a. Digital archaeology and the scalar structure of space and time: Modeling mobile societies of prehistoric Central Asia. In *Digital Archaeology*, ed. T. Evans and P. T. Daly, 128–147. London: Routledge.

———. 2006b. Ancient nomads of the Andronovo Culture: The globalization of the Eurasian steppe during prehistory. In *Of Gold and Grass: Nomads of Kazakhstan*, ed. C. Chang and K. Guroff, 21–28. Bethesda: Foundation for International Arts and Education.

———. 2006c. The Dzhungar Mountains archaeology project: Reconstructing Bronze Age life in the mountains of Eastern Kazakhstan. In *Beyond the Steppe and the Sown*, ed. D. L. Peterson, L. M. Popova and A. T. Smith, 122–141. Boston: Brill Academic Publishing.

———. 2008. Variability and dynamic landscapes of mobile pastoralism in ethnography and prehistory. In *The Archaeology of Mobility: Nomads in the Old and in the New World*, eds. H. Barnard and W. Wendrich. Cotsen Advanced Seminar Series 4, 366–396. Los Angeles: Cotsen Institute of Archaeology (UCLA).

———. In press. Differentiated landscapes and non-uniform complexity among Bronze Age societies of the Eurasian steppe. In *Monuments, Metals And Mobility: Trajectories of Social Complexity in the Late Prehistoric Eurasian Steppe*, eds. Bryan Hanks And Katheryn Linduff. Cambridge: Cambridge University Press.

Frachetti, Michael D. and Christopher Chippindale. 2002. Alpine imagery, Alpine space, Alpine time; and prehistoric human experience. In *European Landscapes of Rock-Art*, ed. G. Nash and C. Chippindale, 116–143. London: Routledge.

Frachetti, Michael D. and Alexei N. Mar'yashev, 2007. Long-term occupation and seasonal settlement of Eastern Eurasian pastoralists at Begash, Kazakhstan. *Journal of Field Archaeology* 32(3):221–42.

Frank, A. G. 1992. *The Centrality of Central Asia*. Amsterdam: VU University Press.

Fuhrmann, J. T., E. C. Bock, and L. I. Twarog. 1971. *Essays on Russian Intellectual History*. Walter Prescott Webb Memorial Lectures. Austin: University of Texas Press.

Galaty, J. G. and D. L. Johnson.1990. Introduction: Pastoral Systems in global perspective. In *The World of Pastoralism*, ed. J. G. Galaty and D. L. Johnson, 1–32. New York: The Guilford Press.

Gaul, J. A. 1943. Observations on the Bronze Age in the Yenisei valley, Siberia. In *Studies in the Anthropology of Oceania and Asia*, ed. C. Coon, J. Andrews, and C. Ashenden, 149–186. Cambridge (MA): The Museum Press.

Gellner, E. 1980. A Russian Marxist philosophy of history. In *Soviet & Western Anthropology*, ed. E. Gellner, 59–82. London: Duckworth.

———. 1988. *State and Society in Soviet Thought*. Oxford: Blackwell.

Gening, V. F., G. V. Zdanovich and V. V. Gening. 1992. *Sintashta*. Chelyabinsk: Yuzhnoe-Uralskoe Knizhkoe Izdatel'stvo.

Germain, R. D. 2000. *Globalization and its Critics: Perspectives from Political Economy*. New York: St. Martin's Press, in association with the Political Economy Research Centre, University of Sheffield.

Giddens, A. 1984. *The Constitution of Society: Outline of a Theory of Structuration*. Cambridge: Polity Press.

Gimbutas, M. A. 1958. *Middle Ural Sites and the Chronology of Northern Eurasia*. Gloucester: J. Bellows.

————. 1965. *Bronze Age Cultures in Central and Eastern Europe*. Paris: Mouton.

Golden, P. B. 1992. *An Introduction to the History of the Turkic Peoples: Ethnogenesis and State-Formation in Medieval and Early Modern Eurasia and the Middle East*. Wiesbaden: Turcologica O. Harrassowitz.

————. 2003. *Nomads and Sedentary Societies in Medieval Eurasia*. Washington DC: American Historical Association.

Goloskokov, V. P. 1984. *Flora Dzhungarskogo Alatau*. Almaty: Nauka Kazakhskogo SSR.

Gomboev, B., I. Sekulich, T. Pykhalaoava, O. Anankhonov, A. Tysbikova, O. Mognonova, T. Borisova, and A. Beshentsev. 1996. The present condition and use of pasture in the Barguzin Valley. In *Culture and Environment in Inner Asia,* ed. C. Humphrey and D. Sneath, 124–140. Cambridge: White Horse.

Gorodtsov, V. A. 1927. *Tipologicheskii metod v arkheologii*. Ryazan: Nauka.

Görsdorf, V. J., H. Parzinger, A. Nagler, and N. Leont'ev. 1998. Neue 14C-Datierungen fur die Sibirische Steppe und ihre Konsequenzen fur die regionale Bronzezeitchronologie. *Eurasia Antiqua* 4:73–80.

Görsdorf J., H. Parzinger and A. Nagler. 2004. 14C Dating of the Siberian Steppe Zone from Bronze Age to Scythian time, in E. Scott, M. Alekseev and A. Yu. Zaitseva, eds., *Impact of the Environment on Human Migration in Eurasia*. Chelyabinsk: Chelyabinsk Gosudarstvenyi Universitet.

Görsdorf, Jochen, Hermann Parzinger, and Anatoli Nagler. 2001. New radiocarbon dates of the North Asian steppe zone and its consequences for the chronology. *Radiocarbon* 43(2):115–120.

Goryachev, A. A. 2001. O Pegrebal'nom Obryade v Pamyatnikakh Kulsaiskogo Tipa. In *Istoriya i Arkheologiya Semirech'ya,* ed. A. N. Mar'yashev, Yu. A. Motov, T. A. Egorova, and A. A. Goryachev, 45–61. Almaty: "XXI vek".

————. 2004. The Bronze Age archaeological memorials in Semirechie. In *Metallurgy in Ancient Eastern Eurasia from the Urals to the Yellow River,* ed. Katheryn M. Linduff, 109–138. Lewiston: Edwin Mellen Press.

Goryachev, A. A. and A. N. Mar'yashev. 1998. Nouveaux sites du Bronze Recent au Semirech'e (Kazakhstan). *Paleorient* 24(1):71–80.

Greenfield, H. 1999. The advent of transhumant pastoralism in temperate southeast Europe: A zooarchaeological perspective from the Central Balkans. In *Transhumant Pastoralism in Southern Europe: Recent Perspectives from Archaeology, History and Ethnology,* ed. L. Bartosiewicz and H. J. Greenfield, 15–36. Budapest: Archaeolingua.

Gryaznov, M. P. 1929. *Pazyrykskoe kniazheskoe pogrebenie na Altae*. M. P. Griaznov.

_____. 1969. *The Ancient Civilization of Southern Siberia*. New York: Cowles Book Co.

Gryaznov, M. P., O. I. Davidan, K. M. Skalon and Gosudarstvennyi Ermitazh (Soviet Union). 1955–1956. *Pervobytnaia kul'tura*. Moskva: Putevoditeli po vystavkam Iskusstvo.

Gryaznov, M. P. 1955. Nekotorye voprosy istorii slozheniya i razvitiya rannikh kochevykh obshchestv Kazakhstana i Yuzhnoi Sibiri. *Kratkie Soobshchennia Institut Etnografii* 24.

Grousset, R. 1970 (1939). *L'empire des Steppes: Attila. Gengis-Khan. Tamerlan*. Paris: Bibliothèque Historique Payot.

_____. 1969. *The Ancient Civilization of Southern Siberia*. London: Barrie & Rocklift.

Gvozdetskii, N. A. and V. A. Nikolaev. 1971. *Kazakhstan Ocherk prirody*. Moskva: Mysl.

Hägerstrand, T. 1967. *Innovation Diffusion as a Spatial Process*. Chicago: University of Chicago Press.

_____. 1975. Space, time and human conditions. In *Dynamic Allocation of Urban Space*, ed. A. Karlqvist, L. Lundqvist, and F. Snickars, 3–14. Lexington (MA): Lexington Books.

Halstead, P. and J. O'Shea. 1989. *Bad Year Economics: Cultural Responses to Risk and Uncertainty*. New York: Cambridge University Press.

Hanks, B. K., A. V. Epimakhov, and A. C. Renfrew. 2007. Towards a refined chronology for the Bronze Age of the Southern Urals, Russia. *Antiquity* 81(312):353–67.

Haydar, Mirza and W. M. Thackston. 1996. *Mirza Haydar Dughlat's Tarikh-i-Rashidi: A History of the Khans of Moghulistan*. Cambridge (MA): Harvard University Press.

Heady, H. F. and R. D. Child. 1994. *Rangeland Ecology and Management*. Boulder (CO): Westview Press.

Hemphill, Brian E. and James P. Mallory. 2004. Horse-mounted invaders from the Russo-Kazakh steppe or agricultural colonists from western Central Asia? A craniometric investigation of the Bronze Age settlement of Xinjiang. *American Journal of Physical Anthropology* 124:199–222.

Hiebert, Fredrik T. 1994. *Origins of the Bronze Age: Oasis Civilization in Central Asia*. Cambridge (MA): Peabody Museum of Archaeology and Ethnology, Harvard University.

_____. 2002. Bronze Age interaction between the Eurasian Steppe and Central Asia. In *Ancient Interactions: East and West in Eurasia*, ed. K. Boyle, C. Renfrew, and M. Levine, 237–48. Cambridge (UK): McDonald Institute Monographs.

Hodder, I. 1990. Archaeology and the postmodern. *Anthropology Today* 6:13–15.

Hole, F. 1978. Pastoral nomadism in western Iran. In *Explorations in Ethnoarchaeology*, ed. R. A. Gould, 127–167. Albuquerque: University of New Mexico Press.

Honeychurch, William and Chunag Amartuvshin. 2007. Hinterlands, urban centers, and mobile settings: The "new" Old World archaeology from the Eurasian Steppe. *Asian Perspectives* 46(1):36–64.

Hopkirk, P. 1994. *The Great Game: The Struggle for Empire in Central Asia*. New York, Tokyo: Kodansha Globe Kodansha International.

Hudson, A. E. 1938. *Kazak Social Structure*. New Haven, London: Yale University Press, Oxford University Press.

Humphrey, C. 1996. *Shamans and Elders: Experience, Knowledge, and Power among the Duar Mongols*. Oxford: Oxford University Press.

Humphrey, C. and D. Sneath. 1996. *Culture and Environment in Inner Asia*. Cambridge: White Horse.

―――. 1999. *The end of Nomadism? Society, State, and the Environment in Inner Asia*. Durham (NC): Duke University Press.

Huntington, E. 1907. *The Pulse of Asia: A Journey in Central Asia Illustrating the Geographical Basis of History*. Boston, New York: Houghton, Mifflin and Company.

Ingold, Timothy. 1985. Khazanov on Nomads. *Current Anthropology* 26(3):384–387.

―――. 1993. The temporality of the landscape. *World Archaeology* 25:152–174.

―――. 2000. *The Perception of the Environment: Essays on Livelihood, Dwelling and Skill*. London, New York: Routledge.

Irons, W. 1974. Nomadism as a political adaptation: The Case of the Yomut Turkmen. *American Ethnologist* 1:635–657.

Jasny, N. 1949. *The Socialized Agriculture of the USSR: Plans and Performance*. Stanford: Stanford University Press.

Jettmar, Karl. 1965. *L'art des Steppes; Le Style Animalier Eurasiatique, Genèse et Arrière-plan Social*. Paris: A. Michel.

―――. 1966. *Traditionen der Steppendluturen bei indoiranischen Bergvol/kern*. 18–23. Heidelberg: Universität Südasien-Institut-Jahrbuch.

Johnson, Douglas L. 1969. *The Nature of Nomadism: A Comparative Study of Pastoral Migrations in Southwestern Asia and Northern Africa*. Chicago: Department of Geography, University of Chicago.

Johnson, Matthew. 2007. *Ideas of Landscape*. Oxford: Blackwell Publishing.

Jones-Bley, K. and D. G. Zdanovich. 2002. *Complex Societies of Central Eurasia from the Third to the First Millennium BCE: Regional Specifics in Light of Global Models*. Washington: Institute for the Study of Man.

Juvaynī, 'Alā'-al-Dīn 'Aṭa' Malik, Qasvini, mirza Muhammad, and John Andrew Boyle. 1997. Genghis Khan: the history of the world conqueror. Manchester, England: Manchester University Press.

Kadirbaev, M. K. and Ch. Kurmankulov. 1992. *Kul'tura Drevnik skotovodov i metallurgov Sari-Arki*. Almaty: Akademiya NAUK Kazakhstana.

Kalieva, S. S. and V. N. Logvin. 1997. *Skotovody Turgaya v tret'em tysyacheletii do nashei ery*. Kystanai: Akademiia Nauk.

Kalinina, A. W. 1974. *Osnovnye tipy pastbishch Mongol'skoi Narodkhoi Respubliki (ikh struktura i produktivnost')*. Leningrad: Nauka

Karabaspakova, K. M. 1987. K voprosu o kul'turnoi prinalezhnosti pamyanikov epkhi pozdnei bronzy Severo-Vostochnogo Semirech'ya i ikh svyaz' s pamyatnikami Tsentral'nogo Kazakhstana. In *Voprosy Periodizatsii Arkheologicheskikh Pamyatnikov Tsentral'nogo i Severnogo Kazakhstana*, ed. Kh. G. Omarova, 90–101. Karaganda: Karaganda Gos. Univ.

―――. 1989. Etnokul'turnye svyazi naseleniya Epokhi Pozdnei Bronzy Semirech'ya (Po materialam mogil'nika Arasan). In *Margulanovskie Chteniya: Sbornik Materialov Konferentsiya*, ed. K.M. Baipakov. Alma-Ata: Nauka.

Kavoori, P. S. 1999. *Pastoralism in Expansion: The Transhuming Herders of Western Rajasthan*. Studies in Social Ecology and Environmental History. New Delhi, New York: Oxford University Press.

Kharitonov, Yu. D. 1980. *Kormovaya Tsennost' Stepnykh Pastbishch Yugo-zapadnogo Zabaikal'ya.* Novosibirsk: Nauka.

Khazanov, Anatoly. 1978. Characteristics of communities in the Eurasian Steppes. In *The Nomadic Alternative,* ed. W. Weissleder, 119–126. Paris: Mouton Publishers.

———. 1994. *Nomads and the Outside World.* Madison: University of Wisconsin Press.

Khlobystina, M. D. 1972. Paleosotsiologicheskie problemy yuzhnosibirskogo eneolita. *Sovetskaya Arkheologiya* 1972(2):32–41.

———. 1973. Proiskhozhdennie i razvitie kul'tury rannei bronzy yuzhnoi Sibiri. *Sovetskaya Arkheologiya* 1973(1):24–38.

Khotinskiy, N. A. 1984a. Holocene climatic changes. In *Late Quaternary Environments of the Soviet Union,* ed. A. A. Velichko, H. E. Wright, and C. W. Barnosky, 305–309. Minneapolis: University of Minnesota Press.

———. 1984b. Holocene vegetation history. In *Late Quaternary Environments of the Soviet Union,* ed. A. A. Velichko, H. E. Wright, and C. W. Barnosky, 179–200. Minneapolis: University of Minnesota Press.

Khudyakov, Yu. S. 1986. *Vooryzhenie srednevekovykh kochevnikov Yuzhnoi Sibiri i Tsentral'noi Azii.* Novosibirsk: Nauka.

Kiselev, S. V. 1951. *Drevniaia istoriia IUzhnoi Sibiri.* Moskva: Izd-vo Akademii nauk SSSR.

Kislenko, A. M., 1993. Opyt rekonstruktsii eneoliticheskogo zhilishcha, in *Problemy rekonstruktsii khozyaistva I tekhnologii po dannym arkheologii.* Petropavlovsk: Nauka.

Kislenko, A. and N. Tatarintseva. 1999. The eastern Ural steppe at the end of the Stone Age. In *Late Prehistoric Exploitation of the Eurasian steppe,* ed. M. Levine, Y. Rassamakin and A. Kislenko, 183–216. Cambridge (UK): McDonald Institute for Archaeological Research.

Klimanov, V. A. 1997. "Late Glacial Climate in Northern Eurasia: The Last Climatic Cycle". *Quaternary International : the Journal of the International Union for Quaternary Research.* 41/42:141.

Knapp, A. B. and W. Ashmore. 1999. Archaeological landscapes: constructed, conceptualized, and ideational. In *Archaeologies of Landscape: Contemporary Perspectives,* ed. W. Ashmore and A. B. Knapp, 1–30. Oxford: Blackwell.

Kohl, Philip L. 2007. *The Making of Bronze Age Eurasia.* Cambridge World Archaeology. Cambridge, UK: Cambridge University Press.

Kohler-Rollefson, I. 1992. A model for the development of nomadic pastoralism on the Transjordanian Plateau. In *Pastoralism in the Levant,* ed. O. Bar-Yosef and A. Khazanov, 11–18. Madison (WI): Prehistory Press.

Kopytoff, I. 1986. The cultural biography of things: Commoditization as process. In *The Social Life of Things: Commodities in Cultural Perspective,* ed. A. Appadurai, 64–94. New York: Cambridge University Press.

Koryakova, L. N. 1998. Cultural relationships in north-central Eurasia. In *Archaeology and Language II: Correlating Archaeological and Linguistic Hypotheses,* ed. R. Blench and M. Spriggs, 209–219. London: Routledge.

———. 2002. Social landscape of Central Eurasia in the Bronze and Iron Ages: Tendencies, factors, and limits of transformation. In *Complex Societies of Central Eurasia from the Third to the First Millnnium BCE,* ed. K. Jones-Bley and D. G. Zdanovich, 97–118. Washington DC: Institute for the Study of Man.

Koryakova, L. N., and A. V. Epimakhov. 2007. *The Urals and Western Siberia in the Bronze and Iron ages*. Cambridge World Archaeology. Cambridge: Cambridge University Press.

Kosarev, M. F. 1981. *Bronzovyi Vek Zapadnoi Sibiri*. Moskva: Nauka.

———. 1984. *Zapadnaia Sibir' v drevnosti*. Moskva: Nauka.

Koster, Harold Albert. 1977. *The Ecology of Pastoralism in Relation to Changing Patterns of Land Use in the Northeast Peloponnese*. Unpublished PhD Dissertation: University of Pennsylvania.

Krader, L. 1963. *Social Organization of the Mongol-turkic Pastoral Nomads*. Ural Altaic Series. Bloomington: Indiana University Publishing.

———. 1980. The orgins of the state among the nomads of Asia. In *Soviet and Western Anthropology*, ed. E. Gellner, 135–150. New York: Columbia University Press.

Kremenetski, C. V., and Olga A. Chichagova and Nathalia I. Shishlina. 1999. Palaeoecological evidence for Holocene vegetation, climate and landuse change in the low Don basin and Kalmuk area, southern Russia. *Vegetative History and Archaeobotany* 8:233–246.

Kremenetski, C. V. 2003. Steppe and forest-steppe belt of Eurasia: Holocene environmental history. In *Prehistoric Steppe Adaptation and the Horse*, ed. M. Levine, C. Renfrew, and K. Boyle, 11–28. Cambridge (UK): McDonald Institute for Archaeological Research.

Krivtsova-Grakova, O. A. 1948. *Alekseevskoe poselenie i mogil'nik*. Trudy Gosudarstvennogo Istoricheskogo Muzeya XVII. Moskva: Nauka.

———. 1955. *Stepnoe Povolzhe i Prichernomore v epokhu pozdnei bronzy*. Materialy Issledovaniya Arkheologii No. 46. Moscow: Nauka.

Kuftin, B. 1926. *Kirgiz-Kazaki: kul'tura i byt*. Ethnologicheskie ocherki no. 2. Moskva: TSentral'nogo muzei narodovedeniia.

Kurylev, Vadim P. 1977. Osnovnye tipy skotovodcheskogo khozyaistva Kazakhov (konets XIX–nachalo XX v.). In *Areal'nye Issledovanuya v Yazykoznanii i Etnografii*, ed. M.A. Borodina, 241–242. Leningrad: Nauka.

Kuz'mina, E. E. 1964a. Andronovskoe poselenie i mogil'nik Shandasha. *Kratkie Soobshcheniya Instituta Arkheologii* 98:102–108.

———. 1964b. Periodizatsiya mogil'nikov elenovskogo mikroraiona andronozhskoi kul'tury. In *Pamyatniki kamennogo i bronzovogo vekov Evrazii*, 121–140. Moscow: Nauka.

———. 1986. *Drevneishie skotovody ot Urala do Tian'-Shania*. Frunze: Ilim.

———. 1988. Kulturnaya i etnicheskaya atributsiya pastusheskikh plemen Kazakhstana i srednii Azii zpokhii bronzu. *Vestnik Drevnei Istorii* 185(2):35–59.

———. 1994. *Otkuda prishli indoarii? material'naia kul'tura plemen andronovskoi obshchnosti i proiskhozhdenie indoirantsev*. Moskva: MGP "Kalina".

———. 1998. Cultural connections of the Tarim Basin people and pastoralists of the Asian steppes in the Bronze Age. In *The Bronze Age Peoples of Eastern Central Asia*, ed. V. Mair, 63–98. Philadelphia: University of Pennsylvania Museum Publications.

———. 2004. Historical Perspectives on the Andronovo and early metal use in Eastern Asia. In *Metallurgy in Ancient Eastern Eurasia from the Urals to the Yellow River*, ed. Katheryn M. Linduff, 37–84. Lewiston: Edwin Mellen Press.

Kuz'mina, E. E., and A. A. Marushchenko. 1966. *Metallicheskie izdeliia eneolita i bronzovogo veka v Srednei Azii*. Arkheologiya SSSR, vyp. V4–9. Moskva: Izd-vo "Nauka".

Lamberg-Karlovsky, C. C. 2002. Archaeology and language: The Indo-Iranians. *Current Anthropology* 43(1):63–88.

Larin, Iu. V. 1937. *Kormovye rasteniya estestvennykh senokosov i pastbishch SSSR.* Leningrad: Lenin Academy of Agricultural Sciences.

———. 1962a. *Pasture Rotation: System for the Care and Utilization of Pastures.* Jerusalem: Israel Program for Scientific Translations.

———. 1962b. *Pasture Economy and Meadow Cultivation.* Jerusalem: Published for the National Foundation, Washington, D.C.

Lattimore, O. 1934. *The Mongols of Manchuria: Their Tribal Divisions, Geographical Distribution, Historical Relations with Manchus and Chinese, and Present Political Problems; with Maps.* New York: The John Day Company.

———. 1940. *Inner Asian Frontiers of China.* Boston: Beacon Press.

Lavrenko, E. M. and Z. V. Karamysheva. 1993. Steppes of the former Soviet Union and Mongolia. In *Ecosystems of the World: Natural Grasslands,* ed. R. T. Coupland, 3–60. New York: Elsevier.

Lees, S. H. and D. G. Bates. 1974. The origins of specialized nomadic pastoralism: A systemic model. *American Antiquity* 39(2):187–193.

Leslie, Paul W., and Michael A. Little. 1999. *Turkana Herders of the Dry Savanna: Ecology and Biobehavioral Response of Nomads to an Uncertain Environment.* Research Monographs on Human Population Biology. Oxford: Oxford University Press.

Levin, M. G. and N. N. Cheboksarov. 1955. Khozyaistvenno-kulturnye tipy i istoriko-etnograficheskie oblast. *Sovetskaya Etnologiya* 4:3–17.

Levine, Marsha (ed). 1999a. *Late Prehistoric Exploitation of the Eurasian Steppe.* McDonald Institute Monographs. Cambridge: McDonald Institute for Archaeological Research.

———. 1999b. Botai and the origins of horse domestication. *Journal of Anthropological Archaeology.* 18(1):29.

———. 2003. Focusing on central Eurasian archaeology: East meets west. In *Prehistoric Steppe Adaptation and the Horse,* ed. M. A. Levine, C. Renfrew and K. Boyle, 1–8. Cambridge: McDonald Institute for Archaeological Research.

Levine, M., C. Renfrew, and M. Boyle (eds.) 2003. *Prehistoric Steppe Adaptation and the Horse.* McDonald Institute for Archaeological Research: Cambridge.

Levshin, A. I. 1840. *Description des Hordes et des Steppes des Kirghiz-Kazaks ou Kirghiz-Kaïssaks, par Alexis de Levchine.* Paris, Ann Arbor (MI): Imprimerie Royale.

Loman, V. G. 1987. Dongol'skii Tip Keramiki. In *Voprosy Periodizatsii Arkheologicheskikh Pamyatnikov Tsentral'nogog i Severnogog Kazakhstana,* ed. Kh. G. Omarova, 115–129. Karaganda: Karaganda Gos. Univ.

———. 1990. Osobennosti goncharnoi tekhnologii epokhi pozdnei bronzy Tsentral'nogo Kazakhstana. *Kratkie Soobshchenniya Instituta Arkheologii* 203:47–53.

———. 1993. *Goncharnaya Tekhnologiya Naseleniya Tsentral'nogo Kazakhstana Vtoroi Poloviny II-ogo Tysyacheletiya do n. e.* Moscow: Nauka.

Lunin, B. V. 1973. *Russkie puteshestvenniki i issledovateli o kirgizakh.* Frunze: Ilim.

Lyonnet, B. 1996. *Sarazm (Tadjikistan) céramiques (Chalcolithique et Bronze ancien).* Paris: Mémoires de la Mission Archéologique Française en Asie Centrale De Boccard.

Mair, Victor H. 1998. *The Bronze Age and early Iron Age peoples of eastern Central Asia.* Journal of Indo-European studies, no. 26. Washington DC: Institute for the Study of Man in collaboration with the University of Pennsylvania Museum Publications.

Maksimova, A. G. 1961. Mogil'nik epokhi bronzy v urochishche Karakuduk. In *Novye Materialy po Arkheologii i Etnographii Kazakhstana*. Alma-Ata: Nauka.

Maksimova, A. G., A. I. Ermolaeva and A. N. Mar'yashev. 1985. *Naskal'nye Isobrazheniya Yrochishcha Tamgaly*. Alma-Ata: Nauka.

Mallory, J. P. 1989. *In Search of the Indo-Europeans: Language, Archaeology, and Myth*. New York: Thames and Hudson.

Mallory, J. P. and V. H. Mair. 2000. *The Tarim Mummies: Ancient China and the Mystery of the Earliest Peoples from the West*. New York: Thames and Hudson.

Mar'yashev, A. N. 1994. *Petroglyphs of South Kazakhstan and Semirechye*. Almaty: Akademiia Nauk.

Mar'yashev, A. N. and A. A. Goryachev. 1993. Voprosy tipologii i khronologii pamyatnikov epokhi bronzy semirechiya. *Rossiyaskaya Arkheologiya* (1):5–20.

————. 1996. *Otchet: o polevykh issledovaniyakh otryada otdepa arkheologicheskoi tekhnologii v 1995 g (Delo #2316/sv 181)*. Almaty: Archive of the Institute of Archaeology.

————. 1998. *Naskal'nye Izobrazheniya Semirech'ya*. Almaty: Akademiia Nauk.

————. 1999. Pamyatniki Kulsaiskogo tipa epokhi pozdnei i final'noi bronzy Semirechie. In *Istoriya i Arkheologiya Semirechiya*, ed. A. N. Mar'yashev, Yu. A. Motov, A. E. Rogozhinski, and A. A. Goryachev, 44–56. Almaty: Institute of Archaeology.

————. 2002. *Izobrazheniya Semirech'ya*. Almaty: "Fond" XXI c.

Mar'yashev, A. N. and K. M. Karabaspakova. 1988. Novye Pamyaatniki Epokhi Bronzy Vostochnogo Semirech'ya. In *Drevnie Pamyaatniki Severnoi Azii i ikh Okhrannye raskopki*, ed. V. E. Medvedev and Yu. S. Khudyakov, 24–39. Novosibirsk: Nauka.

Mar'yashev A. N and M. D. Frachetti, 2008. Issledovanie mogil'nikov i poseleniya u sela Bigash v vostochnom Semirech'ye. *Istoria i Arkeologiya Semirech'ya* 3: 100–105.

Margulan, A. Kh. 1979. *Begazy-Dandybaevskaya kul'tura Tsentral'nogo Kazakhstana*. Alma-Ata: Nauka-Kazakhskoi SSR.

————. 1984. Ocherk zhizn i deyatel'nosti Ch. Ch. Valikhanova. In *Sobranie sochinenii v piati tomakh*, ed. Ch. C. Valikhanov, Z. M. Abdil'din, and A. K. Margulan, 9–103. Alma-Ata: Glavn. red. Kazakhskoi Sov. entsiklopedii.

Margulan, A. X., K. A. Akishev, M. K. Kadirbaev and A. M. Orazbaev. 1966. *Drevnaya Kul'tura Tsentral'nogo Kazakhstana*. Almaty: NAUKA Kazakhskoi SSSR.

Marr, Nikolai I. 1920. *Yafeticheskii Kavkaz i tretii etnicheskiye element v sozdanii sredizemnomorskoi kul'tury*. Materialy po Yafeticheskomu Yazykoznaniyu, 11. Leiptsig: Rossiiskaya akademiya nauk.

————. 1926. *Po etapam razvitiia iafeticheskoi teorii; sbornik statei*. Moskva: Izdaniia.

Marshall, Fiona and Elisabeth Hildebrand. 2004. Cattle before crops: The beginnings of food production in Africa. *The Journal of World Prehistory* 16(2):99–143.

Marx, K. and F. Engels. 1967. *Capital: A Critique of Political Economy*. New York: International Publishers.

Masanov, N. E. 1995. *Kochevaia tsivilizatsiia kazakhov osnovy zhiznedeiatel nosti nomadnogo obshchestva*. Almaty, Moskva: Sotsinvest. Gorizont.

Masson, V. M. and N. I. Merpert. 1982. *Eneolit SSSR*. Moskva: Arkheologiia SSSR Nauka.

Matyushin, G. N. 1982. New data on the Neolithic and Eneolithic of the Voga-Ural region. *Kratkiye soobshcheniya o dokladakh i polevykh issledovaniyakh* 169, 86–94.

McGlade, J. 1995. Archaeology and the ecodynamics of human modified landscapes. *Antiquity* 69:113–32.

Mei, J. 2000. *Copper and Bronze Metallurgy in Late Prehistoric Xinjiang: Its Cultural Context and Relationship with Neighbouring Regions.* BAR international Series, Oxford: Archaeopress.

————. 2003. Cultural interaction between China and Central Asia during the Bronze Age. *Proceedings of the British Academy* 121:1–40.

Mei, J. and C. Shell. 1998. Copper and bronze metallurgy in Late Prehistoric Xinjiang. In *The Bronze Age Peoples of Eastern Central Asia*, ed. V. Mair, 581–603. Philadelphia: University of Pennsylvania Museum Publications.

Miller, M. 1956. *Archaeology in the USSR.* New York: Praeger.

Miller-Rosen, A., C. Chang, and F. Grigoriev. 2000. Paleoenvironments and economy of Iron Age Saka-Wusun agro-pastoralists in southeastern Kazakhstan. *Antiquity* 74(285):611–23.

Molodin, V. I. 1992. Studies in the Bertek River valley on the Ukok plateau. *Altaica* 1:23–34.

Mongait, A. L. 1951. Krizis Burzhuaznoi Arkeologii. *Kratkie soobshcheniya IIMK 42.*

————. 1955. *Arkheologiia v SSSR.* Moskva: Izd-vo Akademii nauk SSSR.

Morales-Muniz, A. and E. Antipina. 2003. Srubnaya fauna and beyond: A critical assessment of the archaezoological information from the East European Steppe. In *Prehistoric Steppe Adaptation and the Horse,* ed. M. Levine, C. Renfrew, and K. Boyle, 329–52. Cambridge: McDonald Institute for Archaeological Research.

Myres, John L. 1941. Nomadism. *The Journal of the Royal Anthropological Institute of Great Britain and Ireland* 71(1):19–42.

O'Connell, Tamsin, Marsha L. Levine, and Robert Hedges. 2003. The importance of fish in the diet of central Eurasian peoples from the Mesolithic to the Early Iron Age. In *Late Prehistoric Steppe Adaptation and the Horse,* eds. M. Levine, C. Renfrew and K. Boyle, 253–268. Cambridge: McDonald Institute for Archaeological Research.

Okladnikov, A. P. 1959 *Ancient Population of Siberia and its Cultures.* Russian Translation Series of the Peabody Museum of Archaeology and Ethnology, Harvard University, v. 1, no. 1. Peabody Museum, Cambridge.

Olsen, Sandra L. 2003. The exploitation of horses at Botai, Kazakhstan. In *Prehistoric Steppe Adaptation and the Horse,* ed. M. Levine, C. Renfrew and K. Boyle, 83–104. Cambridge: McDonald Institute for Archaeological Research.

————. 2006. Early horse domestication in the Eurasian Steppes. In *Documenting Domestication: The Intersection of Genetics and Archaeology,* ed. Melinda A Zeder, 245–269. Berkeley: University of California Press.

Olsen, Sandra L., B. Bradley, D. Maki, and A. Outram 2006. Copper Age community organization in Northern Kazakhstan. In *Beyond the Steppe and the Sown: Proceedings of the 2002 University of Chicago Conference on Eurasian Archaeology,* eds. D. L. Peterson, L. M. Popova, and A. T. Smith, 89–111. Leiden: Brill.

Olsen, Sandra L., M. A. Littauer, and Ingrid Rea. 2006. *Horses and Humans: The Evolution of Human-Equine Relationships.* BAR International Series, 1560. Oxford: Archaeopress.

Ong. 1999. *Flexible Citizenship: The cultural logistics of Transnationality.* Duke Univeristy Press: Durham.

Pal'gov, N. N. 1949. *Krupneishii uzel sovremennogo oledeneniya v Dzhungarskom Alatau.* Almaty: Izv. VGO.

Pallas, Peter Simon, Gauthier de la Peyronie, Jean Baptiste Pierre Antoine de Monet de Lamarck, L. Langlès, and J. B. L. J. Billecocq. 1794. *Voyages du professeur Pallas, dans plusieurs provinces de l'empire de Russie et dans l'Asie septentrionale.* Paris: Maradan.

Parpola, A. 1998. Aryan languages, archaeological cultures, and Sinkiang: Where did Proto-Iranian come into being and how did it spread? In *The Bronze Age and Early Iron Age Peoples of Eastern Central Asia,* ed. V. Mair, 114–147, vol. 1. Philadelphia: University of Pennsylvania Museum Publications.

Paskevich, Galina. 2003. Palaeoethnobotanical Evidence of Agriculture in the Steppe and the Forest-steppe of East Europe in the Late Neolithic and Bronze Age, in Levine, M., C. Renfrew, and M. Boyle (eds.), *Prehistoric Steppe Adaptation and the Horse.* McDonald Institute for Archaeological Research: Cambridge

Pastner, S. 1971. Ideological aspects of nomad-sedentary contact: A case study from southern Baluchistan. *Anthropological Quarterly* 44(3):173–184.

Peregrine, P. N. 1996. Ethnology versus ethnographic analogy: A common confusion in archaeological interpretation. *Cross-Cultural Research* 30(4):316–329.

Petrova-Averkieva, Yu. 1980. Historicism in Soviet ethnographic science. In *Soviet and Western Anthropology,* ed. E. Gellner, 19–28. London: Duckworth.

Popova, Laura Michele. 2006. *Political Pastures: Navigating the Steppe in the Middle Volga Region (Russia) during the Bronze Age.* PhD Dissertation, Department of Anthropology, University of Chicago.

Potemkina, T. M. 1983. Alakulskaya kul'tura. *Sovetskaya Arkheologiya* 2:13–33.

———. 1995a. Problemy Svyzzei i smeny kul'tur naseleniya Zaural'ya v Epokhu Bronzy (Pozdnii i final'ny Etapy). *Russkaya Arkheologiya* 2:11–20.

———. 1995b. Problemy Svyzzei i smeny kul'tur naseleniya Zaural'ya v Epokhu Bronzy (rannii i srednii Etapy). *Russkaya Arkheologiya* 1:14–27.

———. 2002. The Trans-Ural Eneolithic Sanctuaries with Astronomical Reference Points in a System of Similar Eurasian Models, in Jones-Bley, K. and D. G. Zdanovich, eds., *Complex societies of Central Eurasia from the 3rd to the 1st millennium BCE: Regional specifics in light of global models,* 269–282. Washington: Journal of Indo-European Studies Institute for the Study of Man.

Provenza, F. D. 1991. Viewpoint: Range science and range management are complementary but distinct endeavors. *Journal of Range Management* 44(2):181–183.

Raab, L. M. and A. C. Goodyear. 1984. Middle range theory in archaeology: a critical review of origins and applications. *American Antiquity* 49:255–268.

Radlov, V. V. 1882–1902. *Sibirskie Drevnosti.* Sankt Petersburg: Arkheologicheskoi komissii.

Rashīd al-Dīn Tabīb. 2000. *Jāmi al-tawārīkh. Tārīkh Ghāzān Khān.* al-Qāhirah: al-Dār al-Thaqāfīyah lil-Nashr.

Rassamakin, Y. 1999. The Eneolithic of the Black Sea steppe: Dymanics of culture and economic development 4500–2300 BCE. In *Late Prehistoric Exploitation of the Eurasian Steppe,* ed. M. Levine, Y. Rassamakin, A. Kislenko and T. N. Kislenko, 59–182. Cambridge (UK): McDonald Institute for Archaeological Research.

Redman, R. E. 1992. Primary productivity. In *Ecosystems of the World: Natural Grasslands,* ed. R. T. Coupland, 75–93. New York: Elsevier.

Renfrew, C. 2002. The Indo-European problem and the exploitation of the Eurasian steppes: Questions of time depth. In *Complex Societies of Central Eurasia from the Third to the First Millennium BCE,* ed. K. Jones-Bley and D. G. Zdanovich, 3–20. Washington, DC: Institute for the Study of Man.

Rhodes, T. E., F. Gasse, L. Ruifen, J.-C. Fontes, W. Keqin, P. Bertrand, E. Gilbert, F. Melieres, P. Tucholka, W. Zhixiang, and C. Zhi-Yuan. 1996. A Late Pleistocene-Holocene lacustrine record from Lake Manas, Zunggar (northern Xinjiang, western China). *Palaeogeography, Palaeoclimatology, Palaeoecology* 120:105–121.

Ripley, E. A. 1992. Grassland climate. In *Ecosystems of the World: Natural Grasslands,* ed. R. T. Coupland, 7–24. New York: Elsevier.

Roe, E. M. 1997. Viewpoint: On rangeland carrying capacity. *Journal of Rangeland Management* 50(5):467–472.

Rogers, J. Daniel. 2005. Urban centers and the emergence of empires in eastern Inner Asia. *Antiquity* 79 (306):801–818.

Rogozhinski, A. E. 1999. Mogil'niki epokhi bronzy urochishcha Tamgaly. In *Istoriya i Arkheologiya Semirech'ya,* ed. A. N. Mar'yashev, Yu. A. Motov, A. A. Goryachev, and A. E. Rogozhinski, 4–43. Almaty: XXI vek.

———. 2001. Izobrazitel'nye ryad petroglifov epokhi bronzy svyatilishcha Tamgaly. In *Istoriya i Arkheologiya Semirechiya—Vypusk 2.* ed. A. N. Mar'yashev, Yu. A. Motov, A. A. Goryachev, and A. E. Rogozhinski, 7–44. Almaty: Fond (Rodnichok).

Rudenko, S. I. 1927. Ocherk byta kazakov basseina rek Uila i Sagyza. In *Kazaki; antropologicheskie ocherki,* ed. S. F. Baronov, 7–32. Leningrad: Nauka.

Sal'nikov, K. V. 1948. Andronovskii Kurgannii Mogil'nik u. s. Fedorovki Chelyabinskoi Oblast. *Materialy Issledovaniya po Arkheologii SSSR* 1:58–68.

———. 1952. Kurgany na ozere Alakul'. *Materialy i isseldovaniya po arkheologii SSSR* 24:51–71.

———. 1967. *Ocherki drevnei istorii IUzhnogo Urala.* Moskva: Izd-vo "Nauka".

Salzman, P. C. 1967. Political organization among nomadic peoples. *Proceedings of the American Philosophical Society* 111(2):115–131.

———. 1972. Multi-resource nomadism in Iranian Baluchistan. In *Perspectives on Nomadism,* ed. W. Irons and N. Dyson-Hudson, 60–68. Leiden: E. J. Brill.

———. 2002. Pastoral nomads: Some general observations based on research in Iran. *Journal of Anthropological Research* 58(2):245–264.

Samashev, Z. S. 1993. *Petroglyphs of the East Kazakhstan as Historical Sources.* Almaty: Rakurs.

———. 1998. Shamanskie syuzhety petroglifov Kazakhstana. In *Voprosy Arkheologii Kazakhstana.* Almaty: Gylym.

Sandford, S. 1983. *Management of Pastoral Development in the Third World.* New York: John Willey and Sons.

Sarkozi, A. 1976. A Mongolian manual of divination by means of characteristics of the land. In *Tractata Altaica Denis Sinor, sexagenario optime de rebus altaicis merito dedicate,* eds. Sinor, Denis, and Walther Heissig, 584–96. Wiesbaden: Harrassowitz.

Savina, S. S. and N. A. Khotinskiy. 1984. Holocene paleoclimatic reconstructions based on the zonal method. In *Late Quaternary Environments of the Soviet Union*, ed. A. A. Velichko, H. E. Wright, and C. W. Barnosky, 287–304. Minneapolis: University of Minnesota Press.

Savinov, D. G. 1997. Probelmy izucheniya Okun'evskoi kul'tury v istoriograficheskom aspekte. In *Okun'evskie Seornik: kul'tura, iskusstvo, antropologiya,* ed. D. G. Savinov and M. L. Podoliskie, 7–19. St. Petersburg: Akademiia Nauk.

Scarnecchia, D. L. 1985. The animal-unit and animal-unit equivalent concepts in range science. *Journal of Range Management* 38(4):346–349.

Schortman, E. 1989. Interregional interaction in prehistory: The need for a new perspective. *American Antiquity* 54(1):52–65.

Schortman, E. and P. Urban. 1987. Modeling interregional interaction in prehistory. *Advances in Archaeological Method and Theory* 11:37–95.

Schortman, E. and P. Urban. 1992. The place of interaction studies in archaeological throught. In *Resources, Power, and Interregional Interaction,* ed. E. Schortman, E. and P. Urban, 3–15. New York: Plenum Press.

Semenov, Iu. I. 1980. Socio-economic formations and world history. In *Soviet and Western Anthropology,* ed. E. Gellner, 29–58. London: Duckworth.

Shahrani, M. Nazif Mohib. 1976. Kirghiz pastoral nomads of the Afghan Pamirs: an ecological and ethnographic overview. *Folk* 18:129–43.

———. 1979. *The Kirghiz and Wakhi of Afghanistan: Adaptation to Closed Frontiers.* Seattle: University of Washington Press.

Shilov, V. P. 1975. Modeli skotovodcheskikh khoziaistv stepnikh oblastei Evrazii v epokhu eneolita i rannego bronzovogo veka. *Sovetskaya Arkeologiya* 1:5–16.

Shishlina, Nataliya I. 1999. *Tekstil' epokhi bronzy Evraziiskikh stepei.* Moskva: Trudy Gosudarstvennogo istoricheskogo muzeia Gosudarstvennyi istoricheskii muzei.

———. 2001. The seasonal cycle of grassland use in the Caspian Sea steppe during the Bronze Age: A new approach to an old problem. *Journal of European Archaeology,* 4(3): 346–366.

———. 2003. Yamnaya culture pastoral exploitation: A local sequence. In *Late Prehistoric Steppe Adaptation and the Horse,* ed. Marsha Levine, Colin Renfrew and Katie Boyle, 253–266. Cambridge (UK): McDonald Institute for Archaeological Research.

———. 2004. "North-west Caspian Sea steppe; environment and migration crossroads of pastoral culture population during the third millennium B.C.," in E. Scott, M. Alekseev and A. Yu. Zaitseva, eds., *Impact of the Environment on Human Migration in Eurasia.* Chelyabinsk: Chelyabinsk Gosudarstvenyi Universitet, 91–105.

———. 2005. North-west Caspian Sea steppe: Environment and migration crossroads of pastoral culture population during the third millennium BCE. In *Impact of the Environment on Human Migration in Eurasia,* ed. E. Scott, M. Alekseev and A. Yu. Zaitseva, 91–105. Chelyabinsk: Chelyabinsk Gosudarstvenyi Universitet.

Shishlina, N. I., A. L. Alexandrovsky, O. A. Chichagova, and J. van der Plicht 2000. Radiocarbon chronology of the Kalmykia Catacomb culture of the west Eurasian Steppe. Antiquity 74(286): 793–799.

Shlapentokh, D. 1996. *The French Revolution in Russian Intellectual Life, 1865–1905.* Westport (CN): Praeger.

Shnirelman, V. A. 1995. From internationalism to nationalism: forgotten pages of Soviet archaeology in the 1930s and 1940s. In *Nationalism, Politics, and the Practice of Archaeology,* ed. P. Kohl and C. Fawcett, 120–38. London: Routledge.

Sinor, Denis. 1969. *Inner Asia: History, Civilization, Languages; A Syllabus.* Bloomington: Indiana University.

Smith, A. T. 2003. *The Political Landscape: Constellations of Authority in Early Complex Polities.* Berkeley: University of California Press.

Sobolev, L. N. 1960. *Kormovye Resursy Kazakhstana.* Moscow: Akademiya Nauk.

Sokolov, A. 1968. *Agrokhimicheskaya Kharakteristika Pochv SSSR—Kazakhstan i Chelyabinskaya Oblast'.* Moskva: Nauka.

Sokolov, S. I. 1975. *Soils of the Almaty Oblast (translated from the Russian: Pochvy Alma-atinksoi Oblast).* Delhi: INSDOC.

Sorokin, V. S. 1962. *Mogilnik bronzovoi epokhi Tasty-Butak l v zapadnom Kazakhstane.* Moscow: Nauka.

Sorokin, V. S., and M. P. Gryaznov. 1966. *Andronovskaya kul'tura.* Leningrad: Nauka

Soucek, Svatopluk. 2000. *A history of inner Asia.* Cambridge: Cambridge University Press.

Spooner, B. 1973. *The Cultural Ecology of Pastoral Nomads.* Addison-Wesley Modules in Anthropology No. 45.

Stahl, A. B. 1993. Concepts of time and approaches to analogical reasoning in historical perspective. *American Antiquity* 58:235–260.

Stein, Aurel. 1925. Innermost Asia: Its geography as a factor in history. *The Geographical Journal* 65(5):377–403.

Stein, G. 2002. From passive periphery to active agents: Emerging perspectives in the anthropology of interregional interaction. *American Anthropologist* 104(3):903–916.

Stepanova, N. A. 1961. *Climatological Aspects of the Virgin Soil Project in the U.S.S.R.* Washington DC: U.S. Weather Bureau.

Stoddart, L. A. and A. D. Smith. 1943. *Range Management.* New York, London: McGraw-Hill Book Company.

Stoddart, S. 2000. *Landscapes from Antiquity.* Cambridge (UK): Antiquity Publications.

Stone, Glenn Davis. 1996. *Settlement Ecology: The Social and Spatial Organization of Kofyar Agriculture.* Arizona Studies in Human Ecology. Tucson: University of Arizona Press.

Swell, W. H. 1999. The concept of culture. In *Beyond the Cultural Turn,* ed. V. E. Bonnell and L. Hunt, 35–61. Berkeley: University of California Press.

Tanner, G. W. 1983. Determining grazing capacity for native range. In *Document SS-WEC-31, Wildlife Ecology and Conservation Department.* Gainesville: University of Florida.

Tapper, R. 1979. *Pasture and Politics: Economics, Conflict, and Ritual among Shahsevan Nomads of Northwest Iran.* New York: Academic Press.

Telegin, D. I. and J. P. Mallory. 1986. *Dereivka, a Settlement and Cemetery of Copper Age Horse Keepers on the Middle Dnieper.* BAR International Series, 287. Oxford (UK): BAR.

Teploukhov, S. A. 1927. *Drevnie pogrebeni ya v Minusinkom krae.* Materialy po etnografii T.III, vol. 2.

————. 1989. *A History of Archaeological Thought*. Cambridge (UK): Cambridge University Press.

Tsalkin, Veniamin I. 1964. Nekotorye itogi izucheniia kostnykh ostatkov zhivotnykh iz rskopok arkheologicheskikh pamiatnikov pozdnego bronzovogo veka. *Kratkie Soobshcheniia Instituta Arkheologii* 101:24–34.

————. 1966. *Drevnee zhivotnovodstvo plemen Vostochnoi Evropy i Srednei Azii*. Materialy i issledovaniia po arkheologii SSSR, no. 135. Moskva: Nauka.

————. 1970. *Drevneishie domashnie zhivotnye Vostochnoi Evropy*. Moskva: Nauka.

Upham, S. 1992. Interaction and isolation: The empty spaces in panregional political and economic systems. In *Resources, Power, and Interregional Interaction*, ed. E. Schortman and P. Urban, 139–152. New York: Plenum Press.

Utesheva, A. S. 1959. Klimat Kazakhstana. Leningrad: Gidrometeorologicheskoe Izd.

Vadetskaya, E. B. 1980. Afanas'evskii kurgan u s. Vostochnogo na Enisee. *Kratikie Soobshchenniya* 161:101–7.

————. 1986. *Arkheologicheskie Pamyatniki v stepyakh srednevo Yeniseya*. Leningrad: Akademiya Nauk CCCP.

Vainshtein, S. I. 1978. The Problem of origin and formation of the economic-cultural type of pastoral nomads in the moderate belt of Eurasia. In *The Nomadic Alternative: Modes and Models of Interaction in the African-Asian Deserts and Steppes*, ed. W. Weissleder, 127–36. Paris: Mouton.

————. 1980. *Nomads of South Siberia*. Cambridge (UK): Cambridge University Press.

————. 1991. *Mir Kochevnikoe Tsentral'nye Azii*. Moskva: NAUK.

Valikhanov, Ch. C. 1961–1972. *Sobranie sochinenii (vol 1–4)* Alma-Ata: Izd-vo Akademii nauk Kazakhskoi SSR.

Valikhanov, Ch. C., J. Michell, R. Michell and M. I. Venyukov. 1865. *The Russians in Central Asia: Their Occupation of The Kirghiz Steppe and the Line of the Syr-Daria; Their Political Relations with Khiva, Bokhara, and Kokan; Also Descriptions of Chinese Turkestan and Dzungaria; By Capt. Valikhanof, M. Veniukof and [Others]*. London: E. Stanford.

Vallentine, John F., and Phillip L. Sims. 1980. *Range Science: A Guide to Information Sources*. Natural World Information Guide Series, v. 2. Detroit (MI): Gale Research Co.

Velichko, A. A., H. E. Wright, and C. W. Barnosky. 1984. *Late Quaternary Environments of the Soviet Union*. Minneapolis: University of Minnesota Press.

Vinogradov, N. B. 1984. Noviye Alakul'skii mogil'nik v lesostepyakh Yuzhnogo Zaural'ya. *Sovetskaya Arkheologiya* 3:

————. 1995. Khronologiya, soderzhanie i kulturnaya prinadlezhnost pamyatnikov sintashtinskogo tipa bronzovogo veka v Yuzhnom Zauralye. *Vestnik Chelyabinskogo gosudarstvennogo pedagogicheskogo universiteta. Istoricheskie nauki.* 1:16–26.

Vinogradov, A. V., M. A. Itina, L. T. Iablonskii, and V. P. Alekseev. 1986. *Drevneishee naselenie nizovii Amudar'i arkheologo-paleoantropologicheskoe issledovanie*. Moskva: Trudy khorezmskoi arkheologo-etnograficheskoi ekspeditsii "Nauka".

Watson, P. J. 1995. Archaeology, anthropology, and the culture concept. *American Anthropologist* 97(4):683–694.

Wells, R. Spencer, NadiraYuldashevaa, Ruslan Ruzibakievc, Peter A. Underhilld, Irina Evseevae, Jason Blue-Smithd, Li Jinf, Bing Suf, Ramasamy Pitchappang, Sadagopal

Shanmugalakshmig, Karuppiah Balakrishnang, Mark Readh, Nathaniel M. Pearsoni, Tatiana Zerjalj, Matthew T. Websterk, Irakli Zholoshvilil, Elena Jamarjashvilil, Spartak Gambarovm, Behrouz Nikbinn, Ashur Dostievo, Ogonazar Aknazarovp, Pierre Zallouaq, Igor Tsoyr, Mikhail Kitaevs, Mirsaid Mirrakhimovs, Ashir Charievt, and Walter F. Bodmera. 2001. The Eurasian heartland: A continental perspective on Y-chromosome diversity. *Proceedings of the National Academy of Science* 98(18):10244–10249.

Whittle, A. W. R. 1996. *Europe in the Neolithic: The Creation of New Worlds.* New York: Cambridge University Press.

Woods, N. 2000. *The Political Economy of Globalization.* New York: St. Martin's Press.

Workman, J. P. and D. W. MacPherson. 1973. Calculating yearlong carrying capacity: An algebraic approach. *Journal of Range Management* 26(4):274–277.

Wylie, A. 1985. The reaction against analogy. In *Advances in Archaeological Method and Theory,* ed. M. Schiffer, 63–111. New York: Academic Press.

Yablonsky, L. T. 1995. The material culture of the Saka and historical reconstruction. In *Nomads of the Eurasian Steppes in the Early Iron Age,* ed. J. Davis-Kimball, V. B. Bashilov, and L. T. Yablonsky, 201–235. Berkeley: Zinat Press.

Zarins, Juris. 1990. Early pastoral nomadism and the settlement of lower Mesopotamia. *American Schools of Oriental Research Bulletin* 280:31–65.

Zdanovich, D. G. 1997. Arkaim–kur'turnii kompleks epokhi srednei bronzi Yuzhnogo Zaural'ya. *Rossiiskaya Arkheologiya* 2:47–62.

————. 2002a. Introduction. In *Complex Societies of Central Eurasia from the Third to the First Millennium BCE: Regional Specifics in Light of Global Models,* ed. K. Jones-Bley and D. G. Zdanovich, xix–xxxviii. Washington: Institute for the Study of Man.

————. 2002b. *Arkaim: nekropol' (po materialam kurgana 25 Bol'shekararanskogo migil'nika).* Chelyabinsk: Yuzhno-Ural'skoe knizhmoe izdatel'stvo.

Zdanovich, G. B. 1984. K voprosu ob Andronovskom kulturno-istoricheskom edinstve. *Kratkie Soobshcheniya* 177:29–37.

————. 1988. *Bronzovyi Vek Uralo-Kazakhstanskikh Stepei (osnovy periodizatsii).* Sverdlovsk: Uralskogo Universitet.

Zdanovich G. B. and D. G. Zdanovich. 2002. The 'Country of Towns' of southern Trans-Urals and some aspects of steppe assimilation in the Bronze Age. In *Ancient Interactions: East and West in Eurasia,* eds. K. Boyle, C. Renfrew, and M. Levine, 249–65. Cambridge (UK): McDonald Institute Monographs.

Zdanovich, S. Ya. 1970. Mogil'nik epokhi bronzy Burluk-I. In *Po Sledam Drevnikh Kul'tur Kazakhstana,* ed. M. K. Kadirbeav. Alma-Ata: Nauka KSSR.

Zhu, T. 1993. Grasslands of China. In *Natural Grasslands,* ed. R. T. Coupland, 61–80. Amsterdam, New York: Elsevier.

Zaibert, V. F. 1993. *Eneolit Uralo-Irtyshskogo mezhdurechya.* Petropavlovsk: Nauka.

Ziablin, Leonid P. 1977. *Karasukskii mogil'nik Malye Kopeny 3.* Moskva: Nauka.

INDEX

Boldface numbers refer to figures and tables.

forage, 89
forage productivity
    in Barguzin valley, 99–101
    Chinese grasslands, **98**
    components of, 89, 91
    in Dzhungar Mountains, **90**, 91–92
forest steppe zone, 76, 79

Galaty, J. G., 113
geology, 87–88
geomorphology, 88
German archaeologists, 39–40
Giddens, A., 17–18
gifting, 121–122
globality, 29
globalization, 28–29
globalizing, 29, 174
global landscape, 28–29
goats, 48, 49, 94, 131
"Golden Man," 144
Goloskokov, V. P., 91
Gomboev, B. I., 101–102
Gorny, **3**, 41, 49
Gorsdorf, Jochen, 40
graves. *See* burials
grazing capacity, 88–89, 92–98, **98**, 155
Great Zhus, 113–114, 117
Grousset, R., 1, 5–6

Han dynasty, 109
Han shu (Ban Gu), 109
Haydar, Miraz Muhammed, 109
historic period, 145–149
Holocene, 79
Honeychurch, William, 178*n3*
horses, 7, 46–47, 56, 94, 97, 117, 119, 121, 160
Hou han shu (Fan Ye), 109
houses and settlement structures, 33, 55–56,
    57–60, 132, 145
hunting and fishing, 46, 160
Huntington, Ellis, 5
hydrology, 87–88

identity, 25, 26, 175–176
Ikpen'-I, 60
Ili River, 51, 112
Indo-European language, 7, 70
Indo-Iranian language, 7, 70

Inner Asia, 2, 4–5
interaction
    Bronze Age, 24–25, 27, 70–71
    definition of, 17–18
    local context, 174
    model for, 174–175
    Semirech'ye/Dzhungar Mountains,
        117–123
Iron Age, 19, 21, **129**, 141–145
irrigation, 18, 112, 113
Irtysh River Basin, 77
Issyk, 117, 144

Johnson, Douglas, L., 73, 113
Juvayni, al-, 109

Kadirbaev, M. K., 53
Kalmukia region, 79
Kara-khitai, 109
Karasuk culture, 34, 42, 54, 63, 65, 67, **68**
Kargaly, **3**, 41, 45, 49, 51
Kashgar, 109
Kazakh-Kyrgyz, 111
Kazakhs
    burials, 119, 146
    definition of, 177*n1*
    Great Zhus, 113–114, 117
    "New Kazakh" identity, xiv
    seasonal camps, 116
Kazakhstan, present day, xiii–xiv
Kharitonov Yu. D., 101
Khazanov, Anatoly, 19
Khotan, 109
Khvalynsk, **3**, 44
Kirghiz, 118, 119
knives, 52, **53**
Koksu River, **4**, 10
Koksu River valley
    archaeological features, 127–130
    Bronze Age, 130–141, 151
    burials, 127–128, 133–135, 142–144, 146,
        161, 163–164
    ceramic diversity, 165–167
    economic landscape, 38, 151–157
    geography, 126–127
    hydrology and geology, 87–88, 105
    interaction, 24
    Iron Age, 141–145

Srubnaya culture, 40, **41**, 49, 52
Stein, Aurel, 5
steppe vegetation, 79, 80, 81
stone-constructed settlements, 50
stone monuments, 147–148
Suany, 113
subalpine pastures, **90, 91**, 92, **93, 96, 104**, 117
subsistence economy, 46, 50, 151
Surtandy culture, 39, 56
survey data, 13, 127

Talapty, **3**, 127, 131, 132, 135, 153, 158, 159, **166**
Tamgaly, **3**, 138, **166**, 168
Tarikh-i al-Rashidi (Haydar), 109
Tarikh-i jahan gusha (al-Juvayni), 109
Tasty-Butak, **3**, 34, 59–60
Teploukhov, S. A., 31
Tersek culture, 39, **40**, 55
Tian Shan Mountains, 48, 61, 78, 80, 99, 109, 115
time-geography, 172
tin, 51
Tobol region, 34, **43**, 56, 77
tools, 33, 50, 52–53
trade, 120–122
transhumance, 7, 10, 157
trans-Urals, **43**, 48, 49
tribal groups, of Great Zhus, 113–114
tribute, 121–122
Tripol'ye, 44
Turgen, **166**
Turkic people, 109, 117, 118
Turkic period, **130**, 144, 145–149
Turkish ethnohistorical sources, 109

Upais, 69
Ural Mountains, 31, 50, 77, 79
Urban, P., 25
Ushkatty, **3**
Utesheva, A. S., 86

Vadetskaya, E. B., 45–46
Vainshtein, S. I., 21
Valikhanov, Chokan Ch., 111, 115, 119, 120–121
Vasilkovka IV, **3**, 46, 55
Volga River, 77
von den Dreisch, A., 47

wells, 59–60
western steppe zone, 20, 39, 42, **43**, 44, 48, 77, 79
wheat, 50
women, 162, 167
Wusun, 109, 112, 117, 144

Xinjiang, 37, 45, 51, 99
Xiong-Nu, 117

Yamnaya culture, 39, **40**, 44–45, 55
Yavlenka, **3**, 60
Yazevo, **3**, 60
Yenisei River, 31, 42, 77

Zailisky Alatau Mountains, 78
Zdanovich, G. B., 61
Zhalairy, 114
Zhetisu. *See* Semirech'ye
Zhu, T., 98–99
Zibbershtein, Monsieur, 120

Composition:	Michael Bass Associates
Text:	9.5/14 Scala
Display:	Scala
Printer and Binder:	Thomson Shore, Inc.